Lyman M

Get Smart!

Make Your Money Count in the 1990s

Prentice-Hall Canada, Inc., Scarborough, Ontario

Canadian Cataloguing in Publication Data

MacInnis, Lyman, 1938–
Get smart! : make your money count

2nd ed.
ISBN 0-13-355942-4 (bound) ISBN 0-13-355959-9 (pbk.)

1. Finance, Personal. 2. Investments. I. Title.

HG179.M26 1989 332.024 C89-094055-X

The Gold Maple Leaf Coin on the front cover is reproduced with the permission of The Royal Canadian Mint.

Prentice-Hall Inc., Englewood Cliffs, New Jersey
Prentice-Hall International, Inc., London
Prentice-Hall of Australia, Pty., Sydney
Prentice-Hall of India Pvt., Ltd., New Delhi
Prentice-Hall of Japan, Inc., Tokyo
Prentice-Hall of Southeast Asia (Pte.) Ltd., Singapore
Editoria Prentice-Hall do Brasil Ltda., Rio de Janeiro
Prentice-Hall Hispanoamericana, S.A., Mexico

ISBN 0-13-355942-4 (bound) ISBN 0-13-355959-9 (pbk.)

Production Editor: Kirsten Hanson
Interior Design: Monica Kompter
Cover Design: Anita Macklin
Manufacturing Buyer: Luca Di Nicola
Composition: Typografix Inc.

1 2 3 4 5 6 THB 94 93 92 91 90 89

Printed and bound in Canada by T.H. Best Printing Co.

Get Smart!

Make Your Money Count in the 1990s

Table of Contents

Acknowledgments ix

Preface xi

PART ONE — Money Management

Chapter 1 *The Ten Most Common Personal Financial Planning Mistakes* 3

Chapter 2 *Attitude and Action* 10

Chapter 3 *Personal Budgeting* 13

Chapter 4 *Financial Planning Is a Family Affair* 21

Chapter 5 *Choices* 26

Chapter 6 *Registered Retirement Savings Plans* 33

Chapter 7 *Registered Retirement Income Funds* 56

Chapter 8 *Registered Education Savings Plans* 59

Chapter 9 *Estate Planning* 62

Chapter 10 *Insurance* 71

Chapter 11 *Powers of Attorney* 85

Chapter 12 *Borrowing Money* 87

Chapter 13 *Buying a Car* 91

Chapter 14 *Marriage Contracts* 97

Chapter 15 *A Couple of Thoughts on Changing Jobs* . . . 101

Chapter 16 *Investing in Real Estate* 103

Chapter 17 *Winning a Lottery* 119

Chapter 18 *Swiss Banks* 122

PART TWO — Income Tax

Chapter 19 *Prelude to Income Tax* 129

Chapter 20 *Filing Your Income Tax Return* 131

Chapter 21 *What's Taxed* 139

Chapter 22 *Some Common Income Tax Deductions and Credits* 150

Chapter 23 *After You File Your Return* 162

Chapter 24 *Tax Shelters* 167

PART THREE — The Market

Chapter 25 *Introduction to Investment* 171

Chapter 26 *Investment Clubs* 173

Chapter 27 *Investing in Securities* 180

Chapter 28 *Types of Market Players* 184

Chapter 29 *Investment Objectives* **187**

Chapter 30 *Operating an Account* **190**

Chapter 31 *Choosing and Dealing with a Broker* **194**

Chapter 32 *Common Shares* **203**

Chapter 33 *Preferred Shares* **221**

Chapter 34 *Bonds and Debentures* **232**

Chapter 35 *Annuities* **247**

Chapter 36 *Treasury Bills* **251**

Chapter 37 *Options* **256**

Chapter 38 *Diversification* **260**

Chapter 39 *Commodities, Collectibles and Precious Metals* **268**

Chapter 40 *The Right Way to Play the Stock Market* ... **272**

Afterword **275**

Glossary **277**

Appendix A **291**

Index **311**

Acknowledgments

My very special thanks to my good right arm, Kathryn Evelyn, without whose dedicated attention to *her* work *this* work would never have been completed on time, nor as well. Thanks, too, to Anna-Claire Mertei who came on board at exactly the right time. I also appreciate the cooperation of Tanya Long and Ed Brewer of Prentice Hall.

Preface

Since the original version of this book was published, many things have changed in the financial world. Entirely new investment vehicles such as zero coupon bonds, mortgage-backed securities, and registered retirement income funds have been created. There's been a stock market crash. The Income Tax Act has undergone many, many changes. Interest rates and inflation are (at least when this is being written) under control. And, of course, we are all more experienced with money management. The result is a revised, expanded, and updated version of *Get Smart! Make Your Money Count*.

Many familiar features are retained. There are items of interest, both old and new, for everybody. The book is still written in a layperson's terms. Where technical jargon couldn't be avoided, it is clearly defined. This is still a personal financial management book. In addition to including new material relevant to recent developments in the financial world, all of the old material has been updated and much of it expanded. For example, a lot of material on investment strategy and objectives has been added.

A whole new section on income taxes has been included; not the type of material that is out of date by the time you read it, but rather an overview designed to ensure that you consider the many implications and ramifications of personal income tax on just about everything we do in our financial lives. Sometimes even doing nothing has income tax implications. And, as in the original edition, throughout the entire book, whatever the subject, where income tax considerations are of special importance, you are urged to seek specific advice.

Although much has changed over the past few years, much has remained the same. Managing money in the most appropriate way still depends very little on how much of it you have. Whether you scrape by from payday to payday or have surplus funds to invest, there are countless considerations in handling money which don't depend on where the decimal point falls.

As in the original work, parts of this book apply only to the person faced with investment decisions. But the book now includes even more for the person who is simply trying to make ends meet. You will be surprised at how much of this book applies to both people.

There are still chapters on subjects ranging from what to do if you win a lottery right up to opening a Swiss bank account. New topics ranging from giving your kids an allowance to how to save money on your Christmas shopping have been added.

This edition will also be of great interest to the many people who, in the course of their everyday activities, advise others on money management. Bank managers, stockbrokers, insurance agents, real estate brokers, accountants and lawyers will all find something of interest. Teachers and students who are interested in personal financial management will find a wealth of resource material in these expanded pages.

Although no book could cover every personal financial planning situation, this one deals with the most common and the most important financial decisions that face people from all walks of life. Each suggestion in this book has been tested time and time again. The advice and information are based on my quarter-century-plus of experience in helping people manage their personal affairs. Mistakes I haven't made myself, I've seen others make; which means I've seen the consequences of just about every good and bad financial decision.

This book is specifically designed to help *you* get smart, and make *your* money count.

PART ONE

Money Management

Chapter 1

The Ten Most Common Personal Financial Planning Mistakes

THE LIST IN ORDER

I've been helping people manage their personal financial affairs for over thirty years. This help has ranged all the way from advising them on specific points in their money management to actually handling all their finances for them. During that time I've seen just about every mistake that can be made in personal financial planning, and the consequences thereof. Some of the mistakes I've made myself — and that's the best teacher of all.

Drawing on my experience, I've compiled a list of what, in my opinion, are the ten most common personal financial planning mistakes. By "most common" I mean those that are made most often by most people. That's the order in which I'll present them here — the order of frequency, not the order of devastation. Because, you see, the degree of devastation depends very much on an individual's particular circumstances. What might put only a small dent in Aunt Martha's finances could well wipe me out. What I might be able to overcome could just as easily be devastating for Uncle Martin.

Another important thing to remember about these mistakes is that people at all levels of wealth and income make them. The same mistakes cause financial difficulties for the millionaire and the blue-collar worker alike. The only difference is in the number of zeroes and where the decimal point falls in the amounts involved. So whether you're a person who barely makes it from payday to payday or a multi-millionaire, the following are the mistakes to avoid.

Number One

There's no doubt in my mind as to what is the most common financial planning mistake made most often by most people. It's *buying too much on credit.* I've seen more people, rich and poor alike, get into financial difficulty because of buying too much on credit than for any other reason. Now, the key words here are *too much*. It's a rare person indeed who never has to borrow or buy on credit. The problem arises when we overdo it. A good rule of thumb is to borrow only for what you need. Wait until you have cash for the things you simply want. Why? Because buying on credit often doubles or triples the cost by the time you pay off the debt and interest.

Number Two

Mistake number two is *borrowing at the wrong place*. I must quickly explain what I mean by this. I'm not suggesting one bank or trust company is better than another. Nor am I saying you should always borrow at a credit union, or from a rich relative for that matter. What I am saying is if you must borrow, then borrow where the loan is going to cost you the least by the time it's all paid off.

Let's take an example. Suppose you have to borrow $5,000 to buy some much-needed furniture, and you intend to pay it off over three years. How much difference would it make if you borrowed the money at, say, 10% rather than from another source at, say, 15%? Well, over the three years it would be a difference of over $400.

You should also find out how often the interest is going to be compounded — which means how often the interest is going to be calculated and added to the amount you owe. Let's take another example. In the first year of a $5,000 loan with interest at 10% compounded *quarterly,* the total interest would be $519.07. With an interest rate of 10¼%, but compounded annually, the interest would only be $512.50. You can see that a rate of 10% compounded quarterly is the same as an annual rate of 10.38%. Over the long life of a large loan this can make quite a difference. Another point to always check out when borrowing money is to determine whether there are any costs described as something other than interest, such as administration fees, registration fees, repayment bonuses, or whatever.

What has to be compared is the *total cost* of paying off the loan at one place compared to the *total cost* of paying off the loan at another place, whatever the cost happens to be called, whether it's interest, fees, or something else altogether.

Number Three

Mistake number three is *not paying off debts as quickly as possible,* particularly charge accounts and credit card balances. People often forget that if you don't pay off the balance in full every month, it's the same as borrowing at very high interest rates.

In my opinion, you should pay off your mortgage as fast as you can, too. Here's another example. If you paid off a 15%, $50,000 mortgage over 15 years rather than 25 years, how much do you think you would save? Well, you would save about $70,000! And remember, these are whole dollars. Go out and earn an extra $70,000 and you have to pay income tax on it. But save $70,000 of interest and the money is all yours.

Let's go back to those charge account and credit card balances for a moment. Not only are you committing mistake number three if you don't pay off the balances in full each month, but you're also right into the middle of mistake number two. Not paying off charge account and credit card balances in full each month is the most common form of borrowing at the wrong place. Make no mistake about it, when you don't pay off the balances each month you are *borrowing*. Credit cards and charge accounts were meant to be substitutes for cash, not substitutes for borrowing. When they're used as substitutes for cash they're wonderful. But when they're used as substitutes for borrowing, they are disastrous.

There are two reasons why credit cards and charge accounts should never be used as substitutes for borrowing rather than as substitutes for cash. The first is you pay a horrendous rate of interest on the balances, often double what you'd pay on a consumer loan. You will always be better off to take out a consumer loan and pay off these monthly bills. The second reason is there's no discipline employed in the borrowing — you don't have a set payment schedule and you have no idea how much it's going to cost you. If you apply for a consumer loan you're going to have to consider and come to grips with the amount of the monthly payment and exactly how long it's going to take you to pay it off. This might well keep you out of mistake number one as well as mistakes numbers two and three.

Number Four

In my opinion, the fourth most common personal financial planning mistake that people make is *renting living accommodation rather than buying it.*

Now, hold it! Don't get upset yet. I know there are lots of you who would far rather rent than own, and that's a personal decision I'd never argue against. With rent controls and high interest rates, you might even be better off in the short haul renting rather than owning. But from an economic standpoint, over the long term, it's a personal financial planning mistake to rent rather than own your living accommodation.

There are several reasons for this. First of all, your home is the only investment you can sell for a profit and pay absolutely no income tax. Second, residential property is about as good a hedge against inflation as you'll find anywhere — especially over the long term. Third, your home is one of the very few investments you can make that also fills an absolute need. Everybody needs a roof, four walls, and a place to go to the bathroom. Last, but certainly not least (although it is often the most overlooked factor), your home provides more potential for continuous enjoyment than any other investment possible. With the increased used of VCRs, satellite dishes, and other recreation facilities such as swimming pools and gym equipment, the importance of this factor is increasing.

Number Five

Not budgeting for once-a-year expenditures such as insurance, vacations, subscriptions, and even Christmas, constitutes mistake number five. When this mistake is committed people suddenly find themselves mired in numbers one, two and three — the borrowing mistakes.

Number Six

Not budgeting at all.

Most people shy away from personal budgeting because they think personal budgets have to be very formal documents prepared by chartered accountants that basically have the effect of hamstringing their activities. As you will see in Chapter Three, nothing could be further from the truth.

Personal budgeting simply involves sitting down and comparing your planned expenses with your income over, say, the next year. It will help you decide what you can afford, and when you can afford it, thereby cutting down on interest expense and keeping you out of mistakes one, two and three. Everyone I know who has tried personal budgeting has found that it gives them greater financial freedom, not less.

Number Seven

Mistake number seven is *buying on impulse.*

Now, I'm not referring to burning two dollars' worth of gas to save thirty cents on a jar of peanut butter, although that makes no sense either. What I am referring to are big-ticket items like cars, furniture, jewelry, registered retirement savings plans and the like. Don't buy out of habit, in a rush, or at some place simply because that's where you bought the last time. Always shop around and look for the best deal.

Remember that this rule cuts both ways. On big-ticket capital goods that you expect to own and use for a long period of time, the most expensive, high-quality item is very often the cheapest in the long run. It is a fact that a four-hundred-dollar suit will last longer than two two-hundred-dollar suits.

Be especially wise when making a big purchase, like an automobile or a major appliance. It sometimes takes years to overcome the negative financial effects of one major, bad impulsive purchase.

Number Eight

Mistake number eight is *when investing, trying to make a quick buck instead of going for a lower but surer return*. If you're faced with two identical investment choices, and the rate of return on one is much higher than the other, it's because the chance of losing your money in the one with the higher rate is a whole lot greater than if you go for the more conservative investment.

Number Nine

Mistake number nine — and this is a fairly recent one, much more prevalent in recent years than earlier — is *making investments that you can't really afford*, such as borrowing to buy stocks or to invest in mutual funds. Increases in interest rates, drops in the market or the need to get your cash back for other purposes could all force you into panic moves, prompting you to sell at a loss. On the other hand, if you could really afford the investment you could wait out any financial storms.

The only investors who were badly hurt in the October 1987 stock market crash were the ones who had borrowed heavily to invest. Those who had not been using borrowed money didn't have to sell at fire sale prices, and simply waited for the eventual, and certain, turnaround.

Number Ten

Mistake number ten is *thinking the future will take care of itself.* It never has and it never will.

We have to plan prudently for long-term requirements such as children's education and retirement. We should also prepare as well as we can for emergencies such as the death of a breadwinner, the collapse of a business, or the return of run-away inflation or high interest rates. As a matter of fact, a little more self-reliance is just the right economic tonic at any time.

Summary

Here they are again, the ten most common personal financial planning mistakes:

1. Buying too much on credit.
2. Borrowing at the wrong place.
3. Not paying off debts as quickly as possible.
4. Renting living accommodation rather than buying it.
5. Not budgeting for irregular expenditures.
6. Not budgeting at all.
7. Buying on impulse.
8. When investing, trying to make a quick buck instead of going for a lower but surer return.
9. Making investments that you can't really afford.
10. Thinking the future will take care of itself.

WHAT CAUSES THESE MISTAKES

So there's my list of what I think are the ten most common personal financial planning mistakes. Now a few words about what causes people to make these mistakes.

There are as many causes, I suppose, as there are people, and sometimes the mistakes can't really be avoided. But the avoidable ones can be categorized under the following headings.

Trying to keep up with the Joneses: this drives many people into life styles which they simply can't maintain in the long run. Then the mistakes start to compound.

Thinking that the world owes you something: these people tend to sit back and wait for someone — probably the government — to bail them out. In the meantime others are fending for themselves and outstripping the laggards.

Trying to get something for nothing (or listening to the "Buddy, have I got a deal for you" line): there never has been, there isn't now, and there probably never will be such a thing as a free lunch.

Thinking the future will take care of itself: this is not only one of the causes, it's one of the mistakes, too. Always remember that what we do today in large measure determines what will happen to us tomorrow.

Chapter 2

Attitude and Action

Getting smart and making your money count requires both thought and work. It requires a combination of the right attitude and the correct action. Let's deal first with attitude.

ATTITUDE

The first point you have to get into your head is that you are perfectly capable of getting smart and making your money count. There isn't a magic formula that accomplishes it for you, but there are a number of fairly basic rules that, if followed consistently, can make an enormous difference in your financial well-being. Money management is a skill, not an art. You can learn it. You don't have to be born with a Midas touch.

The next point to remember, always, is that no one (with the possible exception of your heirs) cares as much about your money as you do. It's important to always remember this point, for two reasons. You have to be skeptical about opportunities for the quick buck or the free lunch, and in the final analysis the responsibility for your financial condition is yours and yours alone.

The third point to accept in adopting the right attitude for effective money management is that it will take longer than a week or two to whip your finances into shape. Don't expect overnight miracles or weekend windfalls. Money management is a long-term, on-going project that really never ends until you do. Even then someone will have to pick up where you left off. Over a period of time, however, you can enhance your skills and improve your results enormously, accomplishments which make managing your money a much more enjoyable and rewarding task.

ACTION

Depending on the circumstances of each individual, the action steps in effective money management are virtually unlimited. But there are a few money management activities, such as budgeting, that apply to everyone. These are dealt with under various headings in the balance of the book. Some action steps need to be taken even before setting out to perform the most basic task of all, preparing a budget. These preliminary action steps will have to be repeated time and time again over your lifetime, but if you want to make your money count you must take them.

There are only three such steps. Some of you may consider them to be part of the *attitude* phase of money management because they require more thought than movement. But they need to be more than just a part of your attitude. You must actually take these steps by committing them to paper. This doesn't have to be done too formally — but it has to be done. Here they are.

Set Goals

You must set some financial goals. There are as many possible goals as there are people, multiplied by income and expenses. Your financial goals need to be very personal. They might include reducing debt, saving for a house down-payment, early retirement, a vacation, a new state-of-the-art CD player, and the kids' education. Your goals might include all of the above plus any number of others. But you must have goals. And they must be realistic goals.

A sure-fire formula for failure in money management is to set unrealistic goals for yourself. What inevitably happens is that you don't reach them, then you get discouraged and give up. So be sure your goals are realistic.

Reconcile Wants and Needs

You have to reconcile your wants and needs. Plan first for your needs and then turn your attention to your wants. To do otherwise will often have the same effect as setting unreasonable goals. You end up disillusioned and give up on your financial management program. Often this happens when success is just around the corner.

The key to reconciling wants and needs is setting your priorities. Which goals are most important to you? Be sure your activities are consistent with reaching those particular goals. It's best to have a strategy as well, but you definitely need goals.

When reconciling your wants and needs, don't overlook the possibility of trade-offs. For example, if you can't afford the house you *want*, then buy the bare minimum that you *need*. This way you'll be in the real estate market and will profit from future increases in prices rather than lose ground while sitting on the sidelines. It may well be worth commuting for two or three years in order to be able to afford the house you want, rather than forever living in rented accommodation and never achieving your dream. Or perhaps you can take that special vacation you've always dreamed about by keeping the car a couple of years longer. And so on.

Look around you. Usually, trade-offs can be made. But first you need to set your goals and reconcile your wants and needs.

File It

You must have financial records. Keep your records on the backs of napkins if you wish, or keep them in a personal financial affairs binder (there are lots of them on the market), or on a computer program if you're at the opposite end of the stick than the napkin doodler, but have them!

You should be able to look up your goals, budget, assets and liabilities and other relevant financial information. If you don't already keep some sort of financial file, start right now. Just start your file in whatever form you understand. You can hone your record-keeping skills as you go along. But get started.

Chapter 3

Personal Budgeting

DISPOSING OF THE MYTHS

Successful personal financial planning begins with budgeting and depends on it just as much as does the successful operation of a business. Yet even sophisticated business people, who wouldn't dream of trying to run their business affairs without a budget, will stagger along year after year managing their personal financial affairs on a hit-and-miss basis, avoiding the preparation of a personal or family budget like the plague.

This attitude exists because of some myths about personal budgets. Let's dispose of those myths right now.

A Budget Doesn't Cramp Your Style

A personal budget does not cramp your life style — quite the contrary. By forcing you to appraise your financial situation realistically and allocate available resources on a reasonable basis, the preparation of a personal budget will result in a certain peace of mind throughout the year. With a budget, you know exactly what type of vacation you can afford, when you can trade the car, or whether you can have that pool installed.

No Paper Pollution

Burdensome records need not be kept nor constant comparisons made to the budgeted figures. Actually, the budget itself is the only document you need add to your personal papers. Cancelled cheques, charge card slips, ordinary receipts, and memory (all of which you already have) are the only records required. As for making comparisons with the budget, this need only be done periodically: say, every three months; when you wish to check on a particular item; or when there's a significant change in your income or expenses.

Changes

Here goes another myth. Of course the budget can be changed — and it should be. Whenever a significant change occurs in your income or expenses, the budget should be revised. As a matter of course, many people prepare and revise their budgets on a sliding-year basis. Here's how it works.

Suppose a budget is prepared for a given year and at the end of August it becomes necessary to revise the figures. Don't merely revise the remaining four months of the year. Instead, prepare a new 12-month budget covering the period from September to the following August. The merits of this approach are obvious. You will always be reasonably current in your forecasts. You will always have handy the necessary financial information to plan your life style many months ahead, which tends to help prevent financial emergencies. You will find it easier and more interesting to prepare budgets this way.

No Special Skills Required

You don't have to be a chartered accountant to prepare a personal budget. By following the suggestions in this chapter, anyone, including older children, can work out a budget. Indeed, the entire family *should* participate in the exercise. This inspires adherence to the budget by all concerned — after all, they helped prepare it, thereby giving tacit agreement to live within it. In addition, if everyone participates in the budget's development each person develops an understanding of the family's financial circumstances and a feeling of responsibility, both of which tend to promote harmony in the home.

One approach which often works well is for each family member (including children) to prepare his or her own budget for items over which he or she has control. Then a budget meeting is held — after dinner some evening — and the individual budgets are consolidated into an overall family budget. In circumstances where some secrecy is in order, the procedure can be tailored to meet those particular needs.

HOW TO DO IT

A personal budget is really very uncomplicated. Many of us have been brainwashed by the complexity of government or business budgets into thinking that doing our own budget will be almost as difficult. Believe me, it is not. A personal budget consists simply of listing in an orderly fashion the amount of money we expect to receive and pay out over the next year, or whatever other period you decide to budget for. It is really a summary of when cash is received and paid out, and for what. That's the basis on which you should prepare it. For example, if you buy furniture for $1,000 to be paid for $100 a month for 10 months, you enter the $100 items, not the $1,000.

Here are a few suggestions for the actual preparation of the budget. The equipment requirements are a couple of sharp pencils and a few sheets of paper with fourteen columns drawn on them. An adding machine or pocket calculator would be helpful, but not absolutely necessary.

The first column is used for a description of the expected items of receipts and disbursements. The use of the second column will be described shortly. The next 12 columns will represent the 12 months being budgeted.

Divide the sheet horizontally into two sections. The first few lines, whatever number is necessary, will be used for cash receipts, and the rest of the lines (the second section) will be for cash disbursements. The only exceptions are the first line on the sheet, which should always be used for cash on hand at the end of the previous month, and the very last line on the sheet, which will be used for cash on hand at the end of the particular month.

The expected types of receipts and disbursements should be listed on the lines in the first column of the appropriate section. The appropriate totals for the year should be entered in the second column and then broken down under the respective months in columns 3 to 14. In some cases you will have to fill in columns 3 to 14 first in order to arrive at the total for column 2.

Cash receipts are apt to be fixed amounts and should be entered first. Remember it's your net income that's available for this purpose, not your gross.

When entering disbursements, first enter the ideal level of expenditures. Now the ideal level of expenditures depends on your particular circumstances. Although you often read and hear about suggested guidelines, such as a particular percentage of income, it's really quite dangerous to rely on such guidelines. For example, a family of six will spend a lot more on food than a married couple whose children have all grown up and moved out on their own. It costs a lot less for housing in Charlottetown than it does in

Toronto. What you should do is go back over your actual expenses for the last few months, adjust for increases in costs and obvious changes in circumstances and start from there. Even a good guess is better than not budgeting at all.

If it turns out that the ideal level of expenditures is unaffordable, you have to re-assess your plans. If you intend to borrow money, the loan proceeds should be reflected in cash receipts. Interest and loan repayments must be provided for in cash disbursements.

The most common error in beginning a personal budget is omitting cash on hand (which should be the first entry in the first month) and unpaid bills at the time you start (which should be the first entry under disbursements in the first month only — after the first month the expenses will automatically be included on the relevant disbursement line). When starting out be sure you don't include them twice.

The next most common error is overlooking certain disbursements. Don't forget the following: mortgage or rent payments; groceries; lottery tickets; lunch money; bus fare; laundry; house maintenance and repairs; clothing; furniture; medical, drugs and dental; insurance (life, car, house and other); books, newspapers and periodicals; charitable donations; cable and pay TV; birthdays, anniversaries and weddings; annual payments such as registered retirement savings plan contributions; property taxes; heating; telephone; water; entertainment; school costs; sporting equipment and registration fees for sports; club dues; car operation, licenses and repairs; vacation; and a little bit for that proverbial rainy day.

THE RAINY DAY

Whether you call it a contingency fund, emergency fund, slush fund, or anything else, the amount that you earmark for the rainy day may turn out to be the most important component of your personal budget.

Most people operate on some kind of built-in budget, even if they don't commit it to paper. They know how much their take-home pay is and have a fairly good idea of their major expenses. As mentioned earlier, where they suffer is in missing unusual items and, most important, not being able to handle a financial emergency — that rainy day. For example, you get laid off or the roof springs a $3,000 leak.

If you've been squirrelling away some funds, you're probably going to be able to weather the storm. If not, you may suffer a setback from which it will take years to recover. The best way to handle the rainy day is to consistently put away a little bit every payday into your emergency fund, or whatever else you call it. The best way to ensure you consistently put something away is to regard it as a regular part of your financial planning and an integral part of your budget.

You should have a particular amount in mind to build toward. A good rule of thumb is 10% of annual income. So, if your annual family income is $40,000 per year you should be shooting to build up an emergency fund of $4,000. Once the fund total is reached you can then turn your attention to making investments, upgrading your house or car, or whatever. But until the emergency fund target is reached, make contributions to the fund as a regular budget item, just like rent or mortgage payments.

Setting the goal and making regular contributions to the fund are as important as reaching the target. Without a set goal and without forming the habit of setting aside a regular amount you will probably never establish the emergency fund, let alone build it up to a significant level.

How much can be set aside each payday depends on too many individual circumstances for me to be able to tell you what's appropriate for you. The key is to include some amount in the budget and stick to it, even if it's only a couple of bucks a pay. Remember what I said back in Chapter 2 about setting financial goals. It's far better to set a low, realistic amount than to shoot for an unachievable level and end up with nothing in your fund. People have come up with some intriguing ways to establish their emergency funds. Some are as mundane as putting aside a set amount each pay, but others have scaled heights of innovation. Here are some I've run into that I love.

One person imposes a tax on himself every time he buys what he considers to be a luxury item, such as cigarettes, booze, dinners out, and cable television. He throws 10% of each such expenditure into his emergency fund. Another guy I know puts any two-dollar bill he receives into his fund. Another pretends to buy lottery tickets and instead puts the money into his own pot. Choose a method that works for you, but choose one and get at it.

Although an emergency fund is chiefly designed to handle a financial setback, its mere existence can provide peace of mind.

In the early stages of establishing your emergency fund, a daily interest savings account is probably the best place to put the money. When you accumulate over $1,000 you should consider buying a Canada Savings Bond every fall with the money in the savings account. If your fund has $5,000 or more you can consider investing in government treasury bills. The main point to remember when investing your emergency fund is to never invest in stocks or in anything else where you can't get all your money back quickly. Stocks, even if they're blue chip, might be down in value exactly at the time you need the money. The interest penalty on early cancellation of a guaranteed investment certificate could hurt, and there are all sorts of short-term dangers inherent in mutual funds.

BUDGETS WITHIN THE BUDGET

Once you get into the swing of personal budgeting you will find there are at least two occasions during the year which lend themselves to the preparation of their own budgets, in effect, two budgets within the budget. These occasions are vacation and Christmas.

By carefully budgeting these two events you are bound to save money, if for no other reason than you're more likely to stay out of debt if you budget them properly. Even if you end up borrowing for one or the other, a proper budget will help you to plan the borrowing and repayment so as to minimize interest expense.

There are so many variables involved in a vacation that it's virtually impossible to give you any guidelines on specific items. The main point, however, in preparing the vacation budget is to be sure no item of expense is overlooked. For example, people often work out all travel and accommodation costs but forget to include sales taxes and tips. When it comes to Christmas budgeting, though, there are some very definite steps that everyone can take for their own benefit and profit.

Controlling Christmas Costs

Christmas is a jolly but expensive time. Following are a number of suggestions which, if followed diligently, will help control the costs of Christmas.

There's really no magic to controlling Christmas costs. It's pretty much the same as trying to keep any cost centre under control. First we have to recognize what the costs are. Then we have to budget for them realistically. Next we have to resolve to stick to that budget. Finally, if we need to borrow for Christmas we should do it smartly (meaning wisely, not quickly).

Let's deal first with recognition of costs. Most of us make the mistake of budgeting only for the cost of gifts. Even that we do wrongly more often than not; but I'll come back to that shortly.

Christmas costs a lot more than what we spend on gifts. Our Christmas budget has to take into consideration other traditional costs such as: cards;

postage (for both cards and packages); extra food and drink; additional baby sitting costs; tree and decorations; new outfits for Christmas parties or extra laundry and dry cleaning; and extra cab fares (remember the RIDE programs).

Long distance telephone costs tend to balloon around Christmas because our calls increase in both frequency and length. And the telephone bill, like many others, doesn't hit us until January. Also, if you take a Christmas holiday, even a couple of days skiing, that's going to dent your budget. It's a fact that on any occasion when we have extra time off we tend to spend more money.

So you see the Christmas budget has to include many more items than gifts. For many people, however, gifts will represent the largest single item on the overall Christmas budget. That's why a detailed subsidiary gift list should be prepared. This is a *people* and *cost* list. Here's how you do it.

First, list all the people for whom you're going to buy gifts. Then, because there are bound to be changes, pencil in the *ideal* amount you think you can spend for each. Now add up your dollars. Then go back and revise the individual amounts (it never works out right the first time around).

Now that you've got your dollars in line, go over the gift list again, carefully and slowly, jotting down beside the names ideas for appropriate gifts within the price range you've already decided upon. Now you're ready to go shopping.

Go shopping early. With your gift list to guide you and lots of time to browse you can be very selective in choosing particular gifts. This allows you to stay within your Christmas budget and to avoid impulse buying. Be absolutely ruthless when it comes to staying within the list. Remember two things: most people would rather receive a modest, well-thought-out gift than an expensive, impersonal one; and one bad impulse purchase can wipe out your budget. It's also important to remember that if you fill an item on your list for less than the budgeted amount, you shouldn't transfer the saving to someone else on the list. This would just throw off the whole balance (no pun intended). It's better to keep your saving for an emergency. At Christmastime there'll be one along any minute.

Don't carry too much cash with you. Not only will this reduce the risk of losing it or being robbed, but for some strange reason people seem to shop more cautiously with credit cards at Christmastime than with cash. The reverse holds true during the rest of the year. Speaking of credit cards, always be sure it's *your* charge card you get back after the purchase has been rung up. This is a habit we should all acquire for year-round use.

Even if you assiduously adhere to all of the above, there is more to be done. When the charge account and credit card statements start rolling in during January and February, the next major step in financial security must be taken. Pay them off in full as they come in, even if you have to take out a consumer loan at the bank to do so! The interest saving will be enormous. Especially avoid the "no payment for thirty days" offers. These are just ways to increase your interest costs.

Follow these suggestions and next Christmas will be merrier.

EXAMINE OPTIONS

Although each chapter in this book deals with items that have an impact on family budgeting, you will gain most by examining your own family's affairs. Every item of expense should be evaluated to determine first, whether it's really necessary, and, second, whether there might be a more economical way of handling it.

Always remember that an increase of one dollar in your income is reduced by income taxes. But a decrease of one dollar in your personal expenses is a whole dollar more in your pocket.

Chapter 4

Financial Planning Is a Family Affair

The handling and management of a family's financial affairs should be a partnership. The roles children play are relatively minor, such as being consulted on some budget items; but it's important that children be brought into decisions such as the amount of their allowance. It's always been my experience that children are happier, better adjusted, and less demanding when they have a realistic idea of their family's financial status. As I said, their roles may be minor, but they should have roles. When it comes to spouses, though, both should be full partners in every respect in the family's financial affairs.

Unfortunately, whether both spouses are working or only one is bringing home the bacon, the partnership model is seldom followed. It doesn't seem to matter what the circumstances are, one spouse usually takes the dominant role in planning, handling and managing the family's finances. This is a mistake. *Both* spouses should be involved, at least to some extent.

GET YOUR SPOUSE INVOLVED

Married women who make their contributions to the family by staying at home to manage the household rather than going out to work seem to be the main victims of this situation, but even many spouses who contribute to the family's earnings often are not sufficiently involved in managing the family finances. So even though I'm going to refer to wives in this section (because the issues arise primarily for them) there is no sexism involved. In a household where the roles are reversed the issues remain the same.

Simply replace the female gender with the male and act accordingly.

There is a vast difference between *handling* money (for example, looking after the weekly household budget) and *managing* money (for example, planning long-term commitments like children's education and retirement). Both spouses need to be involved in both aspects of the family finances. They usually aren't.

Now, don't get discouraged because one of you enjoys running the finances and is interested in doing so while the other spouse hates the very thought and wouldn't be happy doing it. As you read on you'll see that both don't need to be totally immersed in the family's financial affairs, but both need to be completely aware of them.

The financial side of a family's affairs is like that of a business. Income and expense budgets must be considered (regardless of how informal such considerations might be), capital expenditures must be planned and evaluated, and provision must be made for long-term requirements.

These aspects of family finance should be decided by husband and wife as full partners in an enterprise in every sense of the word. Quite apart from her right to be completely informed of the family's financial affairs and her responsibility to be involved, common sense dictates that every wife be knowledgeable about her family's financial situation. If not, she may find herself in a financial maze when she is least equipped emotionally to cope with it — at the death of her husband. Married couples should realize the odds are overwhelming that the husband will die first. Therefore, at the very least, a wife should be completely aware of all details regarding wills, insurance, banking, assets and liabilities.

Wills

Everyone who owns any assets should have a will. It's the only way to ensure that what you own will go to the person you want it to, how you want it to, when you want it to, after your death. If you don't have a valid will when you die, the government will decide who gets what and when. Even single people with no dependents should have a will, but it is vital in a marriage for *both* the husband and wife to have up-to-date wills.

They both should know where the wills are kept, who the executors are, and the exact provisions of each will. Recourse to the courts is scant relief to the wife who discovers after her husband's death that he left everything to a favourite niece — better to thrash that one out now.

A common error is to make a spouse the *sole* executor of a will.

Having a spouse as a *co*-executor with a strong, knowledgeable second party capable of stepping in and taking charge upon the spouse's death is fine, but the surviving partner is usually in no shape emotionally to perform adequately as a sole executor. Don't make a person an executor just because he or she is a fine family friend. That's not doing anyone a favour. Executors should be chosen on the basis of reliability, competence and knowledge of the family and its affairs. Furthermore, don't name your executors without first obtaining their consent and showing them your wills. They may not want to act.

Wills are covered in more detail in Chapter 9.

Insurance

Both spouses should know how much insurance each has, what the payment options are (annuity, lump sum, etc.), which companies the policies are with, the steps required to collect the insurance and, believe it or not, who the beneficiary is.

Instances have occurred, for example, where the husband was adequately covered with insurance but had never gotten around to changing the beneficiary from his mother to his wife. Mother might well see that wife and kiddies are provided for, but might think it best that she continue to control the funds. The courts would sort it out, but better to solve the problem now.

A surviving spouse should also realize that payment of insurance is not automatic. Steps must be taken to collect it. A death certificate must be obtained and claims filed. Indeed, only a portion of the insurance may be released pending further legal requirements. All these things should be discussed with your insurance agent, the details noted and kept in a safe place.

Banking

Most people don't realize that upon the instant of death the deceased's bank accounts, possibly even joint accounts in some circumstances, may be frozen and safety deposit boxes sealed. The law, which varies from province to province, allows funds to be released for general purposes, with further releases for funeral expenses, etc. The safety deposit box can be opened to remove insurance policies and the will, but other items might remain unavailable until the will is probated. Check out what the law is in this respect in your particular province.

All of this suggests that both spouses should know what bank accounts exist at which branches, and the existence and contents of all safety deposit boxes, and should also know the names of key people at the bank and how to reach such people.

Assets and Liabilities

It seems trite to say that both spouses should be aware of the family's assets and liabilities, but in many cases only one of them knows the whole financial story. It isn't uncommon for investments such as stocks and bonds to languish unnoticed in a secret shoe carton or unknown safety deposit box. It also frequently happens that the surviving spouse is aware of the family assets — house, insurance, etc. — but is completely floored by the discovery of a large broker's margin account and two other bank loans about which only the deceased spouse knew.

HOW TO SOLVE THE PROBLEM

The solution, of course, is for both spouses to participate in all the major financial decisions. One of the best ways to start this is for both spouses to sit down and prepare a list of assets and liabilities, a rough budget for the coming year, and a summary of their wills. You should also prepare a sheet of pertinent data such as the names, addresses, and phone numbers of your lawyer, accountant, bank manager, broker, and insurance agent, the location of important papers, and a description of major assets and liabilities.

The best time to do it is tonight — just before you go to bed.

THE KIDS, TOO

There are two excellent ways to start your kids off on the right foot when it comes to understanding money and learning a bit about managing it properly. Give them an allowance and buy them some stock.

Although it is an excellent idea to give kids an allowance, some definite rules should be observed. First of all, make the allowance a reasonable amount taking into consideration the child's age, the area where you live, and the items which the allowance is expected to cover.

Next, and probably most important of all, the allowance should be absolutely unconditional — no strings attached. Don't give your kids an allowance and then tell them how to spend it, or not spend it. Let them learn by their own mistakes. If Sammy blows the whole allowance the first day on bubble gum, then he has to realize there's no more money available until next week.

Because an allowance, to be any kind of a teaching tool, should be used completely at the child's discretion, a child should not be expected to pay for necessities out of it, such as clothing and school supplies. Those items are your responsibility as parents. It's best to keep it that way. It's also a mistake to pay kids for doing chores around the house which they should be expected to do anyway. Everyone in the family should have responsibilities that have to be fulfilled without being paid for fulfilling them. It's fine if you want to pay a child for an extra effort. But you're not doing your kids a favour by paying them to keep their rooms neat or to help with the dishes.

Your children will learn a lot more about responsibilities and money management if you follow the above rules for allowances. Now to buying them some stock.

The next time your son or daughter has a birthday, or on some other special occasion, consider giving them a few shares of a public company as a gift. There's a lot to be said for it. First, if you restrict yourself to well-established, public corporations, your gift will increase in value over the years. But stay away from speculative stocks. Otherwise, the side benefits of the gift are apt to turn into negatives. Next, it's those side benefits that make the gift really worthwhile. Your son or daughter can learn a lot about how the Canadian economy works by following the stock in the financial press.

Register the shares in their names so they'll receive interim and annual reports from the company. They could even attend the company's annual meeting if they want to. These are also opportunities to learn about how companies, the market, and the economy work.

If the stocks pay dividends, *you* will be taxable on the dividends, but the child will receive the dividend cheques. These dividend cheques represent another important event for the child — often quarterly — and another opportunity to learn more about the economy. It's important that the dividend income remains theirs to do with as they wish, even though you pay the tax on it.

You don't need a whole lot of money to do it — ten shares of a ten-dollar stock can open up a whole new world for a kid.

Chapter 5

Choices

At the end of Chapter 3, I mentioned that every item of expense should be evaluated to determine, first, whether it's necessary and, second, whether there might be a more economical way of handling it. It's worth reminding you that an increase of a dollar in your income will be reduced by the income tax you have to pay on it, whereas a reduction of a dollar in an item of personal expense is a whole dollar that you get to keep or use somewhere else.

Effective money management often comes down to making choices. In this chapter, three such choices will be examined as examples of items of expense where savings might be easily made or at least where different courses of action should always be considered.

The first choice, whether to lease or buy, is a major consideration which could have a tremendous effect on one's financial well-being. The second, whether to use one of the bank plans for banking, is typical of a small item that could mean a saving of only a few dollars a year. But every little bit helps. Find 10 ways to save $100 and you're ahead $1,000 per year, which could mean a great deal when put toward, say, an insurance policy or your retirement fund. The third, whether to take out a long- or a short-term mortgage, is an example of where money may be saved, but perhaps an even more important factor should determine your decision.

LEASE OR BUY

Nothing is cheap these days. And as all consumers know, the purchase price of any object — from a toaster to a new car — is only the beginning. The buyer has to reckon with maintenance and service costs. There's also depreciation to worry about. Moreover, ownership involves hidden costs such as insurance and storage space. Bearing this in mind, should you really go out and spend $700 on a carpet cleaner when you could rent it for $25 some weekend? Does it really make sense to buy a car for $15,000 when you could lease it for around $450 a month?

There is no one answer. The decision whether to lease or buy is based as much on emotion as it is on rates of depreciation or utility factors. The point is that almost anything that can be bought can also be leased.

Whether it be a cactus plant, a mobile car telephone, an inflatable tennis court or a $5,000 oil painting, you probably have a choice of leasing it or buying it. The point is the comparison of the total cost between leasing and buying should always be made, particularly when a big-ticket item is involved.

As attractive as the monthly rate may be when compared to the purchase price, there is always the chance that leasing is not the more economical alternative. There is a fairly high mark-up involved in a leased item. Leasing is not for people who can't afford to buy. A person who can't afford to buy an item probably can't afford to lease it either. The exception is, of course, if financing the downpayment is the only impediment to being able to afford the object. In fact, to make sure that prospective lessees (that's you; the company you lease from is the lessor) can afford their monthly bills, the major leasing companies issue guidelines on the minimum income qualifications for their customers.

If you can afford to lease big-ticket items, a lease can offer advantages — often in terms of service and, sometimes, in terms of cost. For example, in the case of automobiles, lessors can usually offer you a saving because they can, through volume purchases, eliminate the car dealer's often substantial mark-up on new cars.

That doesn't mean that as the lessee you will automatically realize such savings. Unlike an outright purchase, the true costs of a long-term lease may be hidden in the fine print of a contract. Experienced lessees know that most leasing contracts read as if they were written by a team of lawyers trying to impress the law society. That's because they were. But stripped of legalese, there are basically two types of leases.

The Operating Lease

The first and more expensive is the operating lease, a typical example of which is a daily car rental. In this kind of arrangement, the company offering the equipment for lease looks after all transactions and maintenance.

The lease is usually relatively short-term, is cancellable (normally involving a penalty) and does not include an option to purchase the item when the lease is up. Most rentals of tools, boats and other equipment needed on a short-term basis, and particularly by individuals, are of this type.

The Financial Lease

Compared to the operating lease, the financial lease offers less of a service to the lessee. Financial leases are usually long-term (up to 75 or 80 percent of the economic life of the leased item), are non-cancellable without the payment of a fairly stiff penalty, and often include an option to purchase or renew at the end of the lease period. This form of lease is generally used for equipment leased by businesses and covers items ranging from fax machines to airplanes.

An individual is most likely to encounter the financial lease as the lessee of a car. Arrangements to lease a car are fairly standard these days. First, the leasing company will want to know how you intend to use the car: for personal or business use. If for the latter, what kind of business is it? After that, the car must be chosen — make, model, styling, colour and equipment extras. Then a contract will be drawn up.

You should resist the "standard contract." Insist on a contract tailored to suit your circumstances. A key factor in determining the cost will be how much the car will probably be driven. Taking this into account, and based on the cost of the car to the lessor, the estimated wholesale value of the car at the end of the lease period will be calculated, and a monthly leasing cost established. The key to making the right decision is whether that cost will be cheaper, overall, than buying the same car.

Let's take a look at a sample lease-buy decision. These aren't actual figures — just an example, but they will show you what you must take into account. The list price of the car is $15,000 plus sales tax of, say, 10%. Don't forget the sales tax. So the total cost is $16,500. If you took out a 14% loan to cover the purchase price, the total cost of the car over two years would be about $19,000. In two years, allowing for depreciation, the car would be worth about $8,000. Assuming that you can obtain that price for the car when you resell it, your net cost of ownership would be $11,000.

If you leased the same car, your monthly rate would vary, depending on the company you leased it from. You should keep in mind the importance of shopping around to obtain the best possible rate. Let's assume you could lease this car for $450 a month plus a tax of 10%. Your total cost of leasing for the two years would be about $12,000. So in this situation you would be $1,000 worse off by leasing.

Let's say you have the cash to buy the car. When making the comparison, instead of adding an interest cost to the purchase cost of $16,500, add the after-tax interest income you would have received if you had invested the money rather than buying the car.

As I mentioned, this example is just that — an example. In real life leasing often works out to be cheaper.

If you usually keep a car for three years or more before trading it, you will probably find an outright purchase more economical than leasing.

The value of a car depreciates at a much faster rate in the first two years than thereafter. In the above example, the car would probably depreciate about $11,000 in the first two years. In its third year, however, it would by normal standards only depreciate a further $2,000 or so. So if you drive at least 24,000 kilometres a year and trade in your car every two years, leasing may be economical. If you keep your car for three years or more, you will probably be further ahead to purchase it.

These calculations are based on a net lease. Another alternative is the open-end lease. With this type of lease, you agree — in return for a slightly lower monthly rental — to make up the price difference if your car, because of excess mileage, poor maintenance or any other reason, sells for less than the pre-arranged price when the lease expires. You could stand to gain from this type of lease if your car fetches more than the previously set amount.

The lease variations, like others involving maintenance and repair plans, are part of various packages that have developed in the car leasing business since leasing first became popular about twenty-five or thirty years ago.

MORE THAN CARS

As mentioned earlier, almost anything that can be bought can also be leased. Suppose, for instance, you move from Montreal to Toronto, but you aren't sure how permanent your stay will be. Furniture leasing companies will lease you furniture on a long-term basis with an important option: the lease can be cancelled at any time. Determining how much this privilege costs is difficult because of the discount rates involved in furniture selling. Certainly, if furniture leasing suits your needs, then it would be worthwhile to explore it. But it is not — and it is not made out to be — a bargain.

Leasing can be advantageous, however, if you are just starting out in business. One of the most novel alternatives offered in the field is the short-term rental of fully staffed and equipped offices. There are companies operating in all major cities offering clients very nice office space complete with furniture, telephone, fax and copying facilities, a receptionist and secretary, and the use of a boardroom — all for a monthly cost comparable to the salary and fringe benefit costs of one good secretary. This service is used mainly by firms which want to test out new market areas and by individuals who want to start a new business without making a heavy investment in rent and services.

If such a complete package is not required, you can still rent only what you need. Office furniture, fax and copying machines, word processors, telephone answering devices and other equipment can be leased at a cost that works out, over a long-term lease, to be only somewhat higher than the purchase price of the equipment.

You can also rent many other kinds of equipment, such as hand drills, chain saws, garden implements, scaffolding and trailers, on a short-term basis. While the cost is high compared to the usage time, rental firms do offer a definite service. They supply equipment that people use infrequently, have no room to store, or in some cases, no desire to look after. If you rent a boat trailer, for instance, it might cost you $100 for the weekend. Still, it may be more economical in the long run than buying one. The majority of people who buy trailers usually use them very few times in a year. In fact, the trailer often ends up being a storage facility rather than a transportation facility.

Most lease-buy decisions depend on your particular needs. Convenience, after all, is what most rental and leasing firms are selling, and when it suits your purposes to pay a premium for that convenience, it makes sense to lease or rent. Otherwise, if you can afford it, you may be better off to buy.

Always consider the alternative of leasing versus buying. On complicated and expensive lease decisions, you should shop around until you are satisfied you have the best leasing arrangement possible. Then establish the cost of purchasing the item. Work out the annual depreciation and anticipated maintenance costs involved in ownership over the terms of the proposed lease. Don't forget to add additional financing charges you may incur if you elect to buy. A comparison of these figures will give you an indication of the real costs involved in either leasing or buying. On a large item, to be absolutely sure, give your chartered accountant a call. There may be important considerations that you've overlooked in making the comparison.

SHOULD YOU JOIN A BANK PLAN?

Now let's turn our attention to an item far less significant in terms of dollars, but which is indicative of the everyday choices which individuals face. When decisions are made without proper consideration, costs result which could have been easily avoided.

Should you continue to pay a fee each time you use the services offered by your bank, or should you join a bank plan: the package of services offered for a flat fee? Well, as with leasing versus buying, it depends.

If you write more than 15 to 20 cheques a month, pay a lot of monthly bills, buy traveller's cheques at least once a year, and use a safety deposit box, having a bank plan is probably worth the monthly cost.

In some cases, it also helps if you tend to run out of cash on the weekend and aren't afraid of using one of the thousands of banking machines located all over the world.

However, if you don't fit this profile and still subscribe to a bank service, you're probably subsidizing some of the other subscribers.

Most financial institutions offer customers some form of service package. While the benefits of each are strikingly similar, there are some differences that could determine which plan you should choose, if you are one of those who could benefit from participating in a plan.

To decide whether a bank service plan is for you, analyze your banking habits. First, do you usually write a lot of cheques? All the bank service plans offer free, limited or unlimited cheque-writing privileges, and most people with a bank chequing account write at least five cheques a month. But bank plan users should consistently write 15 to 20 cheques a month to benefit from the free chequing privileges of a bank service plan. If you don't, you should make more use of some other part of the plan to compensate for this. Other services offered by the plans include:

1. overdraft protection;
2. no service charge on money orders or traveller's cheques;
3. free utility bill payment;
4. cheque cashing at any branch up to a limited amount, which varies from bank to bank;
5. a reduction on the personal loan rate (in some circumstances); and
6. a reduction in the charge for safety deposit boxes.

LONG-TERM OR SHORT-TERM MORTGAGE?

Finally, here is an example of a choice which must often be made but is sometimes decided on a non-financial basis.

Back in the good old days of consistently stable long-term interest rates, the choice of how long a term for which to take out a mortgage was a fairly easy decision. These days, though, people with mortgage renewals approaching are faced with the dilemma of whether to go for a short-term mortgage, lock in their rates for three years or more, or choose a variable rate mortgage.

The simple fact is no one can predict exactly what interest rates are going to be over any extended period of time. There is always a risk in opting for any of the available alternatives. If you go short-term and interest rates go up, you lose; if you go long-term and interest rates fall, you lose. The reverse, of course, is also true. Go short-term with interest rates going down and you win; go long-term with rates going up and you win. Variable rates eliminate the gamble, but don't in any way control your cost — you might still be either a winner or a loser.

However, there's another consideration that many people completely overlook. And it may be your most important consideration. It's this. If knowing for sure how much your mortgage payments are going to be over the next two to five years is more important to you than saving a couple of points in interest rates, then opt for the longer term. For many homeowners, knowing for sure how much their mortgage payments will be is more critical than saving every possible dollar of interest. So, for many people, it really comes down to whether they prefer to gamble or know for sure.

Personally, I'm a great fan of certainty.

Chapter 6

Registered Retirement Savings Plans

Banks, trust companies, insurance companies, brokerage firms and credit unions all offer RRSPs. For all I know, the neighbourhood drug store may be offering them by now. The range of types of plans covers everything from those with a safe, guaranteed return, to risky equity plans which could result in significant losses if the fund manager makes poor investment decisions.

Indeed, with so many financial institutions all busily trying to attract potential investors to the myriad plans they offer, it's little wonder many people leave the choice to an expert. Yet a lot of people who lack the necessary knowledge or advice still go it on their own, often ending up with a plan that's totally unsuitable for their age or financial circumstances.

For example, there's an overwhelming tendency to place too much emphasis on the income tax deduction aspect of RRSPs and not enough emphasis on the potential return. Often equally important (because they directly affect the rate of return), administration costs of the plan must be considered.

Many taxpayers wait until the last minute to open an RRSP and drop into the first institution they see with a sign in the window. Others go to a particular institution simply because they know an agent or have always dealt with a particular branch. Just because you had your plan one place last year doesn't necessarily mean you should keep it there this year.

But even if you're not an expert nor receiving professional advice, there are steps you can take to enhance your chances of getting the right plan for you. Whether you have professional help or not, the following points should be considered before choosing your plan.

1. Is it important that you're able to get your money out quickly in case of an emergency?
2. How much risk are you willing to accept as a trade-off for a higher rate of return?
3. Which plans are most compatible with your retirement and investment goals?
4. Which plans are most compatible with your age?

But even before getting into the details of these points, there are some other aspects of registered retirement savings plans to be considered.

SHOULD YOU HAVE AN RRSP?

A good place to start is by considering the question of whether you should even have an RRSP in the first place. Remember, not everyone qualifies for one. I'll deal with who qualifies shortly, but for now, assuming you qualify, should you be investing in an RRSP? There's no doubt whatsoever in my mind. If you have some money to save or invest, and you qualify to make deductible contributions to an RRSP, then you should. Here's why I feel so strongly about it.

First and foremost, you get an income tax deduction for the amount you put in an RRSP — up to certain limits, of course. This means the government becomes your partner in making the contribution. The result is you will have more money earning income for you than you would if you invested outside an RRSP.

Second, income earned in an RRSP is not taxed until you take it out of the RRSP. This, too, means that you will have more money earning interest for you than you could without an RRSP. Let's look at this in more detail.

If you're in a forty percent tax bracket and you contribute $3,500 to an RRSP, you're going to get a $1,400 tax refund. So, although you'll be earning interest in your RRSP on $3,500, you've only had to put up $2,100. Suppose you're going to get 9% interest. If you didn't put the money in the plan, you'd earn $189 in a year. But by putting the money into an RRSP, you're going to earn $315. This is because you've got more money working for you. It's the same as getting about 15% interest instead of 9%.

Then, you don't have to pay tax on the interest that's earned in an RRSP until you take it out. That means you're going to pay less tax by having your savings in the plan.

Let's continue on with the same example. If you don't put $3,500 in the RRSP, after a year you would have $2,289 earning interest. If you had contributed $3,500 to an RRSP, then $3,815 would be earning interest after a year. That's an increase of 67%. Compound that over a number of years and the difference is enormous.

I repeat, there's no doubt in my mind, if you qualify for an RRSP, and can afford it, do it.

NOT EVERYONE CAN

Unfortunately, not everybody *can* have a registered retirement savings plan. Even some of those who could might not get deductions for amounts put into the plan. Here's the situation in a nutshell.

First of all, if you're over seventy-one years of age, you cannot have an RRSP. Now, to the next point. Even if you can have a plan, there's seldom much to be said for putting money into an RRSP if it's not deductible for income tax purposes. It could cause a lot of aggravation and possibly result in penalties being levied.

To get a deduction for income tax purposes for money contributed to an RRSP you have to have had certain types of income. Wages and salaries qualify. So does any net profit you make from operating a business. Net rental income — that is, the profit you make on renting out a property — also qualifies.

Royalty income, if you're an author or inventor, qualifies. Alimony and maintenance payments received *do* qualify for purposes of calculating your RRSP contribution limits. But remember, deductible alimony or maintenance *paid* reduces the base on which you calculate your contribution.

Money received from a pension plan, including Canada Pension Plan and Old Age Security, qualifies for the 1989 taxation year. In fact, for 1989 you can contribute all or any of the amount you receive from pensions without affecting your regular contribution limits. So you might want to look into that. But remember that seventy-one-years-of-age limitation. Remember, too, that the rules regarding the treatment of pension income vis-à-vis RRSPs are slated to undergo a complete overhaul in 1990. As a matter of fact the government can't seem to make up its mind on pension income. So if you're receiving pension income always check the current law.

What's equally important in this list of income that qualifies you for an RRSP is the type of income that's *not* on it. Investment income and capital gains do *not* qualify for RRSP contribution calculation purposes.

1989 LIMITS

I mentioned earlier there are limits on the amount you can contribute. For the 1989 taxation year (remember you can make contributions up to March 1, 1990, and have them qualify for 1989) there is an overall annual limit of $7,500 or 20% of your annual qualifying income, whichever is the smaller amount.

There's another important limitation. If you belong to a pension plan or a deferred profit sharing plan, your overall limit drops to $3,500; and this $3,500 is reduced by any amount *you* contribute to the pension plan or deferred profit sharing plan yourself. The 20% limitation still applies, too. So watch your limits carefully.

POST-1989 LIMITS

At the time of writing it is proposed by the Minister of Finance that the limits on deductible contributions to RRSPs will change dramatically in 1991.

For people who are not members of pension plans or deferred profit sharing plans the percentage of qualifying income used to determine the maximum deduction will drop to 18% and will apply to your *previous year's* income.

As mentioned, there's an absolute dollar limit as well as the percentage-of-income limitation (whichever is the lower amount determines your deductible limit). For people who do not belong to pension plans or deferred profit sharing plans, it is proposed that this limit will be:

1990	$ 7,500
1991	$11,500
1992	$12,500
1993	$13,500
1994	$14,500
1995	$15,500

For example, if you had $30,000 of qualifying income in 1990 your 1991 contribution limit would be the lesser of 18% of $30,000 and $11,500. In this case your limit would be $5,400 (the 18%). On the other hand, if your 1990 qualifying income was $70,000, your 1991 deduction limit would be $11,500, it being lower than 18% of $70,000.

If you belong to a pension plan or a deferred profit sharing plan, for 1991 and subsequent years Revenue Canada will notify you what your allowable contribution to an RRSP will be. This is because the provisions in the Income Tax Act setting out the limitations in these circumstances are such that you need a degree in actuarial science and a mainframe computer to do the calculation.

Another important change that is also proposed to become effective in 1991 affects all RRSP holders. Beginning in 1991, if you are qualified to make a deductible contribution to an RRSP and you do not contribute the maximum amount, you can carry forward the difference and add it to your annual limit for any of the subsequent seven years.

Let's return now to the four key points to be considered in determining the type of plan that's right for you.

FLEXIBILITY

Your ability to make contributions without following a fixed payment schedule is extremely important in any plan. You have to consider whether you'll be able to commit a continuing fixed annual or monthly amount to an RRSP. This becomes extremely important in plans offered by life insurance companies which may require sustained payments over what may be the long life of an RRSP.

You should be aware that with such plans, substantial portions of early payments often go to cover commissions and administrative costs. An investor, forced by an emergency to withdraw funds early in the plan's life, could find the first year's payment gone. Most investors should avoid plans that commit them to following rigid deposit schedules and, instead, choose one or more of the other types of RRSPs available that allow contributions anytime at no fixed rate and withdrawals without a major penalty.

RISK AND COMPATIBILITY WITH GOALS

The next points investors have to consider are risk and compatibility with goals. In the context of RRSPs risk describes the range in rates of return you might expect from different types of plans. Guaranteed plans carry the least risk. With these plans you know in advance how much can be earned over a specific period, which could be anywhere from a few months to many years. Depending on the issuer and the length of the time, rates are usually one or two points below current interest rates.

At the other end of the stick are the equity funds whose returns are based on stock market activity. In theory, these could give a higher rate of return over the long term than other types of RRSPs if the value of the underlying stocks in the plan's portfolio grows.

But not all equity-based funds perform equally. For example, over a three-year period, the average annual compound rate of return for equity funds eligible for RRSPs might be 12%. Yet several would likely earn in excess of 20%, while a few might earn less than 5% annually. Some might lose. Over the long term, however, equity funds, on average, probably return less to investors than the guaranteed funds.

Clearly, stocks are not the best investments for all economic periods. In fact, the best-performing RRSPs during periods of high inflation are guaranteed plans.

The third type of fund, called the fixed income fund, is invested in bonds, mortgages or both. It is most suitable for individuals who are willing to accept some volatility in rate of return in order to get greater long-term gains, but who don't want to accept the extreme swings in value of equity funds. More experienced investors often spread their money among different types of funds, trading off expected return for a reduction of risk.

Remember, the rate of return you earn on your RRSP determines in large part the amount of money you will collect at retirement. An individual who contributes $3,500 annually to a plan for 30 years and earns an average rate of 5%, compounded annually, would accumulate almost $200,000. If that same person were able to earn an average return of 7% on annual contributions, over $280,000 would be available at retirement time. An average return of 9% would result in a total of over $400,000, while an average return of 11% would provide almost $600,000. It's easy to understand why many individuals choose the higher-risk funds even though they have proved poor investments during some periods.

Even small investors who are able to set aside, say, $1,000 a year, should spread the risk. They would be wise to split their contributions between two plans of the same type. By diversifying you reduce the possibility of investing everything in a plan that may not perform as well as others.

AGE

Finally, you have to take into consideration your age.

Because of the wide swings possible in equity fund performance, equity funds should not be considered by people approaching retirement age. They are best suited to taxpayers who can look at a 20-year, or longer, time span and who are not bothered by fluctuations of stock markets. Indeed, equity fund RRSPs should be avoided by people who may be forced to liquidate their plan prematurely for whatever reason.

Now let's look at the different types of plans.

OVERVIEW

There is no one registered retirement savings plan — or institution — that is exactly right for all people. If there was, there would only be one institution offering one type of plan. That's obviously not the case. There are many types of plans, and many different institutions offering them.

I would need to know all about your financial situation and personal investment and retirement philosophies before recommending a particular type of plan, or even a particular institution for that matter. So, I can't do that. What I can do, though, is describe generally the various types of plans which are available. This should help you make your own individual decisions.

Let's start with what's usually referred to as an equity plan. In an equity plan the money you invest is pooled with that of thousands of others, and then invested in the stock market. The value of an equity plan will fluctuate with the value of the shares it holds and the ability of the fund manager to make sound investment decisions.

As you probably have already guessed, the equity fund gives you the best opportunity to make a lot of money in your plan. However, it also offers a real possibility of ending up with less than you contributed — almost an impossibility with most other types of plans. Check some of the plan values on October 20, 1987, against what they were a week earlier, for example.

Because of this, an equity fund is a particularly poor choice during the years just prior to retirement. Its value might be way down at the very time you need the money.

Luckily there are other types of plans, because plans that invest in the stock market are not the best for many people. In my opinion, they're suitable only for gamblers. Anyway, on to some other types.

There's the fixed income fund. The income isn't really fixed, but the plan invests in debt instruments with fixed returns, such as bonds and mortgages. With interest rates so volatile these days, you must have a very astute investment manager for this type of plan to be attractive. As already mentioned, it does offer a middle ground between the risky equity funds and the perfectly secure guaranteed fund. It's probably the best choice for investors who want to take some risk on their rate of return, but also want some protection against erosion of their principal.

Next, there's the guaranteed fund. The guaranteed fund is just that. You are guaranteed a specific rate of return for a specific period of time. This plan's obvious attractiveness lies in the certainty of return. Over the long haul this is your best bet. I love guaranteed funds.

Then there are the specialty funds, those that invest in, say, nothing but oil stocks, or real estate, or the gold fund, and so on. These fall into the same category as equity funds. You might make an awful lot or lose an awful lot. These are definitely not for people nearing retirement. The value of the plan might be down just when you need the money.

Of course, you needn't opt completely for any one type of plan. You can, if you wish, spread your investments among various types of plans. So let's examine the different types of plans in a little more detail.

EQUITY PLANS

Equity plans, which are those that invest in stocks, give you the greatest potential return for your investment, but also carry the highest risk.

The risk factor in these plans was most apparent in the fall of 1987 when the stock market plunge saw many investors scurrying to get their nest egg to a safer place, in many cases too late.

But if you are not upset when the stock market takes a nosedive, and if you can take a long-term outlook for investment, equity funds can be rewarding.

Even during a period of mediocre market performance, for instance, some equity-based plans outperform their more sedate relatives. But many don't. However, as a group, equity funds perform better than fixed income or guaranteed funds in periods of low inflation.

For investors willing to gamble on this scenario, a wide array of equity-based plans is available. Banks, trust companies and insurance companies all sell equity funds. Stock and mutual fund brokers also offer these RRSP alternatives. Even a couple of department stores have entered the field by offering a series of house brand funds, some of which are eligible as RRSPs. Keep in mind that not all mutual funds sold in Canada are eligible for retirement plans; the fund's prospectus will inform you if the units qualify for RRSPs.

Fund performances vary widely. Most funds will have a performance close to the market average with a few either greatly outperforming or underperforming the market index.

If more than one ending date is considered for measurement, the results suggest that very few funds consistently outperform or underperform the market in either rising or falling periods. Of those that are consistently at either end of the performance spectrum, superior or inferior results are usually attributed to the decisions of a single individual. A fund is not apt to disclose to investors who is responsible for deciding what stocks are bought and sold for the portfolio. In any event, a committee makes the investment decisions in many cases, and its membership changes from time to time. Committees rarely outperform the market.

Because of this, the majority of equity funds will have, over time, returns comparable to those of the indexes. The reason is relatively simple.

Most fund management committees try to determine which industry groups or stocks will outperform the market, and which will not. They reach a consensus and buy and sell stocks to fit the model they've created, usually based on a stock market index.

However, most other fund management groups would act in a similar fashion and because they all use the same type of brokers' reports and attend the same meetings, it's no surprise that results don't differ substantially from group to group. Because these fund managers' decisions represent a high percentage of the trading on stock markets, the results of professional management and general stock market performance are similar.

Most fund managers are unwilling to load their portfolios with high-risk stocks because this strategy proves unprofitable during a period of volatile stock market performance. A more common strategy is to increase or decrease the portion of the portfolio held in cash according to the manager's expectations of the market's direction. Again, because most institutional managers use the same information in arriving at their decisions, this strategy also seldom leads to consistently superior performances.

A handful of fund managers have been able to outperform their competition. They've done this by ignoring the performance of the markets as the basis for their portfolio holdings. Rather, they have been bold enough to concentrate the bulk of holdings in stocks or industry groups which they believe to be the most undervalued. Such a strategy might lead to buying a holding of, say, 50% oil shares during a time when these are out of favour, then switching out of these into cash or another industry group as the value of oil stocks comes back.

Managers who are agile enough to use this type of portfolio strategy usually show positive results even in periods when the market falls. The problem facing investors is that this type of manager is a rarity. The best investors can hope for is to sort through the funds' results and spread their money among two or three equity funds that appear more often than not among the better performers.

If you are still committed to investing in equities your first step should be to examine past performance records. Even though the historical results of fund management can't be used to predict future performance with any degree of accuracy, the small investor has few other indicators available. A small investor's account is not large enough to demand detailed information about portfolio managers' experience, size of analytical staffs, or investment strategies.

Such information is readily available only to multi-million-dollar corporate or union pension funds. But there's consolation in the fact that these large investors obtain results comparable to the small investor's.

When you use historical records, begin by rejecting any fund which consistently ranks below the average performance of the group. Once you've narrowed your choice to funds which usually match or beat market performance, examine the size of the fund. Be suspicious of top-performing funds with low assets. Many fund managers have been unable to sustain top performance once their funds grow into millions; the result is that the larger size has forced them to broaden their choice of stocks, leading to a respectable, but average, performance. Also examine the fund's investment objectives to make sure the fund's objectives are compatible with yours.

When you've narrowed the field down to a handful, it's time to compare costs, including registration and redemption fees, if any. Published performance figures tell only part of the story. Beware of funds having high sales charges or front-end loads. If you invest in these funds, out of every dollar you contribute, as little as ninety cents may be invested on your behalf. In most cases, a sales charge does not assure superior performance. But if you are interested in specific funds that can only be purchased through a sales agent, determine if the commission is negotiable. The increased availability of funds which are sold without charges has caused many mutual fund operators and brokers to be flexible about front-end loads. In some instances it's possible to bargain for a lower rate.

If you are unwilling or unable to investigate the various equity RRSPs available, probably your best bet lies with some of the no-load or low-load funds sold by trust companies. While these funds are not usually among the top performers, they also seem to avoid the bottom.

An equity fund RRSP, almost by definition, offers diversification by spreading your money among many different stocks. Even so, it's best not to gamble that any single manager will give consistently superior performance. Rather, spread your retirement savings among two or three funds. This way you lower the chance of having all your money with one manager, who for one reason or other may not keep up with the competition.

FIXED INCOME FUNDS

Fixed income registered retirement savings plans provide a middle-of-the-road alternative to guaranteed RRSPs and equity-based plans. By relying on investments in the bond and mortgage markets, which are generally more stable than the stock market, fixed income RRSPs provide an excellent balance between higher-risk equity-based plans and the very secure guaranteed funds.

Indeed, during periods of high but stable interest rates, when the growth rate of inflation is relatively constant, fixed income RRSPs can be consistently good performers. Although they do poorly during periods when inflation and interest rates are rising, they perform well when both inflation and interest rates are falling.

Fixed income funds are alternatives for individuals who are unwilling to accept the broad variations in rates of return that come with owning a stock-based plan. They are worthwhile investments if you are willing to put up with a little risk as a trade-off for the possibility of a better return than guaranteed RRSPs deliver.

What happens is your RRSP buys units in the fund, becoming a part owner of the bonds and mortgages in the overall portfolio. The financial institution charges a management fee, usually a percentage of the value of the account; any profits or losses are charged to the fund. This differs from guaranteed RRSPs in which investors lend the institution their money for a fixed term at a fixed interest rate. Fixed income funds are available through most financial institutions and many mutual fund dealers.

Units in a fixed income fund are valued at the total worth of the portfolio divided by the number of units outstanding. The number of units changes as new contributors invest in the fund or others redeem their units. The value of the units of any bond or mortgage fund unit changes with variations in interest rates. If rates rise, the value of outstanding bonds or mortgages falls and if interest rates decline, the market value of the portfolio goes up.

Unit prices of fixed income funds move in a similar manner because each fund unit represents part ownership in a portfolio which may contain hundreds of bonds or mortgages that can differ from each other in quality, coupon rate and term of maturity. Each shift in interest rates or change in demand for bonds of a specific quality or term will increase or decrease the value of the total portfolio and, in turn, affect the price of a unit of the fund.

Depending on the type of financial institution managing the portfolio, fund values are calculated on a daily, weekly or monthly basis.

The rate of return earned on a fixed income fund depends largely on how the manager structures different types of bonds and mortgages in the portfolio.

During a period of low inflation a portfolio with a lot of long-term bonds would have a higher return than one with shorter maturities. But even in bond and mortgage portfolios, high-return securities can mean higher risk. If interest rates rise, the fund with the longer maturities would fall in value more than one with a portfolio of shorter maturities.

The shorter bonds, while yielding less, are not as volatile because the date when money can be re-invested is closer. Consequently, a bond manager expecting interest rates to be stable over a long period would include in the portfolio a heavy weighting of high-coupon, long-term bonds to maximize the fund's income.

Bonds issued when interest rates were lower than today's trade at a discount from their issue price. A manager who expects interest rates to remain stable for a long period will not usually hold large amounts of such bonds in a portfolio. Instead, the manager will buy high-coupon bonds which provide high current income now as opposed to a low current income from discount bonds and a large lump sum gain at maturity. The manager would do this because the additional income can be re-invested, giving the fund additional revenues. But a manager who expects a substantial drop in rates over a short period may switch to discount bonds and improve the fund's short-term performance.

If a manager is correct in anticipating the timing and direction of interest rate swings, the fund's performance can be enhanced substantially. On the other hand, errors in judgment could prove costly to the fund's investors.

Mortgages usually pay a higher rate of return than bonds. However, historically there has been little difference in performance between well-managed bond funds and well-managed mortgage funds. The trading flexibility a bond fund manager has relative to poorly marketable mortgages offsets the higher interest rates usually available from mortgages.

Because of the similarity in returns, cost should be given serious consideration along with the fund's historical performance when choosing a fixed income RRSP.

Here are some steps to follow. First, narrow your choice by eliminating any fund which consistently ranks below the average performance of the group. While this judgment should be made on as long a term basis as possible, some funds have only been in existence a few years and should not be eliminated for this reason alone.

Second, examine the size of the fund. Be suspicious of top-performing funds with only a few hundred thousand dollars as assets. The managers of such funds might not be able to sustain top performance if the fund's characteristics change through growth.

Once you've narrowed the field down to a handful, it's time to shop for cost. Registration, administration and withdrawal fees vary widely among institutions. These charges can make a substantial difference on your overall return. On the other hand, don't forget it's net return that matters.

Before you buy, remember the old saying about putting all your eggs in one basket. It's best to hold your retirement savings in more than one fixed income RRSP to reduce the risk of having all your retirement savings with a manager whose luck or judgment turns bad.

GUARANTEED FUNDS

Guaranteed registered retirement savings plans offer the most security and are the only plans that should be considered by individuals approaching retirement age. In fact, anyone in their mid-50s or up whose retirement nest egg is locked into RRSPs should be in this type of plan. Guaranteed funds are also ideal for individuals who are unwilling to assume the risks that come with owning units in equity and fixed income RRSPs.

With a guaranteed plan, a financial institution contracts to pay you a specific rate of interest for a specified period of time. After that term expires, the rate paid can be revised up or down to a new level which remains in effect for an additional period. Depending on the fund, this rate might be guaranteed from one month to a number of years.

In effect, you are lending the financial institution your money for a specified period of time. The institution, in turn, agrees to guarantee you a stipulated rate of interest whether or not they make a profit by re-lending your funds. The advantage to you is knowing in advance that at the end of the period the value of your RRSP will be the principal amount in the plan at the beginning, plus interest on that amount at the rate of return guaranteed by the institution.

You do pay a price for this security. You can usually expect to earn between one or two percentage points below the prevailing mortgage rate; the difference becomes the institution's markup. Still, this sacrifice of higher return in exchange for security is essential for many people.

There is usually a choice between two types of guaranteed plans. One is in many ways similar to a bank account without chequing privileges. This type of plan — a special savings account — can be pulled out anytime without any major penalty. The interest rates paid are relatively low. Interest rates paid in savings account RRSPs are guaranteed for fairly short periods — as little as one month and as long as six months — depending on the institution.

These types of RRSPs are the most flexible as far as withdrawals are concerned, and they are the quickest to reflect changes in interest rates. They are the most suitable plans for individuals within two or three years of retirement or for anyone who doesn't want to be locked into a plan for an extended period.

Savings account RRSPs are also used by individuals who believe that the trend of interest rates is up. These plans are among the best performers of all types of RRSPs during such a scenario. Those who believe rates will rise during the short term can use savings account RRSPs as a temporary haven and later switch to a guaranteed plan with a locked-in period or to a fixed income or equity RRSP.

The other type of guaranteed RRSP, a guaranteed investment certificate RRSP, requires that you agree to leave money deposited for a term of one to five years. This allows the institution to re-lend your money with some knowledge as to how long it will have the use of your funds. For instance, if money is deposited with a trust company which guarantees interest rates for five years, then the trust company can re-lend that money also for a five-year period. Even so, if an emergency develops you can pull your money out of most plans before five years is completed, but be prepared to pay a penalty in the form of a substantial reduction in interest received.

People who invest in plans with long lock-ins when inflation is high get better rates than people who invest when inflation is on the downswing. In the early 1980s when interest rates in Canada were near or at historically high levels, locked-in guaranteed funds had enviable performance records and attracted many investors who, in previous years, put their money into equity funds. Many of them have stayed with the guaranteed plans.

Regardless of whether you choose a guaranteed savings account RRSP or one with a locked-in period, you can save money by shopping around and matching a plan to your own situation. Interest rates, as well as registration, administration and withdrawal fees, vary widely among institutions. And don't just look at interest rates. Fee charges can make a difference on your overall return.

For instance, assume a guaranteed savings account offering a 10½% interest rate for six months. This fund has no other administrative or withdrawal fees. A second fund guarantees 11%, also for six months, but with a 1% withdrawal penalty up to $100 if the plan is terminated. The first plan is the better investment for individuals who have less than $20,000 accumulated when they close their RRSP. For larger amounts, the second plan is preferable.

Another point to consider in choosing a guaranteed RRSP is the frequency of interest compounding. This is important because it can affect the return you can receive. For instance, an institution offering 8½% compounded annually would pay $85 interest on principal of $1,000 at the end of one year. One offering 8½% compounded semi-annually would pay $42.50 interest after six months and an additional 4¼% on $1,042.50 — about $44.13 — six months after that.

Compounding semi-annually has the effect of raising the return to almost 8.7%. Although the increased return seems small, the difference between annual and semi-annual compounding can be tremendous over the life of your RRSP. A few financial institutions even compound interest quarterly and others monthly, so it pays to shop around.

THE INSURANCE RRSP

By any measure, cash value life insurance policies make poor registered retirement savings plans. Indeed, such plans fail in the most critical areas of plan selection: flexibility and rate of return relative to risk. They are also, when registered as RRSPs, an expensive way of buying life insurance.

Failure to keep up premiums on these policies could lead to their cancellation and the loss of insurance coverage which may not easily be replaced. It is under such circumstances that investors discover what poor investments they have chosen. Sometimes people learn to their chagrin that they don't even get back all their investment. In fact, in the early life of such plans, it is common for the cash surrender value to be nil. This is because early deposits go to cover non-refundable commissions and administration costs. Consequently, people who decide to switch plans find that they have paid a heavy penalty for not investigating all options earlier.

Tax laws allow the cash surrender portion, the so-called savings element, of life insurance policies to be registered as RRSPs. As a result, many people buy these plans in the belief they are providing their families with adequate insurance coverage and themselves with good retirement savings plans. These investors fail to realize that these plans were designed to provide life insurance, not be be cashed in for retirement savings.

The worst possible insurance RRSP alternatives are ones involving the registration of whole life insurance policies. Ordinary whole life policies require the payment of premiums every year for life in order to keep the death benefit provisions in effect. Limited-pay life policies are similar except that the premium period is limited to a specific time, usually the age at which the policy holder expects to retire. With both types of policies, the insurance benefit is paid at death.

Tax laws require RRSPs to be terminated when you reach a certain age (71 at the time of writing), but by doing that you cancel your policy and may lose the insurance benefit. Indeed, you may have paid expensive whole or limited pay life premiums for coverage which expires at age 71 — and received a return on your savings as little as half that of guaranteed plans.

A third type, endowment insurance, is the only one designed to mature and pay a benefit during policyholders' lives. These once popular policies have fallen from favour as investors have realized that low rates of return make them an expensive way of saving money.

Investors who want a combination of life insurance and retirement savings are probably better off getting term insurance in the amount they need to suit their individual requirements and then choosing an RRSP to accommodate their financial situation and age.

Such a strategy has several advantages, the most important being a high degree of flexibility in making deposits into the RRSP. Also important is the cost of the insurance element. Term insurance is relatively inexpensive for younger men and women and allows them to purchase large amounts of coverage when it is most needed. Like RRSPs, costs of insurance vary widely among companies so it pays to shop around for coverage.

SELF-DIRECTED PLANS

Self-directed registered retirement savings plans allow you to make all your own investment decisions. The plans can be tailor-made to suit your whims, needs, preferences and hunches. Indeed, a self-directed plan can be as risky as you make it. Properly managed, it can offer rewards exceeding those of institutionally managed RRSPs. However, most self-directed programs are usually mismanaged, resulting in poor returns.

A major advantage of self-directed plans for sophisticated investors is that they allow concentration in certain types of investment, such as high-yield mortgages or stripped bonds, which may not be readily available in institutional funds. Self-directed plans also allow stock investors the flexibility to quickly change industry groups or switch to cash or debt instruments.

A self-directed plan requires some investment sophistication and should be considered as an alternative to professionally managed funds only by individuals with a good knowledge of some of the investment alternatives that qualify for inclusion in the plan. Of course, investors can always retain investment counsel to manage their self-directed plans, but this is an additional expense, and is no guarantee of superior performance.

Setting up a self-directed plan is relatively simple. The arrangements have to be made through an institution which acts as administrator and trustee or as an administrator that deals with a trustee. The institution accepts your deposits and receives or delivers any securities you may have bought or sold.

The cost of operating a self-directed plan can be relatively high compared with other types of RRSPs because of the extensive administrative work needed, particularly where there are only a few thousand dollars in the plan. Charges vary widely among the companies that offer self-directed plans and there may be additional charges for each transaction depending on the particular company's arrangement. For small amounts in a fund — say, under $10,000 — the costs of administering a self-directed RRSP may erode any advantage of using such a plan.

When you have a self-directed plan, keep in mind that there is a penalty for holding non-qualified investments. For example, a stock may come under this category if the company moves outside Canada, becomes private, or its shares are exchanged for non-qualified securities, as in some mergers. With a few exceptions, for as long as such a security is held the plan is subject to a pretty hefty tax penalty.

Most individuals who take out self-directed RRSPs do so because they expect to earn a higher return than that available with managed funds. They expect to do this either through their own idea of having superior knowledge or through the expert advice of their advisors. Some succeed. Many fail.

The successful ones have a number of things in common. They usually concentrate in certain types of securities that are not found in large portions in institutionally managed funds; they are diversified but not overly so; and they sometimes contain relatively high-risk securities.

However, in the case of stocks, the higher risk with a self-directed plan is partially offset by the plan's greater flexibility. The small size of these plans, relative to the multi-million-dollar pooled funds, allows sophisticated investors to switch portfolio mix at will.

A popular strategy is to concentrate stocks in specific industries in the expectation that such industry groups will greatly outperform the whole market. Success in using this strategy depends on your ability to sell and switch to other investments or to hold cash. Many investors who attempt this strategy fail because they put all their money in too few stocks, or they depend on the same advice available to every other player in the market.

The minimum amount needed to justify a self-directed plan really depends on the type of securities mix an individual wants in an RRSP portfolio. For stocks, probably enough diversification can be built into a portfolio worth $30,000. For mortgages, the amount needed for diversification may be in the $50,000 to $60,000 range; some experts use substantially higher figures. The mortgages do not have to be owned by one individual but can be held by several parties.

In theory small portions of mortgages, say only a couple of thousand dollars, could be placed in a self-directed RRSP. However, most of the mortgage brokers, accountants and lawyers who deal in mortgages don't like dividing them into such small amounts because of the administrative costs involved in servicing them. Many prefer minimum investments in the $50,000 range and up.

You should not dabble in a self-directed RRSP without familiarizing yourself with the income tax rules affecting RRSPs. In particular you have to be completely knowledgeable about which investments qualify and which don't.

The main disadvantage of the self-directed RRSP, though, is this. If you get wiped out you have absolutely no one else to blame. And if you're that good at picking investments, why aren't you making your living at it?

SPOUSAL RRSPs

If you qualify for a contribution to an RRSP and you are married, you can make a contribution to an RRSP opened in your spouse's name. You will get a deduction against your income for the amount contributed, up to the amount you could otherwise deduct on your own behalf. You can do this even if your spouse makes contributions to his or her own plan.

You cannot, though, double up on your own contributions. For example, suppose you're entitled to contribute $6,000. If you put, say, $4,000 into a plan for your spouse, you could only put $2,000 into your own plan.

Transfers of amounts from pension plans to a spousal plan are limited to $6,000 per year, and even this is scheduled to disappear in 1994. Transfers from other RRSPs must go into your own plan, not your spouse's.

If you make contributions to a spousal RRSP, any amounts withdrawn from that plan, except on maturity of the plan, will be taxable in your hands instead of your spouse's, up to the amount you contributed to the plan in the year of withdrawal and the two preceding years. This rule does not apply in the event of a marriage break-up.

Why would you want to set up a spousal plan? Well, it would be a good idea if your spouse's tax bracket is apt to be lower than yours when the money comes out. In most families this is probably going to be the case. Or, the plan might allow your spouse to take advantage of the annual pension income credit later on.

Remember, though, it's prepaid alimony. Once the money goes into a spousal RRSP it belongs to the spouse.

PUTTING YOUR MORTGAGE IN YOUR OWN RRSP

A few years ago, Revenue Canada admitted that under certain circumstances you could hold your own mortgage in your own RRSP.

Now before you run out to do this, bear in mind that a number of conditions apply. First of all, you have to have a self-directed RRSP. That's not difficult to arrange, but does cost a bit. Next, the mortgaged property must be in Canada. The mortgage must be administered by an NHA-approved lender; and it must be insured by Central Mortgage and Housing

Corporation or a private mortgage insurance company. Finally, the mortgage must have rates and terms similar to those existing in the general market.

Okay, so should you or should you not have your mortgage in your own RRSP? I wish I could tell you, but I simply don't know the answer. I worked out comparisons on a number of situations and the results were not conclusive. I recommended against doing it based on future uncertainty and the difficulty of getting a good rate of return on re-investing the monthly mortgage payments. However, it's conceivable there could be scenarios which would make it a beneficial move.

The main points to remember are these. First, there are a lot of costs involved, such as appraisal fees, legal fees, mortgage insurance fees, set-up fees, mortgage administration fees and fees for administering your self-directed RRSP. Second, you lose some flexibility.

If you have your RRSP money in a normal self-directed plan, you can switch in and out of term deposits, guaranteed investment certificates, stocks, bonds, and other money market securities very quickly and very easily.

However, as any of you who have ever had to re-mortgage a property know, it takes a lot of time and a fair amount of red tape to pay off a mortgage and take out a new one. There are legal and other fees, searches, registrations and so on to be taken care of. So, if you're holding your own mortgage in your own RRSP, you will simply not be able to act as quickly or as easily as if you had more traditional investments in there.

Remember, if you have your own mortgage in your own RRSP, you have to deal with yourself exactly as you would with a total stranger. Stray from this even a little bit and you may well have Revenue Canada breathing down your neck.

Theoretically you can do it; but from a practical standpoint very few people would gain from having their mortgage held by their own RRSP.

BORROWING MONEY FOR AN RRSP IS PROBABLY NOT WISE

For many years now, interest on money borrowed to put into a registered retirement savings plan has not been deductible for income tax purposes. Money borrowed since November 12, 1981, to be put into an RRSP will not give rise to deductible interest. In addition if you still have some of those pre-November 12, 1981, loans on which you're deducting the interest, don't be surprised if Revenue Canada gets curious about it. After all, it's been quite a while since the law was changed. Anyway, the question now is should you borrow money to contribute to an RRSP. In my opinion, you should borrow *only* if you will be able to pay off the loan fairly quickly.

For example, if you had a guaranteed investment certificate or term deposit coming due in a month or so, it might be better to borrow for the short term so as not to lose too much interest by cashing your GIC or term deposit early. Now, that doesn't mean you would never be better off by borrowing for your RRSP. As a matter of fact, depending on the rate of interest you have to pay on the loan, you would in all likelihood come out further ahead by borrowing, provided you left the money in the RRSP long enough.

There is no doubt it makes sense to borrow money to contribute to an RRSP if you're able to pay off the loan over the next year or so, and you intend to leave the money in the RRSP for a long time, at least for a few years.

However, if you have to borrow to put money into an RRSP, and you can't pay off the loan within the next year or so, then you have to give some serious thought as to whether you can really afford to have an RRSP. As theoretically attractive as a particular investment might be — and RRSPs are investments — if you can't afford it, don't do it. But if you can afford to service the debt, and you can pay off the loan within a reasonable time, and you know you can leave the money in the RRSP for a long time, and that's the only way you can make an RRSP contribution, then go ahead. You'll *likely* be better off — but not *definitely.*

This raises another often debated point about RRSPs: given the choice, should you pay off a part of your debt rather than put money into a plan? Although it is clearly possible to create scenarios in which you would be better off in the long term paying off debt than putting money into an RRSP, in most cases you will be better off putting the money into the RRSP. There are a number of reasons for this. First, you pay less income tax. Second, the tax-sheltered compounding within the RRSP causes your principal to grow at a truly amazing rate (often as much as three times what could be accumulated outside the plan). Finally, there are strict limits on how much you can contribute to an RRSP, so fill that up first and then concentrate on paying off debt.

GETTING YOUR MONEY OUT

The Income Tax Act now allows you to take all or any part of the funds out of an RRSP at any time. If you do, you have to include the full amount withdrawn in income for tax purposes and there will be income tax withheld at the time of withdrawal. Of course, this withholding tax will reduce your ultimate tax bill. Your RRSP itself may have some restrictions on when and how money can be withdrawn.

Before the end of the year in which you reach your 71st birthday, the Income Tax Act (at the time of writing) requires that you do one of four things with the money in your RRSP, or else you will have to pay tax on the full amount in your plan or plans.

The first option is to take the money out. This, too, will result in the full amount being included in income for tax purposes.

The second option is to buy a life annuity. The third option is to buy a fixed-term annuity (say to age 90). The fourth option is to transfer the funds in your RRSP to another investment vehicle called a Registered Retirement Income Fund, which will be the subject of the next chapter.

Two of these options, the two types of annuities and a RRIF, offer an additional deferral of tax. Income tax has to be paid only as money is received from the annuities or is withdrawn from the RRIF. Most people opt for the RRIF because of its greater flexibility and the disadvantages of being completely locked in with annuities.

Actually, any of these options can be chosen at any time up to age 71; but remember, at age 71 you must choose.

MORE THAN INCOME TAX TO CONSIDER

Registered retirement savings plans have been called the most important tax shelter in Canada. That's probably true. The combination of an income tax deduction for your contribution and the sheltering of the income earned inside the plan makes for rapid growth of your capital.

If you invested $1,000 in an RRSP each year for thirty-five years, earning 10% per annum, you would accumulate almost $300,000. If you are in a 50% tax bracket all the way, your total cost is only $17,500. The same amount invested outside the RRSP would net you around $100,000. The earlier you can begin investing in an RRSP the more magnificently your capital will grow.

Although there's more to RRSPs than the income tax considerations, there's a tendency to place far too much emphasis on the tax aspects of registered retirement savings plans. This means not enough time and thought are devoted to deciding on the *type* of plan you should have and *where* you should have it.

The two main questions to be answered are: what's the rate of return on the plan; and how safe is your money.

In determining what the rate of return will be on your plan, don't stop when you find out it's going to be 9%, 11% or whatever. You need to know a few more things as well. For example, are there any costs involved, such as administration fees, entrance fees, or termination fees? Another consideration is how often the interest is going to be compounded (9% compounded monthly will earn a lot more in the long run than 9¼% compounded annually).

There are two main considerations in determining the safety of your RRSP. The first is the type of investment you've chosen. A guaranteed plan is not as risky as a plan that invests in common stocks. The second consideration is how safe the institution is. If this is an area that concerns you, then the bigger and better known the institution, the more comfortable you will likely be.

Always remember that when one possible investment opportunity offers a considerably higher return than the same type of investment with another institution, the difference is very apt to be risk. The main point is: don't just get your RRSP at the most convenient location. Shop around, compare, and check the risk.

A final warning about income tax and RRSPs. Lately the government seems to have had great difficulty making up its mind about RRSPs. Always check the current state of affairs when making RRSP decisions that have an income tax implication.

Chapter 7

Registered Retirement Income Funds

The federal government, although willing to let us defer some income tax by making contributions to registered retirement savings plans, is not prepared to let us defer that tax indefinitely. Sooner or later the RRSP has to be closed. At the time of writing, the Income Tax Act requires that action on your RRSP must be taken no later than December 31st of the year in which you become 71 years old, otherwise the whole amount will be subject to income tax that year. A dismal prospect indeed.

As mentioned in the last chapter, there are four options available: pay the tax; take out a life annuity; take out a term-certain annuity; or transfer the funds into a registered retirement income fund (a RRIF).

Because most people don't like to pay income tax before they have to and many people don't like the locked-in inflexibility of annuities, RRIFs have become the most popular of the available options. Some taxpayers have taken advantage of a combination of RRIFs and annuities to balance the flexibility and certainty of their retirement investments.

HOW RRIFs WORK

In one respect it could be said that a RRIF is the opposite of an RRSP. With an RRSP you make annual contributions which give you tax deductions, whereas with a RRIF you have to take out a minimum amount each year and include it in income for tax purposes.

The minimum amount which must be taken out each year is the value of the funds in the RRIF on January 1st divided by the number of years until you reach 90 years of age. For example, if you have $100,000 in your RRIF and you are 72 years old on January 1st, that year you would have to take out $5,556. You could take it all out if you wanted to, but at least $5,556 would have to come out in this situation.

In other respects RRIFs are very much like RRSPs. They can invest in substantially the same type of securities and are offered by most of the same institutions that offer RRSPs. You can even have a self-directed RRIF. Accordingly, you must bring to bear the same types of considerations in choosing your RRIF as you would in selecting an RRSP.

Needn't Wait

Although you must do something with your RRSP by the time you reach age 71, you don't have to wait that long. You can collapse it, buy an annuity with the proceeds, or transfer the funds to a RRIF at any time you wish. However, there is little advantage to be gained by transferring the funds to a RRIF until at least retirement, and probably not until the year you hit age 71. (Remember that rules like this age requirement often change — so always check the current law.)

Fees

RRIFs are subject to the same types of fees, administration costs, and whatever other names the financial institutions can come up with to call the charges they levy. When comparing RRIF alternatives, be sure to make full inquiries about all costs, exactly as you would with an RRSP.

Direct Transfer

It's critical to note that in order to avoid the payment of income tax, funds going from an RRSP to a RRIF must be transferred directly between the plans without passing through your hands.

Don't Leave It to the Last Minute

It takes time to comply with all the government red tape surrounding the transfer of funds from an RRSP to a RRIF, and it will take some time to choose the right RRIF for you. Don't leave all the planning to the last minute. Get started on it at least a year before the time you plan to make the transfer.

Payments

Payments out of your RRIF can be received in whatever manner you choose, monthly, annually or whatever, provided at least the minimum requirement each year is received. You can also change the amount you receive each year so long as at least the annual minimum requirement is received.

Some people like to take out larger payments during the first five or ten years of their RRIF-life in order to better enjoy their early retirement years. Others, particularly if they have other sources of income, will take only the minimum in order to defer income tax as long as possible, possibly offset inflation, or leave a larger estate for their beneficiaries. You can even take out the same amount each year, provided it's at least equal to the minimum requirement.

In the final analysis there is very little difference right now between an RRSP and a RRIF. Don't be surprised if some time soon the government finds some way to blend them.

Chapter 8

Registered Education Savings Plans

I've put this chapter in the book, not because I like registered education savings plans (I don't), but because some financial institutions have begun to push them pretty hard. I'll give you the facts as they exist at the time of writing (late 1989) and you can make your own judgments. However, you should check out the current rules because this is another area in which the Minister of Finance seems unsure what to do. Accordingly, the rules may change.

PURPOSE OF RESPs

Registered education savings plans are meant to help people accumulate money with which to pay some of the costs of their children's education, their grandchildren's education, or possibly somebody else's children's education. I said "some of the costs" because the rules for these plans are so restricted that there's no way you'd ever be able to accumulate the total cost of post-secondary education. Read on and you'll see why you may end up paying for somebody else's kid's education, and also why I don't like the plans.

CONTRIBUTIONS

Contributions are not deductible for income tax purposes. However, money earned in the plan is not subject to income tax until it is taken out. At that time it's taxed in the hands of the student. The theoretical advantage here is that the student is apt to be in a lower tax bracket then than you are now, and the student would also have tuition fees which will offset some or all of the tax to be paid. Of course, any time you can defer payment of a tax it usually makes sense to do so. But read on. There's a catch.

The total amount which any one taxpayer can contribute to a plan or plans in respect to the same future student is strictly limited. In 1989 the lifetime maximum was about $31,000.

RISK

The risk involved in such plans, and the reason I don't like them, is that if your designated student, for whatever reason, fails to attend a post-secondary educational institution and there is no other student you want or can transfer the funds to, you lose all the income. You get back your initial contributions, but all of the income earned would have to be donated to an educational institution. You'd get no income tax benefit whatsoever and you would have lost the income on your contributions.

EVEN WORSE POSSIBILITIES

The above comments apply to the newest type of registered education savings plans — the self-directed type operated by a number of financial institutions. There is an older type which, in addition to the problems already mentioned, have even tougher restrictions.

There are three of these old types that I'm aware of: The Canadian Scholarship Trust Foundation; Foundation Universities; and The International Scholarship Foundation.

Take the Canadian Scholarship Trust Foundation, for example. In this plan, if you miss making your monthly contribution the whole plan may be forfeited. You can only change your beneficiary up to age 10. After that the only way you can change it is if the original beneficiary dies. So if your child doesn't attend at least one year of university *and pass*, you lose all your income. Again, you'd get back your own contributions.

IF YOU'RE A GAMBLER

If you want to take this gamble and enroll in a registered education savings plan, at least find out the answers to all these questions before you go ahead.

1. What are the fees for entering, administering the plan each year, and getting money out of the plan?
2. Under what circumstances can I get my money back? Under what circumstances can I not get it back?
3. Can I change beneficiaries (the potential students) any time I want?
4. Are there restrictions on who can be a beneficiary?
5. Are there age limits? (At present the money must be taken out after a maximum of 21 years.)
6. Can the interest be withdrawn in a lump sum, over a period of years, or either?
7. Does education outside Canada qualify?
8. Which educational institutions qualify?

If you are satisfied with the answers to the above questions, you just have one more to which you need the answer. It's this: will I have a child who will be attending university? Because if it turns out the answer is "no," kiss the income goodbye.

Chapter 9

Estate Planning

The words "estate planning" usually conjure up a highly technical treatise on the many and varied income tax considerations surrounding the subject of planning what will happen to your estate when you die. Although it's true that income tax plays a major role in any estate plan, a detailed examination of taxes in this context is beyond the scope of this book. There will be some general tax advice later in this chapter, but first we'll discuss considerations which everyone should, and can, bring to bear when planning their estates.

The essence of estate planning (from the standpoint of what happens when you die) is ensuring that, of what you leave behind, the right assets (money included) go to the right people at the right time at the least cost — tax or otherwise.

PLANNING IS THE KEY

A good estate plan needs the same ingredients as any other successful plan. You have to set your goals, choose the people who are going to advise you and carry out the plan for you, then review it from time to time. If you've been following the advice contained in Chapter 3 you've already taken the first step required to develop an appropriate estate plan, that is, drawing up a statement of assets and liabilities and considering your budget requirements, both long- and short-term. Indeed, a major ingredient of your planning is ensuring there will be an estate to deal with on your death.

PROFESSIONAL HELP

At this stage of the game you should call in some help. Throughout this book much is made of getting competent, professional advice. One of the most difficult choices people have to make from time to time is the selection of a professional advisor. What I'm about to say applies equally well whether we're talking about choosing an accountant, lawyer, insurance agent or any other professional.

The main point is don't simply take the first name you run across in the yellow pages or have recommended to you. Even in an emergency you should take the time to consider the three criteria I'm about to lay down. Of course, if it's not an emergency you can be even more selective.

Be sure the advisor you select is duly and appropriately qualified in whatever particular field of endeavour you need guidance. There's no point, for example, in going to a chartered accountant whose specialty is computer auditing if your particular problem happens to be an income tax assessment.

Then, be sure the particular professional deals with problems the size of yours. There will probably be dissatisfaction all around if you take your house purchase to a lawyer who normally acts only for multi-million-dollar shopping centres.

Always remember that the best criterion for the choice of a professional advisor is a personal recommendation from someone whose judgment you trust, who knows the nature of your problem, who's familiar with the type of practice which the professional carries on, and has first-hand knowledge of the professional's competence. Of course the person making the recommendation should also have at least some understanding of the nature of your problem.

Any effective estate plan requires a professional financial advisor and a lawyer to go over your goals with you, advise you on how to best achieve your goals and actually put your plan into action. The choice of financial advisor is not an easy one for inexperienced people. Insurance agents, trust companies, accountants, so-called financial planners, and sundry others are all called upon from time to time to act in this capacity. About the only thing certain is that there are competent and incompetent estate planners in all these categories. The best basis on which to choose your financial advisor is:

1. Obtain referral information; choose someone who has done estate planning work for an acquaintance or comes highly recommended.

2. Stay away from the estate planner who may be trying to sell you something other than professional advice, e.g. insurance, a tax shelter or a shopping centre.
3. Choose someone who has experience in dealing with your size of estate.

BEFORE YOU MEET

You can help keep the cost of professional advice at a reasonable level by considering the following before you meet with your professional advisor:

1. Prepare a statement of assets and liabilities.
2. Prepare three rough budgets: a current-year budget; a long-term budget; and an estimate of how much income your family would need in order to maintain an appropriate standard of living if something happened to you.
3. Consider whether your spouse can adequately manage money. If so, then the suggestions the advisor will make will follow a different approach than if your spouse is not sufficiently capable. You should both come to grips with this question before meeting with your advisor. There's little point in paying a hefty hourly rate to have the advisor as a spectator at a family quarrel.
4. At what age do you want children to receive money? Even if you originally leave everything to your spouse, remember that your spouse should have a will too, and both wills should make provision for the possibility of the two of you dying in a common disaster or within a short period of time.
5. Are there any special bequests required, e.g. charities, friends, handicapped heirs, etc.?
6. Who do you want as your executors? (More on this shortly.)
7. Don't let the tax tail wag the family dog.

QUESTIONNAIRE

Appendix A is a sample questionnaire which I use as a starting point in planning a person's financial affairs. It is reproduced at the back of the book as an example of the various questions and types of data that must be carefully considered in formulating any estate plan. Of course, the questionnaire is designed to cover a wide range of personal situations and any particular person would be unlikely to have to answer all the questions or use all the schedules.

Why not use it now as a record of your affairs. It's very thought-provoking. Not only that, but it's a very useful document to have because it will provide you with a record, in one place, of all relevant personal financial information. This will allow you to better assess your current situation and will make updating the data a lot easier.

The questionnaire will also be an excellent starting point (and money saver) should you decide to engage a professional advisor. It would be of particular interest to the executor of your will. As a matter of fact, it should be treated with the same respect as other important documents, such as wills. Keep a copy handy for easy reference, but also have a copy in safekeeping, such as with your lawyer or in a safety deposit box. Remember, though, when you update, update all copies wherever they may be.

WILLS

There is no doubt the single most important ingredient in any estate plan is the will.

Anyone who thinks only rich people need a will is badly and sadly mistaken. The simple fact is every adult should have a will. Married couples should both have wills. If only one spouse has a will and they both die in a common disaster, or within a short period of time, the effect might well be the same as if neither had a will.

A will is the only means by which you can exercise any control over who gets what and when, should you die. If you die without a will, the government decides who gets what and when. And we all know how good, efficient and compassionate governments are in matters like this. Minor children could be hit particularly hard if the government has to take over. A court-appointed official guardian would be a poor choice of administrator when compared to a loving relative or friend. The relative or friend will know a lot more about your family circumstances than any official guardian ever could.

A lot of people think it's cheaper to die without a will than to incur the legal costs of having one drawn. That's simply not the case. In the first instance, in dealing with estates, it's been my experience — without exception — that it's more costly, in terms of legal fees, let alone taxes (in a large estate the tax cost of dying without a will can be enormous), to die without a will than with one.

Second, lawyers don't charge very much for drawing up a simple will. As a matter of fact, in my view it's a bargain. And be sure to have a lawyer do it. The law doesn't say you have to, but it's silly to draw up a will without a lawyer, no matter how simple it may seem to be.

So, the two major problems caused by dying without a will are the cost and difficulty of winding up the estate and distributing the assets, and having no say whatsoever as to who gets what and when. Let's take a closer look at the latter problem.

For example, at the time of writing here's what happens to an estate in Ontario when a person dies without a will. If there is a surviving spouse but no children or grandchildren, the spouse gets it all. If there's a surviving spouse and one child, the spouse gets the first $75,000 plus half of the remainder. The child gets the other half. If there's a surviving spouse and more than one child, the spouse gets the first $75,000 plus one-third of the remainder. The children share the other two-thirds equally.

If there is no spouse, children or grandchildren, it goes to the parents. If neither of them is alive, the deceased's brothers and sisters are next in line. And it goes on and on to the remotest of relatives. If there's no next of kin, the provincial government gets it. As you can see, a lot of difficulty and unintended hardship can be caused by dying without a will. It's well worth repeating that it doesn't cost as much to have a will properly drawn by a competent lawyer as it will likely cost to have the mess unravelled if you die without one.

Believe me, the costs and aggravations of dying without a will are enormous. Maybe *you* won't care. But your survivors certainly will. However, even though dying without a will is about the most inconsiderate thing you could do to your survivors, you should also be aware that what you say in your will may not be the final word in the matter.

Wills can be contested. If a deceased person hasn't made adequate provisions for the proper support of any person dependent on him or her, that dependant can apply to a court for proper and adequate support. Dependants include a spouse, parents, children, grandchildren, brothers or sisters who were dependent on the deceased immediately prior to his or her death, and, in some jurisdictions, common-law spouses and ex-spouses.

Many parents include provisions in their wills outlining who they want to have control and custody of their children in the event that both parents die, for example in a common disaster such as a plane crash or automobile accident. Although this is a very wise thing to do, and a court would certainly give considerable weight to the expressed wishes of the deceased parents, you should remember that the terms of a will are not binding when it comes to guardianship or custody of children. A court always has the authority to look through any document, including wills, where the welfare of a child is at stake. All of this notwithstanding, you should still have a will, and it still makes sense to set out in writing your wishes regarding guardianship of your children.

If you're still not convinced, how about this: having a will may be the only way you can legally *disinherit* someone.

Another important point to keep in mind when it comes to wills is that any time you make a permanent move from one country or province to another you should have your wills reviewed by a lawyer at your new place of residence. Local laws might negate some of the provisions of your existing will and revisions may be required. For example, in most jurisdictions marriage immediately nullifies a will whereas divorce may not. There may be family law provisions that override your will. Indeed, your will should be reviewed with your lawyer any time your circumstances change significantly. At the very least you should go over your will with your lawyer every five years.

CHOOSING EXECUTORS

The executor is the person (or persons) named in your will who is charged with the responsibility of carrying out the provisions of your will. The law gives them the authority to do so.

As someone once suggested, the perfect executor would be a tactful, diplomatic, loving family member who is both a lawyer and a chartered accountant with a wide background in investing, and who will live forever. Well, let's see who's second best.

Bearing in mind that your executor has, at least for a period of time, complete control over your estate and its assets, honesty and integrity are obvious attributes to look for. Your executor should know your family and share your values and principles. Your executor should live in your area; an estate in Vancouver with an executor in Halifax add up to bad news. Your executor should have a solid knowledge of, or access to, business and financial management; access to legal advice is a must.

All of this strongly suggests that a team of executors is probably the best route to go because you probably won't find one person with all of the needed credentials. Your spouse plus your lawyer or accountant, or other trusted business acquaintance or colleague, often make the ideal team. You should also provide for an alternate executor should one of your first choices be unwilling or unable to act.

If your estate is large or complicated or both, or if there are special circumstances, such as a handicapped dependant to be taken care of, the best choice of an executor for your will is, in my opinion, a trust company. They're in the business, and all the reasons often put forward for not using them — they're conservative, impersonal and tough to deal with — are the very reasons you need them for those kinds of estates. A trust company and a spouse, as co-executors, usually make an ideal team in these circumstances. Your spouse knows the family while the trust company knows all the rules.

On the other hand, there's no point incurring what is usually the highest executors' costs (those of a trust company) for a relatively small bequest; or even a large one if it's easily handled. In these circumstances you should fall back on my earlier suggestion for appropriate co-executors; say, your spouse plus a reliable acquaintance with some financial smarts. The key to the success of this combination is that your spouse will know your wishes and those of the family, while the other executor can add the business knowledge, which can be less than that required for a large, complicated estate.

A spouse alone is usually not a good choice of executor. A spouse is usually too emotionally involved to make all the right decisions. But remember that any executor has the right to engage professional help, such as a trust company, lawyer, accountant, or any combination thereof.

Like so many things financial and legal, there isn't one answer. It depends entirely on your personal circumstances.

Regardless of who you finally choose to be your executors, there are two very important steps you should always take:

1. Check with your executors before actually naming them to determine if they are willing to act and have the time to do so.

2. Show them a copy of your will. There might be some provision in it with which they would not be comfortable, such as complete discretion as to whether a recalcitrant teenager ever inherits anything. Perhaps they have a conflict of interest, real or imagined.

INCOME TAXES

Income taxes play an important role in estate planning. But this is not an income tax book. You've been promised that this book is not rendered obsolete by every new budget. Indeed, this entire book is devoted to managing your financial affairs in the most appropriate manner, income tax notwithstanding. So how do we reconcile these conflicting positions? Well, by keeping the income tax comments in the book to those of a very general nature. Areas to consider are pointed out to you and guidance as to when to seek specific professional advice is given.

Like everything financial, effective estate planning from an income tax standpoint involves a combination of the income tax laws and your particular circumstances, which, for an estate of any appreciable size, should never be undertaken without professional help. This is so for three main reasons: first, no two estates are identical; second, the tax laws in this respect are complex and change frequently; and third, there are often other legal considerations, many of which may vary from jurisdiction to jurisdiction.

The main income tax consideration in most estates is the effect of the tax on capital gains when the owner of property dies. This is one area that you should always discuss with your professional advisors, particularly to determine what needs to be done to take advantage of available exemptions.

If you own a valuable piece of real estate other than your principal residence, shares of a public company or an interest in a business, the possibility of entering into an "estate freeze" will almost certainly come up as a means of minimizing income taxes on death.

The idea of an estate freeze is to freeze the value of the assets in your estate at today's value so that future increases in value will be taxed later in the hands of your heirs, rather than sooner in your hands. Freezes are accomplished in a number of different ways depending on the types of assets involved and the circumstances of each case. Shares might be sold to your children, options to purchase real estate later might be granted, or complete new entities such as holding companies may be formed.

Before agreeing to an estate freeze, however, be sure you fully understand the pros and cons, and the magnitude (both qualitative and quantitative) of each.

There is really only one advantage to freezing your estate. It's the one that's already been mentioned: saving income tax when you die. However, this one advantage can be enormous in some circumstances. It's the negative side, the cons, of an estate freeze that's more difficult to come to grips with. But come to grips with it you must.

First of all, there's no point in freezing the value of assets which are not likely to grow in value. The next thing to consider is that your heirs — children, nieces, nephews, or whoever (you can leave anything you wish to a spouse without income tax problems) — are now going to own a piece or all of the business, land or whatever. Be sure you're ready for this and that you're satisfied you want them as partners, co-owners, or new bosses. That's right, you may have to retire.

Even more important, though, is the fact that after an estate freeze future growth in value and earnings will go to your heirs. This suggests to me that you should never consider an estate freeze until you're absolutely certain you are financially able to live out the rest of your days in an acceptable life style without the future growth in asset value.

Yes, estate freezes can be important from an income tax standpoint. But the financial and psychological factors must be clearly understood and acceptable before you go ahead.

Don't let the tax tail wag the family dog. Ever.

Chapter 10

Insurance

CHOOSING AN AGENT

The right kind of insurance in the right amount is one of the best bargains in the world. The trick, of course, is to find the right kind — and to determine the right amount. This holds true whether we're talking about life insurance, fire insurance, or such esoteric coverage as kidnap insurance. The key to proper insurance coverage is to deal with a reputable, independent agent.

The reasons for dealing with reputable agents are obvious. However, the reasons for dealing with independent agents are not always clearly understood. In order to be able to achieve and sustain their status as independent agents they must have proven themselves to be capable and competent professionals. Even more important to you, independent agents are not tied to one particular company and can shop the market to obtain the best rate available for coverage appropriate to your particular circumstances.

And that's another thing to bear in mind. It's very rare for any two people to have identical insurance needs. What's right for your neighbour is not necessarily right for you. Your circumstances may be similar, but not likely identical. Again, the best person to advise you is an agent. But bear in mind that the agent makes money by selling as much insurance as possible. Your best protection against being ripped off is, as already mentioned, to deal with a reputable, independent agent. How do you find one? Like all other professionals, your best choice is probably the one referred to you by a happy customer. But be sure the agent normally deals with your size and type of account.

Now let's turn our attention to some specific types of insurance.

AUTOMOBILE INSURANCE

Probably the most common mistake in the area of automobile insurance is not having enough. It's a well-known fact that there are people operating automobiles who have no insurance at all.

Public liability insurance — the part of your policy that provides payments to other persons for damages caused by you — is the cheapest component of your automobile insurance policy. These days, it doesn't take much of a personal injury accident to run up damages of hundreds of thousands of dollars. When death is involved that sum can quickly escalate into millions. The potential liability in a multiple-death accident is truly frightening. The lesson is clear. Buy as much public liability insurance as you can.

The other major component of automobile insurance cost is, of course, collision insurance. This is the part of your policy that covers damage to your car. The cost here is heavily dependent on the "deductible amount" — the portion of the repair cost that you agree to pay yourself; say, the first $500, $750, or whatever. A reasonable collision strategy would be to have a fairly low deductible on a new car, increasing as the car gets older and the likelihood of your repairing relatively minor damage diminishes. Indeed, you might even reach a point where you have an old bucket of bolts that you wouldn't bother to repair if it got extensively damaged. In these circumstances you might consider dropping collision coverage altogether. But you should never drop your liability coverage.

Another area to look at is the riders that might be available with your policy. Frequently, very attractive coverage can be tacked on to your insurance policy, at very little additional cost, covering such risks as medical expenses and theft of personal belongings.

HOMEOWNERS' INSURANCE

The main point to remember here is that purchasing insurance on your home and its contents is not a one-time, one-shot consideration. Your homeowners' insurance package has to be reviewed every year. Even if you are one of the lucky ones who happened to get the right coverage first time around, an automatic renewal each year simply won't do.

Common mistakes, for example, including failing to tell your agent when a vaulable extension has been built onto your home, or when some valuable addition — like an expensive painting or a mink coat — has been made to the contents. This could ultimately be a pretty expensive lapse of attention if, upon loss, the agent smiles sympathetically and says, "Sorry, that's not covered."

Here are some key points to discuss with your agent and on which you should be completely clear as to the terms and extent of your coverage.

1. Exactly what risks are covered? You probably should, as a minimum, cover: fire and other accidental causes (such as storms, smoke, etc.) of damage to buildings; fire and theft on contents; public liability and medical expenses (much like your automobile policy); and credit card theft.
2. Be sure to insure for adequate replacement cost. Get your agent to determine current replacement cost data for you each year. The automatic inflation increase factor (a percentage per annum in most policies of this type) may not be enough.
3. By the same token, don't insure your land. It won't burn.
4. Determine whether an inventory of contents is required by the insurance company. This is sometimes, but not always, the case. It's a good idea to have one anyway, even if the insurance company doesn't insist on it. If so, don't keep it (or other proof of cost for that matter) where it too will burn if the house and contents go up in flames. If an inventory is required, a good way of doing it is to take pictures of each room with its contents. Don't forget to take things out of drawers and closets, and don't forget the camera itself.
5. Always determine what proof of loss will be required under your policy for both buildings and contents.
6. Determine the amount and terms of your coverage when personal items are outside the home — for example, in the car or at a hotel while on vacation.
7. What about when you are temporarily away and the house is unoccupied, as during vacation? Does someone have to check it regularly? Does the water have to be turned off? Be sure to determine the relevant period of absence. It will vary in different circumstances.
8. A vacant house is different from a temporarily unoccupied house. Vacant means no people or furniture. Usually you are only covered for 30 days of vacancy and this might not be enough or, say, you're selling your home and there is a significant period of time between when you move and the new owner takes possession. Extended coverage is available in these circumstances and should be obtained.

9. Are contents covered during a move? Maybe not, so specific coverage should be obtained when moving.
10. If you carry on a business in your home it could affect your coverage. Better discuss it with your agent.
11. Be sure your contents coverage is adequate. The automatic "percentage of building coverage" may be inadequate, particularly when applied to specific, valuable items such as works of art, cameras, or jewelry. Additional floater policies can bring you up to adequate coverage at relatively little cost.
12. If appraisals of the home or contents are recommended by the agent, be sure the appraiser is reputable. Appraisal reports, like inventories and other valuable proof-of-loss documents, should be kept outside the home, preferably in a safety deposit box.
13. The installation of alarm systems and smoke detectors will likely reduce your premiums — but only if your agent knows you have them.
14. Get your agent to explain "comprehensive" coverage to you. It's the kind you need. As in the case of automobile insurance, check out the floaters and riders available. Once the basic policy is agreed upon there are some truly great bargains available.
15. Use the same agent for all your general (other than life) insurance needs. This will help avoid costly overlaps of coverage.

LIFE INSURANCE

Canadians spend billions of dollars on life insurance premiums each year, but many have no idea of what product to buy, who to buy it from, or how much to pay for it.

When buying a new car it seems natural for most of us to spend days poring over brochures, visiting showrooms, testing models and checking with friends. But when it comes to buying life insurance — a product that is more important and often more costly than a car — most Canadians can't tell a lemon from a plum. Unfortunately, only their survivors will know for sure.

Canadians already are the most heavily insured people, on a per capita basis, in the world. Despite this almost morbid, though necessary, preoccupation with preparing for death, many Canadians are under-insured, pay too much for their life insurance, and often buy the wrong kinds of coverage.

Who's to blame? Well, just about everybody. Individuals, for being so careless about a product that will cost many thousands of dollars over the years.

Society, for being so nervous about dealing with death. Even though we pay a lot of money for protection, most of us don't like to think about premature death and the hardship it might place on our survivors. The life insurance industry, for not doing enough to make things easier for consumers. The industry surrounds itself with a confusing array of actuarial technicalities, needlessly complex terminology and mind-bending numbers. As a result, most life insurance buyers end up bewildered.

You can save anywhere from a few dollars to a few thousand dollars on life insurance if you follow a couple of basic rules:

1. Ask questions and compare prices. That may seem difficult — there are scores of organizations selling life insurance in Canada, and each uses its own particular names for various kinds of coverage. However, guides are available and it is not necessary to check the pricing structure of every company. Some comparison is worthwhile, though, because prices for the same product often vary widely.
2. Make sure you know what you want to buy — in other words, what you want to protect. This is the most difficult, but most crucial, aspect of buying life insurance.

Most people buy life insurance to replace a source of income that would be eliminated by a death. For example, a thirty-year-old man with a mortgage, car loan and two young children usually takes care of his obligations with a monthly pay cheque. If he dies, his family will still need a pay cheque of some sort to pay the bills.

How much life insurance a person needs is a question that's easy to ask, but very difficult to answer. What I can do, though, is give you some guidelines which will help you arrive at the right amount for you, or at least close to it.

Each individual has different needs, but generally a wage earner with dependants but without substantial assets should consider buying life insurance equal to about twelve times annual salary. The amount can vary, depending on how old you are, what other assets you have and how many dependants you are supporting. The younger you are, if you have dependants, generally the more insurance you need.

The first thing to consider is how much annual income your dependants would need to maintain a reasonable life style should something happen to you. Remember, though, that their life style is very apt to change considerably.

Then determine how much of that income (if any) is already available from other sources such as pensions, existing investments and assets which might be sold upon your death.

When doing these calculations, remember the effect of income tax and that some reasonable allowance has to be made for inflation.

Now, compare the available income after your death to the amount you think your dependants would need. As a very minimum, you should have about ten to twelve times as much life insurance as any shortfall. For example, if your dependants would need $35,000 a year before income tax, and there would be no other source of income available, it's my opinion you should have at least $350,000 to $450,000 of insurance.

Now that will sound like an awful lot of insurance for some of you. However, you can probably get it more cheaply than you think. Talk it over with a knowledgeable insurance agent, one who is willing to discuss group and term coverage as well as whole life.

As I said before, when you buy the right kind and amount for your particular needs, insurance is the best bargain around.

Undoubtedly, a CLU (chartered life underwriter) is most knowledgeable about life insurance matters. If the agent you are dealing with is not a CLU, it would be wise to seek a second opinion from one. Many people also feel it's a good idea to double check any agent's recommendations (CLU or not) with an independent consultant, such as an accountant, lawyer, banker or other knowledgeable person you trust. Indeed, until you find an independent life agent (one who is not forced to sell a particular company's product, but is free to make the best deal for you — which could be the case even if he or she works out of one company's office or branch) whose advice you trust completely, the second opinion route is a sensible one. However, when going this route, you, the agent and your third party consultant should always meet together before a final decision is made. This will save you a lot of time in that any disagreements can be thrashed out by your two advisors directly without you having to ferry arguments pro and con between them. But always remember, the agent is the most knowledgeable about insurance matters.

It isn't that the insurance industry can't be trusted — it can. The problem is that agents are human and some of them occasionally try to sell a product that meets their commission requirements more than it meets your insurance needs. But, as mentioned, an experienced, independent life agent with a solid reputation in the community knows more about life insurance than any accountant, lawyer or bank manager. So you have a tightrope to walk. The approach suggested in the preceding paragraph is probably your best bet.

See page 79 for some tips on dealing with an insurance agent. It will help you deal with the problem if you understand it better.

Whole Life vs Term

There are two basic types of life insurance, both good products, but each created to meet entirely different needs: "whole life" and "term." For most people, term is the one to buy.

Term insurance is cheaper because it provides protection for age groups in which the mortality rate is low. Even at age 60, relatively few policyholders die. Hence, yearly premiums tend to be low. Term premiums are generally much lower than whole life premiums for young people.

While term insurance provides temporary protection, say, for one year, five years, or until a specified age, whole life provides protection for the whole of your life. Premiums are higher because the risk is greater that the insurance company will have to pay a death benefit. In fact, they *will* have to pay unless the policy lapses or is cancelled.

Whole life insurance can be useful for those who have taxable estates, business partners, special care problems (such as a handicapped heir), the possibility of a temporary period during which one might not be able to pay premiums, a real reason to believe that one might someday be uninsurable, or if insurance will always be needed.

However, too many people end up with costly whole life products simply because they don't know any better. Life insurance companies are not about to discourage that flow of extra premiums — especially since many whole life policies never pay a death benefit. They often lapse or are surrendered before the policyholder dies, for example, by policyholders who discover that their policies don't suit their needs, or that they can't really afford them.

Many people don't need insurance in their old age and shouldn't pay for it. Most people plan to retire by age 65 and expect to be financially self-sufficient by then. If they are not, life insurance premiums at that age might only add to the drain on their incomes.

If you're pretty sure you will not need insurance when you're old and grey, why try to pay off steep whole life premiums when you're young? This is not to say that whole life is a bad product. It isn't. But it's expensive and its uses are limited. You should get to know them before you sign on the dotted line.

A final word of caution: beware of life insurance agents who try to sell whole life policies on the grounds that they are good vehicles for saving. In fact, whole life insurance does not provide for any savings, although the cash values that come with these policies may sometimes seem like savings.

The cash value of a whole life policy belongs to the life insurance company, not the policyholder. If you want to take part of your ''savings'' out, the life insurance company will charge interest on what they call a ''loan.'' At the same time the amount of your insurance coverage will be reduced by the amount of the ''loan'' with no reduction in the amount of your premium.

This raises an interesting point. If you have a whole life policy with a cash surrender value (the term given the so-called ''savings'' portion) it is probable that you can ''borrow'' against it at a very reasonable interest rate. You might be able to make money by simply borrowing the maximum amount you can and putting the proceeds into term deposits. But check it out carefully before doing so, and remember that your ''loan'' reduces your insurance coverage.

Now let's examine situations where whole life insurance might be appropriate.

It's often been said there are only two things of which we can be certain — death and taxes. Whole life insurance, however, can make the latter easier for your dependants or business partners when the former happens. This applies to relatively few Canadians as most do not have taxable estates or business partners. However, if you do, or if you fall into one of the other categories explained earlier, take a close look at whole life insurance.

The main reason for buying whole life is to create ready cash at death. The cash can be used to pay taxes arising on death (such as on deemed capital gains), or to look after funeral and burial expenses, or in the case of a business, to provide funds to ease what could be a bumpy transition when a key executive dies. Term insurance doesn't always serve this need because it becomes prohibitively expensive, and ultimately impossible to buy, as you grow older.

But for most people, this is academic, because they won't need the ready cash that whole life will provide in old age, and they shouldn't pay for it.

Most of us don't have to worry about death taxes. As for funeral expenses, many Canadians can provide for that out of a small savings fund. Otherwise, a small $5,000 to $10,000 whole life policy might be worthwhile.

An important application for whole life insurance is in business. Business partners, for example, can insure each other for a large sum, so that if one dies, the other will have the funds to buy the deceased partner's share of the business, pay large company debts and survive the first year.

For example, if one partner needed to borrow to pay for a deceased partner's share of the business, that loan could cost most of a company's pre-tax earnings, whereas a single premium whole life policy might only cost a fraction of that amount. Life insurance meets the need.

Even after you've decided which is the more appropriate form of life coverage — term or whole life; and for the vast majority of people it should be term — you will still have to decide from among a number of alternatives with wonderful sounding names. Examples are single premium plans, joint and last survivor plans, level premium plans, reducing term plans, convertible plans, and on and on.

Books could be, and have been, written about these various options. Space will only allow me to advise you to be absolutely sure you understand exactly what you're buying. The best way to achieve that is to deal firmly, objectively, and appropriately with the agent.

When you've determined the amount and type of life insurance coverage you need, a good place to start is to obtain as much group term coverage as is available to you. This is usually the cheapest form of life insurance coverage you can find. Most employers provide group life plans, and you are often able to obtain more than the minimum coverage provided by paying a low additional premium. Ask about it. Professional organizations, fraternity clubs, and unions, often provide very cheap group term coverage. If you are a member, ask about that, too.

Dealing with a Life Insurance Agent

What can you do to protect yourself when dealing with life insurance agents? The odds are you will be dealing with a competent, sincere agent, but unless you have a thorough and detailed knowledge of the business, or know the agent personally, you can't be sure.

The agent will know more about life insurance than you do. At the very least the agent will have a finely honed sales pitch, and you won't have the ammunition to argue.

But there are a few things you can do.

1. Insist that the agent keep things simple. Don't be ashamed of your lack of knowledge. Ask any and all questions, even if they seem silly.
2. Talk to more than one agent. Invite two or three to your home and make sure at least one favours term insurance. In this way you get more than one side of a life insurance argument (and there are many sides).
3. Talk to each agent about what the others have proposed. There are two main things to consider — cost and benefit.

4. Finally, phone a few other companies to get price quotations on the policy and amounts of coverage you think are best suited to your needs. In this way you foster competition among life insurance agents and their companies, and you will at least have some choice.

Insuring Children

It was almost traditional at one time in Canada to take out endowment life insurance policies on babies before they were even out of the maternity ward. Fortunately this practice is waning, but it's still sufficiently widespread to warrant a cautionary word.

The big selling tool agents use to push a policy on a child is the so-called forced savings aspect. Well, as mentioned earlier, insurance policies are seldom the best savings vehicles.

The simple fact is children don't need life insurance. It would be far better to take out a term policy on the mother, a factor which is often overlooked if she isn't a wage earner.

Non-smokers

Everyone should review their life insurance coverage every year in any event, but if you happen to be a non-smoker you should definitely be talking to your life insurance agent about that very fact.

You see, non-smokers — and some insurance companies will consider you to be a non-smoker even if you take an occasional puff on a cigar or a pipe, so it's really non-*cigarette* smokers I'm talking about — so, as I was saying, non-cigarette smokers can get much cheaper premium rates on their life insurance than people who smoke cigarettes.

This is a relatively new development in the age-old life insurance field, and it is only in recent years that life insurance companies have been pushing the fact. It may well be that you could save a considerable amount of money by letting your agent know that you are a non-cigarette smoker. Don't lie about it, because a lie will void the policy — even if the cause of death is being hit by a truck. Remember, though, if you're going to change your policy, you may have to have a medical examination — but that's not a bad idea either.

Any one person's savings would, of course, depend on considerations such as age, and amount and type of coverage. There's one thing for certain, however. If you're a non-cigarette smoker your life insurance agent should know about it. It's almost certain you can save money on your life insurance.

Changing Policies

Many people still have endowment or whole-life insurance policies which were issued back when interest rates were very low, and on which the return is based on those lower figures. A common question is whether these policies should be cancelled and replaced with so-called "new money" policies, or indeed, replaced with term insurance.

Unfortunately, the answer is "maybe." There was a time when it could be said for sure that once you had an endowment or whole-life policy for a few years it was not in your interest to cancel it. That's not the case anymore. The features of some newer policies are sufficiently attractive that perhaps you should consider switching. But this is still likely the exception rather than the rule. The only way to know for sure is to compare your existing situation to what your replacement coverage, return and cost would be.

What I can tell you for certain is never cancel an existing insurance policy until the replacement coverage is in place. You might now be uninsurable, or your new policy might be horrendously expensive.

Another thing I suggest is that no matter how attractive a new proposal may seem to you, don't go for it until an agent from your existing policy's company has had a chance to explain their side of the story to you.

There's the main point. Always make your insurance decisions based on what reputable insurance agents or brokers tell you in detail — not on some generality.

DISABILITY INSURANCE

For most young breadwinners, the odds are greater that they will become disabled before age 65 than that they will die. Yet, many people who wouldn't for a moment not have life insurance will go merrily along every day with no disability coverage whatsoever. You should be sure that you have some form of disability insurance to cover the situation if you become unable to work. Many employers provide group disability coverage, and many professional organizations and unions also provide such plans. Fraternity organizations or service clubs often provide group coverage as well. Of course, commercial insurance companies have disability plans available.

The technicalities of disability insurance are even more confusing than life insurance rules. Here are a few things to keep in mind when buying such coverage:

1. Always deal only with a reputable agent and company.
2. Make sure you understand each and every provision of your coverage. For example, would you have to be totally disabled to collect, or would you qualify if you were unable to carry on your normal vocation?
3. If you have more than one form of coverage, e.g. a group plan at work and a private or professional organization plan as well, be sure that one doesn't cancel out the other. If they do, you're paying one set of premiums with no hope of getting anything in return.

The main thing to remember, of course, is if you don't have disability coverage, you may be subjecting your dependants to more risk than if you didn't have life insurance.

CANADA DEPOSIT INSURANCE

You may have an insurance policy that you don't even know about — and you should know about it because it might affect your choice of savings vehicles. The Canada Deposit Insurance Corporation (C.D.I.C.) provides protection for people who have deposits with member institutions.

The Canada Deposit Insurance Corporation is a Crown corporation established by a special act of Parliament in 1967. As mentioned, its purpose is to provide, within clearly defined limits, insurance against the loss of deposits with member institutions because of the insolvency of an institution.

Membership in the C.D.I.C. is restricted to banks, trust companies and mortgage loan companies. Any such institution which is incorporated under federal law must be a member. Provincially incorporated institutions become members only after making a formal application, which in turn will be accepted by the C.D.I.C. only if the government of the province concerned has approved the application and if prescribed standards and conditions are met.

If you don't know whether you're dealing with a federally incorporated institution, there are really only three ways to determine whether the institution you're dealing with is a member. You could look for an official membership sign which might be on display; you can ask at the institution; or (the only sure way to find out) you can enquire of the C.D.I.C. itself. It's located in Ottawa and can be reached by a toll-free telephone number.

The C.D.I.C. insures savings and chequing accounts, money orders, deposit receipts, guaranteed investment certificates, debentures and other obligations issued by member institutions.

The maximum amount of deposit insurance in force is, at the time of writing, $60,000 for each person. That limit applies to the combined total of principal and interest. It should be noted, though, that to be insurable, a term deposit must be redeemable no later than five years after the date of deposit. In addition, money held in a foreign currency account — for example, a U.S. dollar account — is *not* covered.

The maximum amount applies to the combined total of all separate deposit accounts any one person has at the same institution. This includes the combined total of all deposits in all branches of the same institution. You can only increase your coverage by spreading your business among various institutions. Spreading it among different branches of the same institution doesn't work. Simply stated, a person's deposits are separately insured to the maximum in each institution which is a member of the Corporation. However, joint deposits are insured separately from deposits in the individual names of the parties to the joint deposit. The joint deposit is essentially looked on as a separate person for this purpose.

An area of great confusion in the context of deposit insurance is whether it applies to registered retirement savings plans and registered retirement income funds with member institutions. The short answer is that it does not apply. But, like almost everything else these days such a straight answer doesn't tell the whole story. So let's try to unravel the mystery a bit.

Neither an RRSP nor a RRIF is itself covered by deposit insurance. Neither are the contributions to such plans covered per se. But remember that when you make a contribution or transfer to an RRSP or RRIF you are really handing over your money to a trustee who invests it on your behalf. Now that trustee, in the capacity of acting on your behalf, is a separate person insofar as deposit insurance is concerned. Accordingly, if the institution invests the contribution in a type of deposit qualifying for deposit insurance — such as term deposits not exceeding five years — the protection, up to the maximum per trustee per institution, is available.

Remember, though, in these circumstances it is the trustee who is insured and not the holder of the plan. If the Canada Deposit Insurance Corporation was called upon to meet the obligations of the member institution, the Corporation would pay the trustee, not the contributor. The contributor would then have to look to the trustee for reimbursement.

This raises the question of what the deposit insurance coverage is on a trust deposit made by a trustee acting for several beneficiaries. If the member institution is notified of the separate interest of each beneficiary in the deposits, then the interests of each beneficiary would be separately insured to the maximum.

This raises another important point. If you are the executor, administrator or trustee of an estate with two or more beneficiaries, the maximum insurance applies to the entire estate unless you notify the member institution of the interest of each beneficiary. If you do so, each beneficiary will be insured up to the maximum.

As is usually the case, things are slightly different in Quebec, but there is really no different effect on the depositors.

Deposits with federally incorporated companies are insured by the Canada Deposit Insurance Corporation regardless of where the deposits are located. Quebec has its own deposit insurance plan (the Quebec Deposit Insurance Board). Under the terms of an agreement between the C.D.I.C. and the Q.D.I.B., deposits made in Quebec with provincially incorporated companies are guaranteed by the Q.D.I.B., while deposits made outside Quebec with such companies are guaranteed by the C.D.I.C.

Always remember that the C.D.I.C. insures against a loss arising only from the insolvency of a member institution. Other losses, such as theft, are not covered.

Chapter 11

Powers of Attorney

Not many years ago a power of attorney was a document very few people had even heard about, let alone ever contemplated becoming a party to. Even fewer people ever signed one. This is changing, however, as powers of attorney are becoming more necessary, and more common.

Simply stated, a power of attorney is an authorization in writing given by one person to another enabling the latter to act on behalf of the former in respect to specific matters or in general. In short, the person who is given the power of attorney can deal with the other person's assets as if they were his or her own; always, of course, within any restrictions the power of attorney itself lays down.

Dealing with assets requires judgment. People often lose that judgment.

Such impairment may come as a result of a stroke, an accident, Alzheimer's disease, or just a general loss of mental competence. But whatever the cause, the consequences can be grave.

Sometimes these people are cheated out of their money. Sometimes they simply make enough bad judgments before the situation is recognized that they seriously deplete their resources. Others do peculiar things such as giving away some or all of their money; or they turn all their assets into cash and hoard it somewhere, often forgetting where.

The answer to these problems is to grant a power of attorney to a trusted person or persons which would become effective upon the occurrence of certain events. For example, the power of attorney could become effective upon the grantor of the power being declared incompetent by two doctors, say the family physician and a specialist.

The time to draw up the power of attorney is while the person granting it is still healthy and lucid. That way they choose to whom it will be given. It's often wise to share the power, say between a family member and a trusted outsider such as a lawyer, chartered accountant, banker, or trust company.

Remember, too, this isn't a consideration just for the elderly. You or I might suffer a stroke tonight, or be in a car accident tomorrow and end up being unable to make rational judgments.

Some people now draw up a power of attorney at the same time they draw up their wills, leaving the document in the hands of their lawyer until the power is triggered, such as by the doctors' decision as outlined above.

Many people shy away from drawing up such a document because they fear control of their financial lives, or more, may be taken away from them when such a result isn't really warranted. Rest assured that any power of attorney can be tailored to fit any particular set of circumstances and to offset any particular concerns you might have.

If a power of attorney hasn't been drawn up and a person becomes mentally incompetent, application to a court can be made to gain control of that person's affairs. This will take time, however, during which a lot can happen; and recourse to the courts is always cumbersome, expensive, and upsetting.

In some circumstances simply having joint accounts requiring two signatures can be an effective power of attorney in itself. It's better, though, to have the real thing.

If you're the person granting the power of attorney always follow these rules:

1. Have it drawn up by a competent lawyer of your own choosing.
2. Have your lawyer explain it fully to you in plain language.
3. Be sure it's tailored to offset your concerns and fit your particular circumstances.
4. Leave the document with your lawyer until the triggering event occurs, if ever.
5. Explain the whole thing to all members of your family, especially where the document is and why you chose the people you did.

If you're the person to whom the power of attorney has been granted, be sure of the following:

1. You're willing to act, taking into consideration the specific terms of the document.
2. The power of attorney allows you to seek professional help.
3. To carefully document every decision and action you take in the execution of your duties.

Chapter 12

Borrowing Money

DO'S AND DON'TS

There aren't too many of us who can go through life without ever having to borrow money. Of course, there are pros and cons, do's and don'ts. There are times we should borrow and there are times we should not.

The advantages of borrowing are that we can often use borrowed money to make money, such as for investment purposes, and it allows us to enjoy things while we earn the money to pay for them, such as a home or car.

The disadvantages of borrowing are that interest adds considerably to the cost of whatever it is we are borrowing for and that cost often has a snowball effect that prevents us from ever getting launched on a savings or investment program.

Although there are many guidelines bandied about as to how much a person should or should not borrow, there are really only two that have universal application: don't borrow money that you can't afford to repay when it is due; and borrow only for what you need, save money for the things you simply want. Even at that, there is a right and wrong way to borrow.

One of the first rules of borrowing is to shop around. A difference of half a percentage point can mean a lot of money over the life of a loan.

Most Canadians still have the mistaken impression that all banks, trust companies and other lending institutions are alike, offering the same services at the same rates with the same criteria for granting loans. Yet anyone who shops for a loan quickly discovers that while lenders are similar, rates do differ, as do lending limits and criteria for granting loans. Often these factors vary even among branches of the same institution.

It's a recognized fact of banking, for example, just how much managers' discretion varies, as does their willingness to take risks. Go where the bank is "hungry." You often have a better chance of getting what you want by going to a new branch in the suburbs than to a bank's main branch.

Even so, your goal is to get an institution to lend you the money you really need. The first step in achieving this is to know what the lending institution will ask for, so you won't be caught off guard.

Be prepared when walking into any lending institution to offer specific and detailed information about your income, debts and monthly payments. Of equal importance, you should know the current value of your home, car, insurance, investment portfolio and any other assets. Also prepare an up-to-date list of your liabilities.

Even if you owe a lot of money at the moment, lenders are usually impressed when applicants for loans walk in with a personal financial statement in their hands. In itself, this will often make the difference in marginal cases. It just might get you the money.

Any lending institution will want a loan application form filled out by either you or the loan officer. This usually consists of a personal statement listing income, assets, liabilities, monthly payments, and employment history. You may also be asked to sign a form giving the lender authority to make inquiries about you to a credit bureau.

Borrowers are often unaware as to how much weight is given to stable employment. An employment history of five to ten years with one company often makes the difference — but obviously not always. A person who switches jobs to gain income, add responsibility, or both, is unlikely to be rejected for this reason alone. Similarly, a stable residency is a good sign that you probably won't skip town without paying back a loan.

Lenders also like to know about a spouse's income and generally want the spouse's guarantee. In fact, many lenders like to discuss a loan with both husband and wife because either may be the one who controls the family budget. Besides, many creditors believe both parties should acknowledge how loan payments will affect their life styles. As a rule, loan officers are reluctant to grant credit where repayments may necessitate cutting back on personal spending, for the simple reason that people find it very difficult to change life styles.

Sometimes lenders will require additional security such as bonds or stocks to protect the loan. On personal loans, this security may take the form of a collateral mortgage on a home or, in the case of a loan to buy a car, a chattel mortgage on the vehicle itself.

While your local bank branch is not in the business of lending risk capital for new ventures, such funds are available for the individual who has income from other sources or a net worth which can provide the bank with some security.

Credit unions have been a growing force across the country and in some provinces, especially British Columbia and Quebec, are major competitors of the banks. So don't overlook this source.

Remember, if you have a history of not paying back your debts, or have a habit of switching jobs or residences for no apparent reason, be prepared to knock on a lot of doors before you get your loan. While lenders want new business, they like to see some stability in your life. As a back-up to the interview, lenders usually obtain a credit report on the applicant.

THERE'S MORE TO INTEREST THAN JUST THE RATE

When borrowing or lending money (and remember we are really lending money every time we put it in a savings account or term deposit), most people have a tendency to concentrate only on the interest rate.

There's another factor in the transaction that is just as important, and of which we should never lose sight. It's this: how often is the interest going to be compounded? Or, another way of putting it: how often is the interest going to be calculated and collected, paid or added to the loan, as the case might be?

If you're borrowing money, you want the interest compounded as infrequently as possible. Shoot for annual compounding if you can. On the other hand, when you're lending money, you want the interest compounded as frequently as possible. Daily would be great.

To illustrate how important the compounding factor is, here are the annual interest figures on a $10,000 loan with interest at 20%.

Compounding	Interest
annually	$2,000
semi-annually	$2,100
quarterly	$2,155
monthly	$2,194
weekly	$2,209
daily	$2,213

So if interest is compounded daily, it would be almost 11% higher than if compounded annually. Or, put another way, on daily compounding you're actually paying 22.13% compared to 20% on an annual basis. Big bucks.

Never overlook the compounding period, whichever end of the loan you're on.

Chapter 13

Buying a Car

Some of us take the purchase of a car far too lightly. Over a lifetime automobiles represent the second highest expenditure for many people. The single biggest expenditure, of course, is accommodation, which is covered in Chapter 16.

Almost every car owner, at one time or another, realizes that a bad purchase has been made. Many car owners continue to make bad purchases. When this happens the total amount of money wasted plus the income that could have been earned on it, or the interest that could have been saved through less borrowing, can mount to an enormous sum over a period of years.

Actually, the rules for making sensible car purchases can be stated quite simply. Until you can afford what you want, buy only what you need.

If you have to borrow for the purchase be sure you get the best loan available and pay it off as quickly as possible. Remember, too, the purchase price is only the beginning of your cash outlays. Don't forget interest, insurance, license, operating costs, parking and repairs.

NEW CAR OR USED CAR?

This isn't really a decision a lot of people have to make. For the most part financial circumstances or personal choice will dictate which way you go. It's a toss of the coin whether a person is better off financially going one route or the other.

Buying a new car, taking care of it, and trading it in on another new car every few years will certainly curtail your repair and maintenance costs. On the other hand, the amounts saved on the sensible purchases of used cars will often more than offset the higher operating and maintenance costs involved with them.

So I can't really tell you which is better. What I can do is point out some things to keep in mind whichever decision you make: new or used.

Buying a New Car

One of the traps to watch for in buying a new car is the opportunity to pay for a lot of features you don't need or even want. The cost of options can add up very quickly. This in turn leads to higher financing costs and the vicious circle is formed. Bear in mind that you get very little return for options on a trade-in or re-sale. You can save a lot of money over your lifetime by refusing to spend it on new-car options. This is particularly true if you're buying a car off the lot. Often they're loaded with expensive toys you certainly don't need and often don't even want. To avoid this trap, order your new car from the factory. You'll have to wait a couple of months, but the money you can save is worth it. Check out demonstrators, too. Sometimes you can get a loaded demonstrator for not much more than a basic brand new model.

Shop around. The difference in price between dealerships can be absolutely staggering. Although it may be desirable to have your car serviced where you buy it, it certainly isn't necessary. So if you can save a few hundred dollars by buying a little farther from home or work, do it. Your neighbourhood dealer will still be happy to service the car for you.

Don't just shop around for the car, shop around for your financing too. Even if the dealership offers a bit off the price if you finance through them, don't automatically jump at it. Check out the total cost (car *and* loan) of various alternatives, such as dealer financing versus bank financing, before making your final decision.

The biggest problem with buying a new car is impatience. We're always so anxious to get behind the wheel and experience that incredible feeling and smell connected with a new car, that we tend to buy impulsively. That's a luxury only the very rich can afford. The rest of us have to adhere to the advice given above: do our homework and shop around. If we do, as I mentioned earlier, the amount saved over a lifetime can be enormous.

One more thought about buying a new car. Dicker and bargain. There's almost always room to shave a few hundred dollars off the price you are first quoted. If the salesperson won't dicker, move on. There's another one out there somewhere who will.

Where to Shop for a Used Car

There are three different places to shop for a used car: private sellers; used-car dealers; and new-car dealers who have used-car lots. There are pros and cons to each.

If you buy privately you're usually getting a car with little or no reconditioning or servicing before the sale. However, this might be an advantage. Because most people don't know how to cover up mechanical faults you can often determine the real condition of the car. Although a privately sold car should cost less than one sold by a dealer, many private sellers are unrealistic in their asking prices, so don't be afraid to dicker with them also. As a matter of fact you probably have more bargaining room in a private sale than with a dealer.

Many people prefer to buy a used car from a reputable dealer who services the car well before the sale and backs it up with a written warranty. Prices may be a little lower at the dealer who sells only second-hand cars, but new-car dealers usually have a better selection of late-model trade-ins, and, of course, have service facilities.

The dealer's advertising methods are often an indication of reliability. If the dealer advertises "repossessed" cars at bargain prices, cars that turn out to have "just been sold," or no-money-down financing, be leery.

If you have a particular make of car in mind, start with a dealer who sells that car.

The simple fact is there are many, many very good used cars on the market. Especially large, luxury cars. As mentioned earlier, what you save in purchase price will often more than offset increased operating costs over your period of ownership.

However, you should bargain hard and be a total skeptic. The only thing you know for sure about a used car is that someone decided to get rid of it. Find out why.

What to Look for When Buying a Used Car

Even if all you know for sure about a used car is that somebody got rid of it for some reason, there are steps you can take — no matter how inexpert you might be — to help determine just what kind of shape the car is in.

Look over the body for signs of major repairs. Tell-tale items include ripples and bumps in the paint and signs of metal replacements. Good spots to check for rust are inside the trunk, underneath the car and on the door sills.

Let the car sit somewhere for a while and then check underneath for oil leaks. If there are any, move on to your next prospect. While on the subject of oil, warm up the car and then check to see if the exhaust is heavy or blue. If it is, it's an oil burner. Move on.

A good way to determine whether the car has been mistreated, or is really more of a used car than you want, is to check for unusual wear and tear.

Areas such as the brake pedal, accelerator pedal, arm rests, driver's seat and floor will often, by their condition, tip you off as to how ''used'' the car really is. The general condition of the carpeting, upholstery and trunk will also provide evidence of hard use or gentle care.

Sometimes, a simple way to check the accuracy of the mileage showing is to check it against the mileage recorded on the last oil change sticker. If there is a huge gap, or no sticker, some enquiries are in order.

Test Driving a Used Car Before Buying

If the used car you're looking at has passed the visual tests outlined above, the next step is to take it for a test drive.

Before getting under way, check the shock absorbers by rocking the car at each corner (corner of the car, that is, not each street corner). Push it down. When you let go it should move up and stop in a level position.

As you start the engine be sure all warning lights go on.

After starting the engine, just sit for a few minutes and listen for unusual noises or uneven idling. Be sure all gauges work.

Put your foot on the brake and hold the pressure steady for a few seconds. If the pedal goes all the way to the floor — even slowly — there may be a brake fluid problem. Check it out.

Make a number of starts, both forward and in reverse. Be sure the automatic transmission slips firmly and quickly in place. There should be no clanking or lurching. If it's a manual transmission, test the clutch. It should grab firmly, not slip.

Now, go where the speed limit allows it, and accelerate briskly up to 90 kilometres per hour. The acceleration should be smooth and quiet. If you hear knocking or other weird noises, forget that car.

Make a few sharp turns in both directions. If the car doesn't turn easily and naturally, move on. Test the brakes a few times, too, to ensure there's no squealing or pulling to the right or left. As already mentioned, the brake pedal should be firm, even under pressure.

When you turn off the key, the motor should stop, quickly and quietly.

Assuming you've satisfied yourself about the used car you're going to buy using the methods described above, there's still one more step to take. It's probably the most important step of all. Have the car checked thoroughly by an unbiased mechanic who will be able to tell you what it will probably cost to put it in shape. Even if you're advised against buying the car, take the advice and consider the cost a good investment.

Making the Used Car Deal

Now the deal itself. Get it in writing and don't sign anything before reading it carefully and making sure you fully understand everything. Don't ever sign an agreement of sale that isn't completely filled in. If you're negotiating with a dealer, don't commit yourself to anything until you have a signed price commitment from an authorized official of the dealer as well as the salesperson. This holds true for new cars, too.

If you've got cash, don't listen to anyone who insists that you just make a small downpayment. You should borrow or finance as little as possible, and, if you do, be sure you know exactly how much the loan is going to cost.

Be sure what's now your car is insured before you drive it away, and licensed, too, of course. As in the case of a new car, don't take insurance or financing offered by a dealer just because it's convenient to do so.

Shop around and take the best deal, the one that costs you the least when you add together the cost of the car and the cost of financing.

Never spend all your money on a used car. You're going to need some for repairs.

Last but Definitely Not Least

When buying a used car, always have a search done to determine who actually owns it and whether there are any liens against it. The same advice applies to buying a boat or any other asset that may have a lien registered against it.

If you find out the registered owner isn't the person you're dealing with, walk away. Deal only with the registered owner. If you find there's a lien on the vehicle, make out your cheque jointly to the owner and the lien holder. They can sort out themselves who gets what, and you'll be protected.

Usually this type of registration (both liens and ownership) falls under provincial jurisdiction. The rules vary from province to province, and the steps required to do your search may also vary. Check with your provincial transportation and consumer affairs ministries to determine exactly what you have to do in order to be completely protected. At the very least you'll need a serial number and name to do a proper search.

Some government departments will carry out such searches for a small fee. Automobile clubs might do it for you. But if the deal is a large one, or a complex one, get legal advice.

Always do the search before signing the deal. If you don't, you could end up with no car and no refund.

Chapter 14

Marriage Contracts

In an era in which almost a third of Canadian marriages fail, the well-worn phrase "what is mine is yours" quickly disintegrates when the time comes to carve up the family assets.

Indeed, many couples whose marriages failed after ten, twenty or even thirty years, with many thousands of dollars of property involved, have found themselves haggling in lawyers' offices over such mundane matters as who owns the television set and who gets the cat.

Aware of these prospects, many Canadian couples are now taking steps to clearly define their property rights. From teenage newlyweds to skeptical oldtimers heading to the altar for the second or third try, spouses are taking the time to visit lawyers' offices long enough to hammer out the fine points of a marriage contract. Their hope is that by drafting their own document, they will be able to earmark clearly and concisely who owns what, how they intend to share their assets during marriage, and how such assets will be divided up if their marriage fails.

Marriage contracts, of course, are not new. Such contracts have been popular for many years in Quebec where the Civil Code, rather than English common law, determines spousal property rights. What is new is that, under family reform legislation in many provinces, it is possible for couples to draw up a marriage contract that anticipates the disposal of property in the event of marriage breakdown. Until the mid-seventies such contracts were legal only if they did not anticipate or tentatively plan for the eventuality of separation or divorce.

Although the very thought of a marriage contract may be repugnant to those of us who hold traditional views, some undeniable facts should be taken into account in appropriate circumstances. For example, in the undeniable category is the fact that many marriages break up and the splits are seldom neat and clean.

Marriage contracts may be particularly attractive to couples who feel current marital laws go either too far or not far enough in sharing property.

People involved in second marriages or common-law relationships might also find contracts particularly useful.

If you and your spouse or future spouse are contemplating a marriage contract, and feel that it may provide you with a clearer definition of your property rights, then your first step should be to sit down and openly discuss all joint and individual assets. You should also include in your discussion the extent to which you wish to share these assets and how you would divide your property.

You may wish to design your contract to include:

1. Full disclosure of assets. This clause should name all sources of income plus existing assets. Include all real estate and personal property as well as income derived from employment and investments such as stocks and bonds.
2. Property acquired before marriage. You may agree that all possessions brought to the marriage will be shared jointly during its course. With a contract you can stipulate that each spouse will retain full ownership of property acquired before marriage even after your vows have been exchanged. (But keep in mind that in most provinces, you cannot deprive your spouse of the marital home during the course of the marriage, even if you own it. If the marriage breaks down, special rules will likely come into play.)
3. Property acquired during marriage. Several options are available here: you may follow provincial reform legislation and agree to share all family assets on a 50-50 basis. Or you may draw up a contract which specifically defines that real property acquired during marriage will not be owned on an equal basis but as "tenants in common," that is, in proportion to each person's original investment.
4. Cash and business assets. If this is not covered by law, then you may contract to share (or not share) cash and business holdings. This clause may include registered retirement savings plans, savings accounts, term deposits, stocks, bonds and insurance earnings.
5. Bank accounts. You may want to contract for a joint bank account to keep the day-to-day practicalities of your marriage running smoothly.

For instance, you may agree to deposit, in direct proportion to each spouse's income, sufficient funds to pay for such expenditures as the mortgage, food, fuel, cable T.V., telephone, home maintenance, furniture and child care expenses. The balance of your net incomes can then be pooled and divided equally between you for your own use.

6. Child support. While under the law you cannot opt out of your obligation as a parent, you can contract to limit your obligation. For instance, if one spouse earns less than the other, a clause in your contract could specify that each spouse will pay for a child's maintenance in direct proportion to earnings.

Since it has not been a widespread practice for Canadian couples to have marriage contracts, most couples don't know the first thing about them.

Many lawyers frankly admit that they have had limited experience in drawing up such documents.

It's worth examining some pitfalls. Make sure you insert a clause which will allow you to reasonably revise the contract. Otherwise, you may run into difficulties later if you want to modify one clause or change the document completely and your spouse won't cooperate. At this point, you may be forced to stay with what you have.

Make sure that you also include a provision which protects the framework of your contract. Include a clause, for instance, stipulating that even if a particular clause is ruled invalid, the remainder of the contract remains enforceable.

Because people and times change, be sure you include the provision that your contract may be terminated by the written agreement of both you and your spouse.

Once you and your spouse have hammered out what you want in the contract, you could legally write your own. But it would not be a very good idea. Most people have no knowledge of family law, and a badly drawn document could create enormous legal problems later. As with wills, the key is to get good legal advice.

A good lawyer, preferably one with experience in family law and specifically in drawing up marriage contracts, will be able to point out areas which you might have overlooked. A lawyer may also be able to give you some obscure but beneficial information. For instance, if you live in a jurisdiction where it's not legal to draw up a contract with a separation clause, then it may be possible to adopt the law of another jurisdiction which does have this provision.

Since lawyers usually charge by the hour, you should reach an agreement on as many points as possible before involving the lawyer. The cost of drawing up a contract doesn't depend on the value of assets involved, but on the time needed to arrive at the finished contract.

Don't settle for legal gobbledygook. Your contract should be written in an ordinary layperson's language so you can understand it.

Even with the trend in Canadian family law to increased freedom for couples to define their personal property rights, drawing up a marriage contract probably won't hurt. In fact, it may help couples to more clearly define their status with each other and with society. With so many of our marriages ending in divorce courts, a contract may be one of the few tangible ways of defining each person's rights and responsibilities in the matrimonial home.

Chapter 15

A Couple of Thoughts on Changing Jobs

One of life's great blessings is having a job that you thoroughly enjoy. One of the most depressing things in life is to have to get up in the morning to go to a job you hate. So it's not surprising that every day there are thousands of people looking for more satisfying, better-paying, better-located, or just simply better jobs — even in times of high unemployment.

Many books and articles have been written on how to look for a job, dealing with topics such as how to prepare a résumé; how to write a letter of application; how to dress; how to be interviewed; and just about everything else imaginable. Now, these are all valid considerations and most, if not all, of these books and articles contain very good advice.

But, if you're looking for a better job, there is one piece of advice which is more important than all the others put together — especially these days. It's this: don't quit the job you have until you find another one.

Unless you're independently wealthy, quitting your present job is bound to cut deeply into your budget, your savings, or both. This alone could have such an effect on your self-confidence and judgment that it more than offsets the possible advantages of having more time to look around and have interviews. Furthermore, people *with* jobs often find it easier to *get* a job than someone who's not working.

Often people who are quite content with their jobs come across opportunities to make a move. If you're going to make a move to enhance your long-term future, that's one thing. But if you're about to change jobs simply because the immediate salary would be higher, you had better stop and think. There is more to the economics of changing jobs than the salary.

A very important economic aspect of a job change is the comparison of fringe benefits. Quite often a salary increase would be more than offset by reduced fringe benefits such as pension plan, group insurance coverage, medical plans, company cars, vacations and the like. So always consider these items when contemplating a job change.

What about location? Travel costs are pretty high these days. If it's going to cost you a lot more in travel — both in terms of money and time — take that into consideration. There are other things to think about: will it cost you an extra $25 a week because there's no cafeteria at the new job; will it cost you more to dress for the new job?

However, these items work both ways. Sometimes you'll be better off with the same, or a lower, salary because the fringe benefits and other considerations are a lot better in the new postion.

Don't change jobs without looking at the economics as well as all the other considerations, such as the effect on your quality of life and the reactions of family members.

Chapter 16

Investing in Real Estate

There are a number of different ways to invest in real estate: owning your own home; owning a recreation property; owning property which you rent to others; owning raw land; owning shares in real estate corporations; and investing in mortgages. The first two — owning your own home or a recreation property — are probably the most common, and certainly the largest, investments that most people make. Ironically, though, many people don't look upon them as investments, but rather concentrate on their usefulness as filling a need or fulfilling a wish. At the same time, they represent the investment vehicle with which most individuals are most familiar. Nevertheless, some points in connection therewith are not well understood. There are some misconceptions.

This chapter will remind you of some things you may have forgotten about real estate as an investment, clarify some others, and maybe even raise some considerations you hadn't thought about at all.

YOUR BEST INVESTMENT

Your residence is probably the best investment you will ever make.

Although not a perfect hedge against inflation (but then, nothing is), over the long run, residential real estate probably comes closest. Couple this with the fact there is no capital gains tax payable on any increase in value throughout the period during which a property qualifies as your principal residence, and you see it's very difficult to find a better long-term investment.

In addition, there is no other investment that carries with it such utilitarian value. As mentioned in Chapter 1, we all need four walls around us, a roof over our heads, and a place to go to the bathroom. Furthermore, there is probably no other investment that consistently contributes as much to our everyday enjoyment. With the coming of age of home computers, VCRs, pay and cable television and the like, the importance of the home in all aspects of our lives will probably increase.

The lesson is clear. If you can afford to buy, don't rent. Even if you have to settle for less attractive accommodation, or a less desirable area, you are far better off being an owner than sitting on the outside looking in while property values continue to rise away from you.

Even though most people buy their homes (particularly their first one) based on what they can afford, there are a number of things to keep in mind. For example, the price of the home itself is only one of the components of its total cost to you. The interest cost of financing it has to be taken into consideration. Furthermore, you're going be directly responsible for a number of additional costs which were previously built right into your rent, such as repairs, insurance, property taxes, water and, in some cases, electricity and heating.

There are also one-time costs involved in buying a house which have to be taken care of. These include legal fees, moving, land transfer taxes in some jurisdictions, and other so-called "closing adjustments" such as oil in the tank and property taxes already paid by the vendor for the period of time during the current year in which you will be the owner.

It's rare to find a house that you can just move into. Usually you'll have to do some decorating and repairing and you'll often need some additional drapes, curtains, furniture and tools. For example, if you live in an apartment you aren't likely to own a lawnmower, rake and snow shovel. All of these costs have to be considered.

Another consideration is what type of a house you want — an old one or a new one? Here are a couple of points to keep in mind when making this decision. With an older house you're usually in a position to negotiate over items like drapes, fixtures, and appliances. If you like the idea of having a new house, remember that you are really starting from scratch.

A new house usually has absolutely nothing in it — no appliances, carpets, fixtures or drapes. These items are very costly if you have to go out and buy them new.

Now, how do you find your house? The two most popular routes to follow when looking for a house are registering with a real estate agency and having them look for you, or looking in the newspaper yourself.

If you register with a real estate agency, you simply tell the agent how much you can afford to pay and the area in which you want to live. The agent will then call you when something comes available. This doesn't cost you anything.

Right about now is the time to get an "Interest Amortization Table."

You'll find this to be a most helpful item to have at hand when you're looking at homes. This book tells you how much your mortgage payments will be each month, at whatever percent of interest you'll be paying over the amortization period you choose. This book is quite simple to get. Most bookstores will have one, and if they don't carry it on the shelf, they will order it for you.

When the agent takes you to look at homes, don't be afraid to look in cupboards and closets. If the people who are selling the home are there, ask them questions, such as how much the heating bills are each month. Is the house insulated? How long have they lived there? What kind of public transportation is available? But remember when assessing the answers that these folks are trying to sell the property. When you find a house you are really interested in, go back and see it at least one more time before you make an offer. Don't ever get pressured into a quick decision; it's very apt to be a wrong one.

After you've seen the house at least twice and you know you can afford the monthly bills and the mortgage payment, make an offer to purchase.

Have the agent write up a formal offer. Make sure you list everything you want left in the house, such as fixtures, broadloom, stove, refrigerator, washer and dryer — don't just say "appliances." You may want to put clauses in your offer such as "this home has never been insulated with urea-formaldehyde." Another clause might be that the people who now own the house must take everything with them when they move out, other than what you have listed in the offer. You don't want to move in and find they've left all the old furniture and garbage they didn't think was worth taking with them to their new home.

Now that you have your offer ready, no matter what the agent says, don't sign anything! See a lawyer. An offer to purchase is a binding legal document that should be carefully reviewed by a lawyer familiar with real estate matters. It is also important that you see a lawyer of your choice. Don't use the same lawyer as the vendor or the real estate agent. A little time and money now could save a fortune in dollars and disappointment later on.

Another thing to keep in mind when planning to purchase a home is that the federal and provincial governments have in recent years introduced many and varied plans to assist homebuyers, particularly first-time buyers. From time to time, both levels of government have introduced temporary purchase assistance grants. Because these plans come and go, and are changed with almost every federal and provincial budget, it could be misleading to get into any details of them here. If you're contemplating the purchase of a home, however, especially if you're a first-time buyer, you should enquire as to what government assistance or income tax breaks might be available. The real estate agent will probably know all about them, but if not, your accountant, lawyer, or bank or trust company manager should be able to advise you.

Many of the comments under the heading of "Buying a Country Property" apply as well to your regular residence, so read on.

Remember that a cheap house in an expensive neighbourhood is a better investment than an expensive house in a cheaper neighbourhood. You never want to own the best house on the block.

RECREATION PROPERTIES

Perhaps you should consider buying a cottage, farm, chalet or other recreation property as protection against the ravages of inflation.

We usually think of such properties in terms of family vacations or a country retreat where we can enjoy the outdoor life. All well-located recreation properties offer these benefits, of course, but they might also be a smart investment.

An example is in order. Say you have $70,000 which you plan to invest, reinvesting the income each year to create a retirement nest egg. The first thing you have to take into account is that the income will be taxable. For many people, this means losing 40 to 50 percent of it.

Say you invest at 8%. Your money would earn $5,600 in the first year — but at a 50 percent tax rate, you would pay $2,800 in income tax. Your investment would total $72,800. After five years you would have about $85,000. Seems okay, doesn't it? Well, it's not — because inflation will likely have eroded the value of your money substantially. If we apply even a 5% inflation loss each year for five years to that $85,000, it turns out that that amount of money would be worth less than your original $70,000. Your nest egg is shrinking fast.

Now, let's say that instead of salting your $70,000 away for a rainy day, you put it toward the purchase of a lakeside cottage. It's a fair assumption that the value of the cottage and lot will appreciate over a period of time. At the very least, you can safely assume that over the long term your cottage will stay even with inflation.

Five years from now, if we take the same 5% annual inflation rate, the $70,000 you sank into the cottage would be worth around $90,000. This is simply the equivalent, in these inflated dollars, of your $70,000 in current dollars.

You would, however, have paid expenses on the cottage, such as property taxes, hydro, and maintenance, which we can estimate to be $1,000. If we apply a five percent inflation rate to this, you would pay about $1,300 in expenses in five years' time — or a total of about $6,800 over the five years. Take that from the inflated value of the cottage, and you have an investment of $83,200.

You should also consider the intangibles.

First, we can assume that over the years you and your family enhance the value of the cottage through your own efforts. Clearing the land, improving the waterfront, and putting in flower beds and shrubbery are all chores you and your family will want to do anyway. These improvements will add substantially to resale value.

Second, you may contribute much of your own labour to improvements to the building itself, by redecorating, constructing built-in furniture, perhaps putting on an addition or even building a guest cottage. You will get far more than just your money back when you sell.

Third, you will not find it difficult to rent your cottage during periods when you aren't using it, to help offset costs.

Fourth, you will save on family vacation costs every year you use your cottage.

Fifth, and most important, desirable real estate in highly popular markets has traditionally increased in value much more rapidly over the long term than general inflation. Population pressures plus the relative scarcity of good vacation land will help push up the resale value of your cottage over the years. Just be certain you choose well — waterfront access on a popular body of water, no more than three or four hours' drive from a major population centre.

Of course no one can predict the future, so you will never be absolutely certain that any financial decision you make today will turn out to be the very best for you five years from now. If inflation were to fall off drastically, for example, things could turn out quite differently — but this is not likely.

An informed guess, based on past experience, is that you could enjoy all the pleasure of cottage ownership and create a retirement nest egg at the same time.

BUYING A COUNTRY PROPERTY

An old home, fresh air, a garden, peace and quiet, and the promise of easy living away from the stress of the city all send people scurrying into the countryside in search of dreamland. Finding your paradise, or knowing it when you see it, is quite another matter.

Locating a country home is not at all like buying one in town. Business in Ruralsville is conducted at a more leisurely and far less exacting pace.

If you're heading in that direction, here are ten suggestions which might make life a little easier for you:

1. Choose an area that interests you and then spend a fair amount of time getting to know it well. Drive around the roads. Call into the stores and service stations and get the owners talking about properties that might be for sale if and when there is a buyer. Watch the local papers and visit properties that are up for sale. Have local real estate brokers show you everything that even vaguely meets your desires; there's no better way to learn about what you like and don't like than actually inspecting properties.
2. Read about old homes, particularly articles that list problems you might encounter and what it may cost you to set them right. It's useful to know, for example, that a beat-up-looking building with a solid foundation may have more life left in it than a beautifully painted ranch style with a leaky basement.
3. Be skeptical about anything good you are told about a property, and remember that if any faults are mentioned, you can bet they will be humdingers.
4. Ask embarrassing questions like: "It's impossible to heat the upstairs in February, isn't it?"
5. Never actually buy a country home in the summer. Look, certainly; probe, by all means; show you are interested if you must; but don't make an offer. October, or even better, a rainy day in November, is the best time to talk money. The country looks good enough during the summer to blind you. Vendors and agents know that and adjust their prices accordingly. In late fall, on the other hand, your July manor may more closely resemble the house from the movie *Psycho*.
6. Don't be enthralled by any one particular aspect of a property. The pond at the bottom of the hill won't keep you warm in January. An old barn can be better enjoyed in a painting on the wall than through a

drafty window. Owning a home ''well back from the road'' is privacy in the summer but a curse in the winter and spring.

7. Check the land. Walk around it with the broker or vendor and determine roughly where the boundaries are. Walking it is also the best way to find the swamp. Find out if anyone has access rights across the property.
8. Check the well and the sewage system. If the well is shallow you will almost certainly have to drill a new one sometime, and that's expensive. If there's no septic tank you will likely need one.
9. Check the house. You should have a contractor inspect any home you intend to buy, but with the help of a few small tools — a flashlight, icepick, measuring tape, binoculars, and paper and pencil, you can get a fair idea yourself of whether you're considering a handyman's delight or the real thing. Begin in the basement. If it's dry, that's a great start. If the foundation looks like it needs a lot of work, thank the owner and move on. Use the flashlight to check the corners and beams. If the beams appear soft, jab them with the icepick. If you hit solid wood without going in too deep they are likely okay. Check the wiring. Chances are it will have to be replaced. Have a look at the plumbing. If it isn't copper it will probably have to be replaced, too. Locate the furnace — if there is one. Unless it's hot water or forced air you will likely need a new one. In the living areas pay close attention to the walls. If the plaster sags or has damp spots you will want to replace it with wallboard after curing the cause. Go over the layout using the tape measure and note any load-bearing walls (they usually run at right angles to the support beam, but not always, and are tremendously expensive to remove). Windows should open and close easily. If there is a fireplace, shine your light up the flue. It should be clear. Ask about insulation: regardless of what you're told you will probably need more. Outside, look at the roof with the binoculars. Unless it seems to be in A-1 shape it will probably need some attention.
10. As you complete this exercise, list all the things the house will require to make it liveable — new roof, wiring, plumbing, furnace, insulation and so on. Make a rough guess at how much it will cost to repair or replace each item. Total the amounts, double the result and add that total to the asking price. Now you have some idea of what paradise will cost you. If country living still appeals to you, make an offer.

PROPERTY TAXES

Many Canadians year after year continue to pay too much property tax. Different municipalities assess their properties and levy their taxes in different ways. There is very little consistency across the country and, even more important, each assessment method relies heavily on the personal judgment of the assessor.

The result is that many taxpayers are paying either too much or too little in property taxes. The municipality will usually adjust your property tax if the facts are drawn to its attention on a timely basis and if an adjustment is actually warranted.

If you think you've been hit with an unfair property tax assessment, this is one time when it may be worth your while to fight city hall. You stand a chance of getting a reduction in assessment on appeal. But the bonus here is that appealing your assessment is free; all it will cost is time and a little leg work.

If you're too busy to spend time researching the market values and documenting an appeal, your spouse or even your older children may be able to do it for you. The fact is that reducing an assessment is relatively straightforward and the chances are you won't need to consult a professional. There are definite steps that you can take yourself to effectively reduce an unfair assessment.

First, make sure your assessment is actually for *your* property. Strange as it may seem, assessments are sometimes addressed incorrectly or refer to the wrong property.

If it is your assessment, the next step is to check out how your home compares in value with others in the neighbourhood. This will take some work on your part, but comparing how your property stacks up with others in the neighbourhood is the main point of an appeal and is usually well worth the effort.

Here are steps you can take to determine if you've been unfairly assessed:

1. Compile a list of some properties in your area that closely resemble yours. Include in your list those that have the same features as yours, such as garage, swimming pool, or similar size. If similar properties are for sale in your area, all the better. This way you can establish the current market value from your realtor.
2. Visit the local Registry Office and confirm that the information about your property is correctly recorded.

3. Ask the local assessment office for your neighbourhood's property rolls. On these rolls you can check out the assessment shown opposite the properties you've listed. Simply write in beside them the sales values.
4. With this information, you should be able to establish ratios of assessments to market values which can be compared to the ratio calculated for your property. When you know these ratios you can determine if you have grounds for an appeal. If yours is out of line, you've got a good case.
5. Determine whether the assessor worked within the rules of the relevant assessment act. This may require the help of a specialist such as a property tax consultant, and such services may cost you a lot of money. It's only worth it in extreme cases.
6. Call the district assessment office and arrange an informal meeting with the assessor. This gives the assessor the opportunity to correct any errors. If the assessment is wrong, the assessor will usually file an amended assessment right away.

By approaching the problem this way, you can avoid spending further time at the appeal stage. But if this negotiation fails, file an appeal.

Count on taking a day off to sit in appeal court prior to your hearing to see what happens; allow yourself another day to collect further data and to attend the appeal itself.

Keep in mind that the appeal court can also raise your taxes as well as lower them, so be sure you have a good case before you go there. Remember, too, that deadline periods for appeals are not flexible; the court will only hear your appeal for the current year's property taxes. This is a very important point to note because the appeal periods are relatively short. Check your assessment notice carefully for the appeal deadline and the address where the appeal must be made.

The appeal process itself is usually pretty straightforward. Start by listing your reasons for appealing on the reverse side of your notice of assessment and send it to the proper authority.

When your appeal date has been set, it will help you to argue your case effectively if you:

1. Take time beforehand to prepare enough copies of your appeal so that all members of the court can follow your argument.
2. Limit your argument to pertinent points. This will retain the attention of the court.

3. Support your case with exhibits, such as charts showing the comparable values of similar homes in your area. Photographs could be helpful, but don't overdo it.
4. Sum up your argument by telling the court what you think the assessment should be, and why.

Even if you are turned down at this level of appeal, you can then go to the provincial court of appeal. But consider this decision carefully. At this point, you'll need a lawyer. What began as a simple, free procedure could end up costing you a lot in legal fees.

Nevertheless, the odds of appealing your assessment might be worth the gamble. Many homeowners who appeal their property taxes effectively chop dollars from their assessment. Last, but not least, remember there is a principle at stake: why pay moe tax than necessary? Remember, a tax dollar saved is a whole dollar.

SELLING YOUR HOME WITHOUT A BROKER

When you consider that brokerage fees will eat up as much as 6% of your proceeds of sale, it's easy to understand the overwhelming temptation to sell your home privately without the help of a broker, real estate agent or consultant. Why, then, do most of the hundreds of thousands of homes sold in Canada each year go through an agent? Because there's more to selling a house than meets the eye.

If you act as your own broker, keep in mind you will need a lot of patience. It generally takes longer to sell on your own than through an agent, because an agent can reach more potential buyers through widespread advertising and listing services and will have more time and energy to devote to the task.

Remember, too, you may have to spend anywhere from several hundred to several thousand dollars to entice buyers to look at your property.

If you decide to sell on your own, begin by making your home as attractive as possible. Nothing turns potential purchasers off more quickly than peeling paint or yesterday's garbage stacked in a corner. Dirty or cracked walls should be replastered or painted; the exterior too, if it needs it. If the shrubbery or grass on your property is ugly, consider hiring a gardener to get it back in shape.

Once your house is spic and span, there are some steps which will help to close your sale successfully.

1. Set your price, and make it the current market value. Don't overprice. Most vendors arrive at the right figure by checking on other sales in the area or by telephoning real estate agents about advertised listings. Some actually entice agents to their homes for opinions under the pretence of enquiring about a listing. It's likely best to hire a professional appraiser. For a few hundred dollars a professionally qualified appraiser will consider all sales in your area and adjust for any differences between your home and ones that have recently been sold. The appraiser will give you a written report detailing the reasons for arriving at the price. Don't be shy about using the appraisal as a sales tool. It's an independent valuation that would be acceptable proof of value to most financial institutions that grant mortgages, an important consideration to possible purchasers.
2. After setting the price, notify the mortgage holder and see if they would be prepared to lend money to a purchaser, and if so, how much and on what terms — all necessary information to prospective buyers.
3. Put up a neat, simple sign. If you're concerned about strangers dropping in at all hours, indicate on the sign "By Appointment." Otherwise, "For Sale" and your telephone number are enough.
4. Your sale will have its widest exposure if you place a classified ad in the newspaper. Count on spending a few hundred dollars if you have to advertise for a long time. Always ask about weekly or monthly rates before placing an ad. The ad should include location, type of house, outstanding features, asking price (raise this if you want to leave room for bargaining) and your phone or box number.
5. Have your lawyer review any offer you are contemplating accepting. Also notify your lawyer of any liens against your property so that arrangements can be made for removing them before your house is sold. A good lawyer will also advise you of any potential flaws in an offer you are considering. Lawyers' fees will vary from transaction to transaction, but fees charged for a relatively simple sale are very reasonable considering the possible costs of a defective sale.
6. When you have cleared a serious offer with your lawyer, consult your mortgage holder to ensure everything is in order.
7. Have the purchaser give your lawyer a deposit with the offer (usually half the down payment). Your lawyer will keep it in escrow until the sale is closed. If your buyer fails to come up with the remainder of the down payment, you usually get to keep the deposit.

8. Your lawyer should deal with any mortgages, make sure taxes have been paid, arrange for any insurance transfers, and answer questions raised by the buyer. After you have sold your home, your lawyer should also provide you with a written report outlining how the mortgages were settled, as well as other details.

When your sign goes up and your advertising campaign is on, expect calls from real estate brokers. They will attempt to persuade you that they can sell your home more quickly than you and obtain a better price. Some might even tell you that they "have a buyer looking for a home exactly like yours and willing to pay your price. Just sign this listing statement." Before changing your mind, check with your lawyer.

If you decide to go it alone, not only will you have the satisfaction of knowing that you did it on your own, but you might end up a few thousand dollars richer.

USING A REAL ESTATE AGENT

On the other hand, most real estate agents are trained to do exactly what you are trying to do — sell your property.

An agent has the resources to provide the widest possible exposure for your house, either through listing your home exclusively with his or her agency for a particular period of time, or through multiple listing services (M.L.S.). With M.L.S., a description of your house with a picture is sent to all members of your local real estate board. In an exclusive listing you agree to list only with that agent for a specified time and at a specified commission rate. It's important to remember that commission rates are now completely negotiable. You no longer have to agree to a rate fixed by a real estate board.

Whether you sign an exclusive or an M.L.S. listing, take time to check the fine print of your agreement. For instance, under some contracts you will have to pay the agent's commission, even if at the last minute the buyer fails to close the sale. Your best bet is to stick with a contract which specifies that you pay your agent's commission only if the deal actually closes. What can you expect from your agent in return for the commission? Here are some of the steps a reputable agent should take to sell your house:

1. Get a general appraisal. After investigating your home, a good agent should be able to counsel you on the price you should be looking for and why. Remember, however, it's up to you to set the price.

2. Develop a marketing strategy for selling your home. Your agent should determine what method of exposure will obtain the best results — either an exclusive listing or M.L.S. These plans should be explained to you in detail. Your agent should also place classified ads in daily newspapers at the agency's expense, although if you've negotiated a very low commission rate you may have to pick up some of these expenses yourself.
3. Interview prospective buyers on your behalf. Potential purchasers contact your agent directly. The agent should personally escort buyers through your property with your consent and at a time convenient to you. Your agent is bound by law to present every offer to you, even if it's far below your asking price. However, you are under no obligation to accept any offer. Although no credit check is usually done on a prospective buyer, your agent should screen potential purchasers by discreetly determining beforehand their probable ability to afford to buy your home. This step alone can save hours of wasted time and much frustration.
4. Negotiate your sale. Although your lawyer will handle most of the transaction, your real estate agent can accept a deposit from a buyer and keep it in escrow until the remainder of the downpayment is made and the sale is closed.

THE MIDDLE GROUND

In recent years a new element has appeared on the real estate scene that allows you to choose a middle ground between going it on your own or completely handing things over to an agent when the time comes to sell your house. This new element can be loosely described as real estate sales consultants.

For a very low commission, or even a flat fee, the consultant will advise you on how to go about acting as your own real estate agent. The degree of assistance varies widely, all the way from answering a few questions and giving very general advice to practically acting as your agent.

These consultants may be just what you need if you can't make up your mind whether to go it alone or list. But if you go the consultant route be sure of the following:

1. You're dealing with reputable, knowledgeable people.
2. You know exactly what they are going to do for you.

3. You know exactly what it's going to cost you.
4. You're confident 2. is worth 3.

BUYING FOREIGN REAL ESTATE

Often people will buy real estate outside Canada, either as a straight investment or to have a place to get away from it all for a while every now and then. Even if you know everything there is to know about Canadian real estate, the minute you step across the border you're into a whole new ball game. Laws differ, habits change and there are always problems and solutions peculiar to that other country — even one whose society closely parallels ours. The United States is no exception.

Here are a few tips to consider when contemplating the purchase of foreign real estate:

1. Investigate the developer. A developer's integrity and stability are often the most important considerations. Speak with previous customers and take a look at the developer's earlier projects if possible. Check also with state authorities and the U.S. Federal Trade Commission (F.T.C.) for outstanding complaints, if you are buying property in the United States. If there is no Canadian prospectus, inspect a copy of the property report filed with the Office of Interstate Land Sales Registration, U.S. Department of Housing and Urban Development.
2. Personally inspect your purchase. Nothing beats a first-hand look. Pretty photos of a project won't reveal the junkyard or expressway behind the camera. Investigate such amenities as recreation and shopping facilities and medical care.
3. Buy a finished unit. Buying a finished unit saves you from surprises in construction quality, general layout and appearance. The same goes for amenities such as golf courses, clubhouses, yacht clubs and tennis courts. In large development projects, these recreation features may be a year or more from completion.
4. Beware of misleading names. A multinational company's name or initials may be on the prospectus, but it may well have no obligations to guarantee the project.
5. Obtain legal advice. While some people believe that taking out title insurance, a common practice in the U.S., may eliminate the need for a lawyer's services, this may prove to be penny-wise and pound foolish.

In any purchase, hiring a lawyer is advisable. Lawyers are trained to read between the lines and track down discrepancies you may miss.

When purchasing property outside the U.S., the same words of caution apply, plus a few others. You should assess the political situation of any country in which you wish to buy property. This may be tricky, but certainly necessary. Blocked currencies, nationalization, violence and revolution are unpleasant side-effects of buying land in the wrong country.

In any foreign country, including the United States, possible income, capital gains, and estate tax implications should be carefully checked out. Frequently, onerous reporting requirements apply even to owning real estate, let alone buying and selling it.

RENTAL PROPERTIES

Many people seem to think that buying property to rent out is a great way to earn income, but the life of a landlord is more than just going to the bank to cash rent cheques.

Before you rush out to buy a house to rent out, or rent out part of the one you already own, there are a few things to consider.

First of all, you will have to take on the responsibilities and aggravations of being a landlord. Your tenants may enjoy listening to hard rock at full volume or they might like throwing wild parties late into the night — it's often hard to tell when they arrive on your doorstep enquiring about your accommodation for rent. What would you do if their rent cheques started to bounce? Would you evict them? *Could* you evict them? You should find out what your rights are as well as the rights of your tenant. You will probably find out that landlords have almost no rights compared to tenants.

What about rent controls? If they apply, forget about being a landlord. In a jurisdiction with rent controls, landlords are soon in a position where they can't raise their rents sufficiently to cover increased costs of owning and maintaining their buildings. The result is a deterioration in value of the building and often an absolute loss on the rental operation itself.

Some of these potential problems may be minimized by setting out certain rules in the lease (if you have one, and you should). But have your lawyer draw up your lease to be sure it doesn't contravene any legislation protecting tenants.

You may also run into problems if there is an excess of rental space in your community. You may not be able to keep yours fully occupied. If the conversion of part of your home to an apartment is going to involve considerable expense, you might think twice. If you want to use it again at some time in the future for your own residence you should consider the additional cost of converting back.

In order to ensure you know the result of your rental activity you should set up a separate bank account. All expenses should be paid out of this and all rental payments should be deposited into it. By setting up a simple set of books you will be able to keep track of all your expenses for the year in one place. This will be much easier than trying to remember in April what expenses you paid the previous August.

In larger urban centres you could hire a rental agent to look after all these administrative matters for you. But if you do, expect to pay anywhere from 6% to 10% of your rental income for the service.

MORTGAGES

Still another way to invest in real estate is holding mortgages. Again, this is not the type of investment that the unsophisticated investor should consider. Unless you have had considerable experience in the field, or act only after getting competent professional advice on all aspects of mortgages, you should leave it to the pros. There are volumes of laws applying solely to mortgages. They represent one of the most complex of legal documents and the rights and obligations of holding mortgages can often be a nightmare. However, in the mid-eighties a new type of security appeared on the market that solved some of these problems. It's called a mortgage-backed security.

MORTGAGE-BACKED SECURITIES

A mortgage-backed security is similar in some respects to a government bond. It's secure and it pays a fixed rate of interest. What the security actually represents is a share of a much larger pool of residential first mortgages, all of which have been insured under the National Housing Act. This means that Canada Mortgage and Housing Corp. will step in and cover any defaults.

Although the rate of return is a bit less than you could get on a mortgage you arranged directly, the security and the fact that you can invest as little as $5,000 make mortgage-backed securities very popular investment vehicles. Indeed, your biggest problem may be finding one. They are gobbled up as quickly as they become available.

You do receive your interest payments monthly, but you might not be able to get all your capital back as readily as you could with, say, short-term T-bills. If you're interested, talk to your stockbroker about them.

Chapter 17

Winning a Lottery

This chapter is not for rich folks who are accustomed to handling vast sums of money. I'm going to make some suggestions as to what you should do if you hit it lucky in one of the lotteries. Of course, no general answer exists which could be appropriately applied in all circumstances to all people and it is obvious that for some people a lottery win wouldn't change their lives a great deal. But here are some practical suggestions for winners.

First the biggy — your number comes up for the multi-million-dollar prize. What you do that night and the morning after might set the course for the rest of your life. So stop and think about it.

The first thing you must do is suppress the urge to go out in the street and announce your good fortune to the world. The next thing to do, even if you are in Tobermory, Summerside, or Moose Jaw, is hop on the first plane to the lottery head office to be there when it opens in the morning. A million dollars earns a few hundred dollars in interest a day — so any delay in picking up the prize means money lost. You may as well have it rather than the government. Don't forget, it's the governments that run the lotteries.

But you've got more to worry about than just money in a multi-million-dollar situation. You may not be able to escape the publicity since the lotteries almost always insist that you agree to have your name publicized in the case of really big wins. This means that a horde of full-time money chasers, including less fortunate relatives and friends, will learn of your good fortune. You will be flooded with requests for money — not only will beggars and crackpots be after you, but so will charities, salespeople, advisors, investment counsellors and hopeful entrepreneurs with plans for a better mousetrap.

Don't forget extortionists. People have been kidnapped for much less than a million.

The next person you have to be wary of is yourself. Resist those urges to go out and buy fancy cars and flashy jewelry. In fact, don't make any rash decisions. After cashing in the ticket and arranging for the money to earn interest, pay off all your debts, particularly your mortgage.

Then, put all the money, except for $20,000, into a three-month guaranteed term deposit with your bank. Follow this so far? Now, take your $20,000, your family and your suntan oil and disappear to an undisclosed haven and have a holiday for a month or so.

Why disappear? To escape the storm of publicity with its temptations and possible dangers, and to take time to adjust to your sudden wealth. Your money is locked into an account you can't touch — and the interest that accumulates will pay for most of your vacation. After the initial euphoria wears off, you'll be in a much better position to decide exactly what to do with the money — what to buy, how to invest, how much to give away. You will certainly need professional help in the conduct of your financial affairs. Get yourself the best advice you can from a reputable professional.

By far the most important thing to remember is not to go off the deep end that first night or next morning. A million or more will certainly change your life, but you want it to change in ways and at a pace that you can control.

Another thing not to do is immediately to begin living like the millionaires who've had their money for some years. If you move to their part of town, and try to move in their circles, you're apt to find your life-long friends (not to mention relatives) don't relate to you any more, and your new colleagues may not accept you either. Make your changes in life style slowly and carefully.

Now, what about winning $100,000? Well, $100,000 is a nice manageable amount of money. It won't fulfill your wildest dreams of wealth and luxury, but it can satisfy your immediate cash needs and bring you a measure of comfort and security. There are a few things you should do and some you should emphatically not do with your hundred grand.

Don't immediately quit your job. $100,000 is simply not enough to retire on, unless you're close to retirement age anyway and have lots of other security. The annual income from perfectly safe investments would be far less than you can live on comfortably. $100,000 is enough to give you a nice head start in life, but not enough to change your whole lifestyle — not enough to run wild on for any length of time.

Don't sell your $90,000 house, add the $100,000 to what you receive and put it all down on a $190,000 house uptown. You will still have your mortgage and other debts, and you may find that the taxes and other expenses of the larger home are more than you can handle.

Now, here's what you should do. First, collect the money immediately and get it into the bank so that it is earning interest. Then pay off all your debts, particularly your mortgage — this alone will put you a good 15 to 20 years ahead of your less fortunate friends and neighbours. You could, perhaps, leave the cash in the bank for five years or so, almost doubling it, but your interest would be taxable. Your mortgage interest, at a higher rate, is probably non-deductible, which means your real interest cost may be almost double the rate you think it is. You're better off to eliminate mortgage interest from your life altogether, especially since your home will continue to increase in value.

Then, but only then, you can buy a few things you need, or want, such as a new car, furniture, a cottage, or an extraordinary vacation.

An alternative that many people might consider is this. If you already own your home, or don't wish to own one at all, and you don't have any debt, use the $100,000 to improve your life. If you're stuck in a job you don't like, or if there's something you've always wanted to do, such as get a degree, learn a trade or write novels, your windfall gives you a golden opportunity to give it a try. By living off the interest and consuming the principal reasonably carefully, you could buy yourself at least three, and maybe more, years of freedom to pursue your personal ambition. Let's face it, this is a chance that very few people ever get.

The most important thing, however, is not to go head-over-heels off the deep end with a $100,000 lottery win. Don't quit your job right away and don't speculate with the money. Pay off all your debts — the key to financial prosperity in the long run — have a little fun, treat yourself a bit, then wisely invest whatever is left, perhaps in guaranteed investment certificates, Canada Savings Bonds, treasury bills and other forms of safe securities.

Chapter 18

Swiss Banks

The very mention of Swiss banks conjures up visions of the Mafia, drug money, the jet set and high rollers. Very little truth about Swiss banks is disclosed in such stories.

Yet there are some truths in the myths. Swiss banks have built a reputation for financial freedom, privacy and stability. The Swiss have enjoyed monetary freedom unparalleled in any other country of the world. When economic conditions deteriorate world-wide, governments tend to impose regulations such as foreign currency restrictions, wage and price controls, and gold ownership bans. The Swiss tend to avoid such over-regulation.

The political and economic stability of Switzerland, demonstrated by its neutrality in world wars and the absence of unexpected government regulation, has given Swiss bankers the opportunity to build a reputation based on reliability, competence and efficiency.

Customers of Swiss banks can rest assured that their business dealings with the bank will remain confidential, except for some situations which will be discussed later. The concept of secrecy was entrenched in the banking laws of Switzerland many decades ago, and has been revised and reaffirmed in more modern times. The laws apply to the banks and their officers and employees. Anyone who divulges information obtained in their capacity as an officer or employee of a bank could be punished by a prison term or a hefty fine. These measures were introduced in response to the bribery, blackmail and other devious means used by the Gestapo during the Nazi regime to obtain information about German citizens' foreign holdings.

The duty of secrecy ends, however, when a higher public interest clashes with the personal interest of the bank's clients in the preservation of their anonymity. Criminal activities of account holders are not protected by banking secrecy legislation. In cases of arson, common and organized crime, murder, narcotics trading and dealing in firearms, following the judgment of a Swiss Court, banks will disclose information to entitled authorities. However, in cases of political, military, exchange control or tax evasion offences punishable in other countries, Switzerland declines legal cooperation.

In recent years Swiss secrecy laws have received a great deal of media coverage as a result of severe criticism aimed at this banking tradition by other countries, primarily the United States. Switzerland has signed several treaties with other countries to provide legal assistance in prosecuting criminal cases where the crime would be a crime under Swiss law. In cases of tax evasion in Canada and the U.S., which is a failure to declare or pay taxes and considered a crime in these countries, revenue authorities have been unable to gain access to information in Swiss bank accounts of the suspects because simple tax evasion is not considered a crime in Switzerland. Therefore, no disclosure; hence the stories of aiding and abetting crime. Switzerland expects its laws to be respected, just as it makes no attempt to impose its laws elsewhere.

With its reputation for freedom, privacy and the stability of its political system and currency, Switzerland has had a significant inflow of capital from investors around the world. The diverse services provided by Swiss banks include commercial banking, portfolio management, mortgages, capital market financing and custodial services. The most highly publicized aspect of Swiss banking, the Swiss numbered account, is the Swiss banking practice that is most misunderstood. Let's clear up some of the misconceptions about the functioning of these fabled numbered accounts.

What's so special about a Swiss numbered account? All bank accounts have numbers. The difference is that the identity of the holder of the Swiss account is not shown on the account itself and is known only by a few top officials in the bank. All instructions for transactions are made by using only the number of the account.

Here's how you open a Swiss numbered account. First, the account usually must be opened in person, and depending on the bank selected this could necessitate a trip to Switzerland. Tough penalty to pay. However, a few of the big Swiss banks have opened branch offices in Toronto and Montreal, and as a result an account could probably be opened here. The bank manager would likely require a reference letter, information about your business, your assets and your family situation. A signature card bearing your coded "signature" is kept on file. If any other family members are authorized to use the account, their coded signatures would also be kept on file. The coded signature is the famous number, which could be either a pure number or a code word and number.

Most of the banks do not specify minimum balances, but might refuse to open an account for a small amount. People have been known to open an account with a couple of hundred dollars, but a few thousand would be more desirable. Some banks refuse to open small accounts because of the administrative cost and paperwork involved. Service charges are minimal.

Subject to the bank's acceptance of you as a customer, you now have a numbered account. Should you desire, it could consist of sub-accounts for foreign currencies and securities, precious metals and art custodial services. Written orders affecting any of these accounts must bear your coded signature. They are never signed with actual names. Transactions may be made by written instruction, by telephone or in person. In the latter case the transaction would take place in a private room with only the manager or other top officials of the bank present. Under Swiss law full signature names must appear on a cheque. If you wish to preserve your anonymity, a bank will issue a cashier's cheque, very similar to a money order, for a nominal fee.

There are several advantages to a numbered account. First, the central location of Switzerland within Europe affords easy communication with other industrialized nations. Switzerland's neutrality during the world wars and years of uninterrupted peace have contributed to economic stability and development. When making an investment these are important factors to consider and this advantage results in a significant inflow of capital into Switzerland when economic, political and social conditions worsen in other countries. Historically, the Swiss have permitted currency freedom to residents and non-residents, which enables people to convert their own currency to any other. However, some restrictive rules were adopted in the mid-seventies with respect to investment by non-residents in Swiss currency.

Unrestricted ownership of gold and other metals is also allowed.

This contributes to the attraction of the numbered account since transfers of an endangered currency to Swiss francs protects the asset value, and the anonymity of the numbered account provides security.

The numbered account also affords freedom from persecution. For example, in countries where foreign exchange restrictions exist, an individual can successfully transfer funds to a numbered account without leaving a trace. When the individual and his or her assets are out of the country of residence, the assets can be disposed of without any risk. To prevent the government of the country of residence gaining any knowledge of such an account, you can request that all correspondence be held at the bank.

In South American, Eastern European, and Middle Eastern countries the nationalization of mines, oil wells and factories has left many disgruntled owners without rewards for their past efforts. In the face of a threat of nationalization, the earnings of foreign participants could be transferred to numbered accounts in Switzerland to avoid loss when nationalization takes place.

The banking secrecy laws furnish protection and confidentiality to holders of accounts. Many people in the public eye, such as politicians, entertainers and movie stars, enjoy the anonymity of the numbered account and hold them for that reason. All Swiss accounts are subject to the secrecy laws and it is this additional feature of numbered accounts that is considered a necessity for many individuals. The pros of holding a numbered account are obvious for individuals in certain circumstances such as those outlined above, but the cons must be considered prior to making a decision.

Some of the disadvantages are strictly psychological. Many of us feel a sense of security in keeping our investments close to home and feel a certain discomfort about having holdings many thousands of miles away, despite Switzerland's strong track record. Numbered accounts offend legality and morality in many countries of the world, and there is that apprehension about the trouble ahead if the authorities discover it.

For Canadian and U.S. residents it is not illegal to hold numbered accounts. However, the U.S. requires that all foreign holdings be disclosed on your annual tax return. As long as the account produces no income, there can be no tax evasion. In Canada, a tax is levied on the world income of residents, so that if there were interest or dividends in the account, this fact would have to be reported. In addition, when accounts holding foreign currencies are closed and funds repatriated, any appreciation of the foreign currency relative to the Canadian dollar might be subject to tax.

Getting back to the U.S. for a moment: even though the penalties for non-disclosure of foreign holdings may not be severe, there is the loss of anonymity upon discovery by the authorities. Weighing the benefits of privacy and the potential consequences of being found out allows each individual to make a decision that he or she can live with.

The transfer of funds to a Swiss account without leaving a trace presents an obstacle. Records of cheques cashed are kept by Canadian banks. However, small amounts could be transferred by money orders, which do not require the sender's signature, and several of these could be sent at one time. The use of cashier's cheques is also a possibility. Of course, you can always stuff a black bag with cash and make a trip.

In countries which impose foreign currency controls, transferring assets can be a costly procedure. First it is necessary to buy hard currency illegally in the black market of the resident country. A stiff premium will be paid for the currency depending on the size of the transaction and the conditions of the local and international currency. A commission is also levied by the broker who arranges the transfer of the funds.

The question of Swiss taxes also arises. On Swiss deposits and securities bearing interest or earning dividends, held by non-residents, a withholding tax is levied and withheld by the banks when the income is deposited to the account. At present there is a tax convention between Canada and Switzerland which eases the tax burden.

As mentioned, Switzerland occasionally imposes restrictions limiting the inflow of foreign funds. You should always keep abreast of the current situation.

Now that the pros and cons of the numbered account have been considered, the decision is yours. It may make no economic sense, but the snob appeal is irresistible to many.

PART TWO

Income Tax

Chapter 19

Prelude to Income Tax

As already mentioned, this is not an income tax book. Rather, it is a book designed to help you better manage your financial affairs regardless of the level of your income or the amount of taxes you pay. This book will not have to be updated every time the federal government introduces a new tax change, and you can be sure that the advice given in other chapters is still valid without having to check to see whether there's been a later edition.

This is not to say, however, that income tax doesn't represent a major component of everyone's personal financial affairs. Of course it does. And wherever income tax is a significant factor in the advice given in this book, you are reminded to seek professional advice.

If your income tax affairs are particularly complex, you should be seeking professional advice in any event. For those of you whose affairs are less complex, but who want to be sure they are consistent with good tax planning, there is a very easy way to keep up-to-date. All large accounting firms, many insurance companies and other financial institutions have up-to-date pamphlets and booklets describing most facets of personal tax planning, which they will be pleased to provide you at no cost. Ask for them and ask for up-dated copies each year.

Even though income tax laws change so rapidly it is almost impossible to keep up-to-date with specific rates, levels of exemptions, and the like, there are enough traditional elements in our income tax system that a fair amount of useful advice can be given. Hence, this part of the book.

The following chapters deal in general terms with a number of basic Canadian income tax provisions which affect many, many individual taxpayers.

Even though the topics chosen are of general interest and have been presented in a manner that should stand the test of time, income tax laws do change every year. So, don't take the following chapters as a substitute for the law. Before acting on the words contained in this part of the book, always check to see if the words are still relevant. They probably will be, but they may not. They are designed to serve as a reminder rather than as an income tax guide.

Anyway, enough warning. Let's get on with this unpleasant but necessary subject.

Chapter 20

Filing Your Income Tax Return

MUST YOU?

Must you file an income tax return each year? Maybe. Maybe not.

Generally speaking you're only required to file a personal income tax return if you have some income tax to pay. If you're entitled to a refund, or have had enough tax withheld to cover your income tax liability for the year, you don't have to file a return unless Revenue Canada asks for one. But as in most things having to do with income tax, there are exceptions.

If you have a taxable capital gain you have to file a return, even if there is no income tax to pay because of a capital gains exemption, or any other reason for that matter. As a matter of fact, you are not eligible for the lifetime capital gains exemption *unless* a return is filed reporting your gains. You even have to file a return if you've had a capital loss.

You have to file a return in order to obtain any of the refundable income tax credits, such as the sales tax credit or the child tax credit. If you are one of the taxpayers who receive a prepayment of such credits you have to file a return, even if there is no other amount being claimed.

If you're entitled to any of the various provincial tax credits that are linked to the federal income tax return, you must file that return to obtain such credits. Similarly, if you're entitled to a refund of an overpayment of unemployment insurance or Canada Pension Plan premiums, the only way you'll get it is if you file an income tax return. And speaking of Canada Pension Plan, if you have self-employed income or pensionable income on which insufficient premiums have been paid (such as commission income or tips), the only way you can contribute additional amounts and get credit for them is by filing an income tax return.

If you're entitled to an income tax refund, no matter how obvious this might be, the only way you're going to get it is if you file an income tax return and claim it.

Even if you feel you're a borderline case, file the return! Quite often you're in for a surprise either way: a pleasant one if you file and get a refund you weren't expecting; or an unpleasant one if you don't file and find out later you should have. This latter situation often results in interest or penalties being levied.

If you have business income you should always file a return. This is the only way to protect certain of your deductions and carry-over amounts.

It's also the best way to protect against unpleasant surprises later when Revenue Canada might decide you owe a few years' tax complete with the aforementioned interest and penalties.

So you see, the odds are overwhelming that most of the people reading this book should be filing annual income tax returns. The next question then is whether you can do your own return or need professional help.

CAN YOU DO IT YOURSELF?

For most people the cost of getting a tax return prepared by a professional — or for that matter by an amateur, for there are lots of amateurs preparing tax returns in the spring of each year — is not deductible. It's only deductible if you have business income, rental income, or a whole lot of investment income.

The simple fact is the vast majority of you who are reading this book could not deduct the cost. But you probably *can* do your own return. The form looks scary, but if you follow the guides carefully, stick to the instructions, *and* double check your work before filling out the return in final form, you can probably do it yourself. The problem is the Income Tax Act is so complicated there is little chance of you knowing for sure your return is correct.

On the other hand, if you have business income or any other complicated income tax situation, or if you want to be absolutely sure your income tax return is correct, then get professional help. But be sure you consult real tax professionals. As mentioned earlier, there are lots of amateurs out there preparing income tax returns each year.

THE PROS AND CONS OF TAX DISCOUNTERS

Each year firms spring up offering you 85% of your income tax refund right away, provided you give them the rights to all of it. Should you? Well, not too many people are neutral about tax discounters. Some consider them loan sharks. Others consider them saviours. Who's right depends on the particular circumstances.

The facts are these. The discounters charge an outrageous rate of interest. Remember what they're really doing is lending you money. On the other hand, banks and other lending institutions must be dropping the ball or there wouldn't be a market for income tax discounters.

The disadvantage of using a discounter is the real cost. Even allowing for the fact most will prepare your tax return free if you discount with them, you're still going to be paying interest at rates of up to 100% or more. The actual rate depends on how long you'd have to wait for your refund.

For example, suppose you're entitled to a refund of $1,000 and the discounter is going to give you $850 now. The $150 is the cost of borrowing that $850 between the time you received it from the discounter and the time you would have gotten your full $1,000 back from Revenue Canada. If that is, say, eight weeks, you've paid $150 interest to borrow $850 for eight weeks. That's an annual interest rate of over 114%! Even if they don't charge you for doing your income tax return you're paying a tremendous rate of interest. In the same set of circumstances, even assuming it was worth $75 to have your return prepared, you're paying interest on the $850 at the rate of 57%.

The advantage of using a tax discounter is you'll get 85% of your money without a lot of hassle and embarrassment. Most lending institutions aren't really interested in granting small loans in these circumstances and discourage them in various ways.

If it's a small refund and you desperately need the money, the tax discounter will probably fulfill your needs. But if it's a large refund, try to borrow the money at conventional lending institutions, or wait for your refund. The tax discounter is just too expensive.

DOING YOUR RETURN

As I've already mentioned, most of you probably can do your own income tax returns. Unless you have business income, or complicated rental or investment affairs, with a little patience and careful study of the tax guides you can, in all likelihood, do your own return and do it right. As I also already mentioned, the problem is that our tax laws are so complicated that it's virtually impossible for you to be *sure* it's right. But, assuming you're an adventuresome soul and intend to go it on your own, the most important points to remember are as follows.

First, read the relevant guides all the way through, referring to the form as you do, *before* you start to fill out the form. Mark the areas in the guides which apply to you so you can easily refer back to them later when actually filling out the return. Second, use the working copy to do the return in draft, in pencil, before trying to fill out the final form for mailing. Next, double check the draft form before transferring the figures to the mailing copy. And, finally, double check the mailing copy before signing and mailing it.

The main ingredient here is patience. Don't try to fill out the form until you've gone over all the parts of both the form and the guides that affect you.

Get Your Forms Early

There are few things as frustrating as getting all settled in to do your income tax return and then discovering there are income tax forms you need that you don't have. Here's a list of some of the forms some of you may need. The time to get them is before you start to work on your T1.

If you're claiming an exemption for a spouse or child who lives outside Canada, you're going to need a form T1E-NR.

If you're claiming moving expenses, you need a form T1-M.

If you're an employee claiming expenses for which you were not reimbursed, such as travel or automobile use, you'll need a T2200. Your employer has to sign this one too. So if you need a T2200, you'd better get after it right after the end of the year.

If you're claiming a disability deduction for the first time, you're going to need a T2201. You're going to have to get this one certified by a doctor. So here's another one you'd better get working on well before you start to fill out your T1.

If you're reporting rental income you'll need a T776 and the Rental Income Tax Guide.

If you're carrying back a loss to a previous year you'll need a T1A.

If you're claiming an education credit you'll need a T2202 or T2202A. This is for the monthly credit, not tuition fees.

If you're claiming tuition fees paid to a Canadian educational institution, your official receipt is all you need. But if you're claiming tuition fees paid to an educational institution outside Canada, you're going to need a special certificate called TL11. This form has to be certified by the educational institution, so it's another one you should chase up shortly after the end of the year if you haven't already received it by then.

If you're reporting income received from a spousal registered retirement savings plan you're going to need a form T2205.

If you're claiming child care expenses you need a form T778 which is included in the Child Care Expenses Tax Guide.

If you're reporting business income (but remember I strongly suggest you should get professional help in these circumstances) you'll need the Business and Professional Income Tax Guide and some of the forms that are in it.

If you're reporting a capital gain or loss you're going to need the Capital Gains Tax Guide and some of the forms in it.

Farmers and fishermen have their own tax rules and, as is to be expected, their own tax guides and special forms. But again, I urge those of you who are in the business of farming or fishing to seek professional tax help.

Some of you will receive some of these forms and guides automatically in the mail. Many of you will not. None of you will receive them by mail the first time you need them. If you need any of these special forms or guides (or any others, as the above list is just the most common of the special forms and guides) and you don't have them, they can be obtained from your District Taxation Office.

Be Sure You Have the Right T1

Don't feel slighted if you don't get a T1 in the mail. Perhaps it wouldn't even have been the right one. Some people get their T1s in the mail, and some don't. If you didn't file a return last year, you'll not get one.

If for some reason your previous year's tax return was very late being assessed, you probably won't get a personalized T1 return for the current year. If you had your previous year's return prepared by someone else for a fee, you'll not get a current year's form in the mail, just some labels.

Whether you received a T1 in the mail, or whether you're picking one up at the District Taxation Office or at the Post Office, be sure you have the right one. There are two things to watch out for.

First, be sure the T1 you're using for your income tax return is for the province in which you were living on December 31st of the year for which you're filing. For example, if you moved from one province to another, you may receive a T1 designed for the province you used to live in. Be sure the T1 you have is for the province you were living in on December 31st.

That's the date which determines which province was your residence for income tax purposes even if you moved there on December 30th. This could be very important. Different provinces have different tax rates and many provinces have particular provincial income tax credits.

Next, there is a T1 General, which *anyone* can use, and a so-called simpler special T1 form, which many people *cannot* use. If you have one of the simpler forms, read the instructions carefully to be sure it's appropriate for you. If in doubt, use the T1 General — it's designed for anyone to use.

You can expect to receive your T4 and T5 slips anytime from the first of the year until about the end of March. Don't file your return without them, even if you know all the amounts. It'll be quicker in the long run to wait.

Also, remember these two things about T-slips. First, you're taxable on the income whether you receive slips or not; and, second, T5s don't have to be issued for small amounts of interest.

What to Do if You Don't Get a T4 or T5

If you worked during the previous year and you don't get a T4 slip from your employer or former employer, that doesn't mean you have no income tax to pay. You're taxable on all income earned, whether you get a slip or not.

If you don't get one by the end of March, here's what you should do. Contact your employer or former employer and tell them you want your T4. Right away. They should, by law, have them out by the end of February.

If you can't track your employer down, or if you have and they simply won't cooperate, here's what to do next. Estimate all the items you're missing: income; CPP contributions; unemployment insurance premiums; and tax withheld. Include these amounts on your tax return and attach a note explaining the situation. List your estimates and give the full name and address of the company or person who didn't issue the T4. If you've kept pay stubs they will help with your estimates and it's a good idea to attach the pay stubs to your tax return.

The same thing applies to T5 slips. You still have to report the income even if you don't get a T5. This is a more common situation because T5s don't have to be issued for small amounts. If you don't get a T5, include the income anyway and, as with a missing T4, attach a note to your return explaining the situation, including the name and address of who paid you the interest or dividend.

Another Thing About T4s

The old song says "little things mean a lot." Kitty Kallin wasn't thinking about T4 slips when she sang that song back in the 1950s, but she could have been. You see there are a couple of little things about your T4 slip that might mean a lot to you later on. They are your social insurance number and name. When you receive your T4 slip from your employer, check carefully to see that your social insurance number and name are on it, and that they're correct. Here's why.

Your employer sends a copy of this T4 slip to the government. The government uses its copy not only to double check the amount of income you report for income tax purposes, but also to update your Canada Pension Plan computer files. This is how the government keeps track of the amount you and your employer have contributed to your Canada Pension Plan account and the amount of earnings recorded in your Record of Earnings information. It's this amount which will ultimately determine the amount of Canada Pension Plan pension you will receive when you retire.

If there's no social insurance number on the T4, or if the *wrong* social insurance number is shown on the T4, or if your name is incorrect on the T4, then your Canada Pension Plan account may not get properly credited.

If the correct social insurance number and name are not on your T4, get in touch with your employer right away and have them issue a new one with the correct information on it. Be sure they send a copy of the amended T4 to the government. A little thing that could indeed mean a lot in the long run.

HOW TO SPEED UP A TAX REFUND — MAYBE

If your income tax refund seems to be always late, it may be your own fault. According to Revenue Canada, each year millions of income tax returns are held up in processing simply because of preparation errors. The odds are most of these would be returns on which refunds are due. Here's how you might reduce the chances of *your* return being included in that category.

First, be sure all the personal information requested has been filled in. Two common omissions are your date of birth and social insurance number. Be sure, too, that your spouse's social insurance number is filled in — provided, of course, you have a spouse.

Another common cause of returns being held up is not attaching the relevant information slips, such as T4s, T5s and necessary receipts. Be sure they're all attached.

If you're claiming a deduction for an RRSP contribution, be sure this official receipt is attached, too. The same holds true for tuition fees, union dues and charitable donations. If you're claiming medical expenses, be sure to attach relevant receipts.

If you're claiming anything on the line "other deductions," be sure to attach a note explaining clearly what these other deductions are.

Before mailing your return, double-check your arithmetic and be sure to sign the T1 and any attachments that need signatures.

These steps won't guarantee a speedy refund, but like chicken soup when you've got a cold, they can't hurt.

FILE YOUR TAX RETURN, EVEN IF YOU CAN'T PAY THE TAX

The deadline for filing your personal income tax return is April 30th (unless that's a Saturday or Sunday, then the deadline is the following Monday). And it's important that you file it on time, even if you don't have the money available to pay any tax you might owe. Here's why. If you're late paying your income tax you're going to pay interest anyway, whether you file or not. But if there's any unpaid tax, there's also a penalty for filing your return late. And this is in *addition* to interest. It's a penalty for just being late.

Now, even if you're only one day late, the late filing penalty is going to be 5% of the unpaid tax. And Revenue Canada will add another 1% for each month you're late until a maximum penalty of 17% is reached.

It's worth repeating. In addition to interest on unpaid tax, there's a penalty for filing late. And it starts at 5% — even if you're only one day late.

Let's take an example. Suppose you owed $1,000 tax and didn't file your return and pay your tax until May 31st. The penalty and interest would be about $60. But if you filed your return by the April 30th deadline and paid the tax on May 31st, your extra costs would be about $10.

So get your return in on time, even if you can't pay the tax until some later date.

Chapter 21

What's Taxed

Although there are a few types of receipts which aren't subject to income tax, they're the exception rather than the rule. So let's examine what has to be included in income for tax purposes.

EMPLOYMENT INCOME

Not surprisingly, income received from employment, whether it's called salary, wages, bonus, commission, or whatever, has to be included in income for tax purposes.

It must be remembered there are many employment income components which are not always visible to the naked eye, or included in your pay cheque for that matter, but on which you do have to pay income tax. Included in this category are items such as the value of board or lodging, personal use of a company car (and in some cases an amount even if the car was merely *available* for personal use), rent-free or low-rent accommodation, interest-free or low-interest loans, the amount of the loans themselves in some cases, subsidized meals, and government hospital and medical premiums paid by your employer.

Employment income will also include any gifts, prizes, awards, trips and other perks you garner by virtue of your work.

It's common practice for spouses to accompany business people on business trips. This situation often causes some income tax problems when the spouse's travelling and accommodation expenses are paid for or reimbursed by the employer.

The question, of course, is whether there's a taxable benefit involved. If there is a taxable benefit, the employer has to include the amount on the employee's T4, and the employee — not the spouse — has to pay tax on the benefit.

So, what determines whether there is a taxable benefit? Well, the policy of Revenue Canada in this respect is very easy to describe, but not so easy to apply.

Revenue Canada's position is that there *is* a taxable benefit, unless: your spouse went on the trip at the request of your employer; *and* the main purpose of your spouse accompanying you on the trip was to assist in achieving the business objectives of the trip.

Of course, it's easy to determine whether your employer requests that your spouse go along; but trying to prove that your spouse was there to help achieve the business objectives of the trip is usually a lot tougher.

Bear in mind that this list is far from exhaustive; it just mentions the most common items normally included in the broad category of employment income. Your T4 slip will usually reflect all of the items of this nature you have to include on your return. But there is one source of income some of you earn which will probably not appear on a T4 — tips.

TIPS

Even though you might argue that a tip is really a gift, and therefore shouldn't be taxed because other gifts aren't taxed, the law is quite clear. Tips are taxable. If you're engaged in an activity where you earn tips, you should keep a record of them and report them on your income tax return.

PENSIONS

Old Age Security and Canada Pension Plan benefits, including survivor benefits, are taxable. But, remember, people 65 years of age or over get extra personal tax credits.

Most pensions from a foreign country are taxable. And don't forget the amounts have to be converted to Canadian dollars on your return. Another thing to remember about pensions from foreign countries is that there might be special provisions in Canada's income tax treaties that apply. For example, you have to include only one-half of U.S. Social Security payments in income for Canadian tax purposes.

War veterans' allowances and veterans' disability and dependants' pension payments are *not* subject to income tax.

Any amounts received from your company pension plan or from a union or professional organization plan are taxable. Any receipts from an RRSP or RRIF are subject to tax, as are amounts received from a Deferred Profit Sharing Plan. If any of these items are in the form of annuities, the amounts are still taxed.

Income averaging annuities are taxed in full. (Yes, there are still some around. If you don't know what they are they probably don't affect you. You can't buy them any more). Other types of annuity income may not be taxed in full; usually your T4A will show the amount you have to report. If in doubt, enquire at the institution that pays you the annuity.

EMPLOYMENT ASSISTANCE

Adult training allowances are taxable. So is unemployment insurance. Speaking of unemployment insurance, if your net income is over a certain threshold (it changes each year, so check your T1 Guide) and you received unemployment insurance, you're going to have to pay some of it back. You do this as part of your tax payable, and how you do it is explained in the tax guide and on the T1.

FAMILY ALLOWANCE

It's taxable, but read on.

A very confusing area of income tax law is who does what with family allowance payments for income tax purposes. I'll try to explain it to you. But you'd better read slowly.

If you are married, the spouse with the higher net income is the one who reports the family allowance payments as income, regardless of which spouse actually receives them. Remember, too, it's the person who reports the family allowance income who must claim the children as dependants.

If you are separated throughout the entire year, the person who actually receives the payments must report them and claim the children.

If you were separated for a period of more than ninety days beginning in a year, the family allowance payments for all months at the end of which you were separated must be reported by whoever received them. For other months it's the spouse with the higher net income who reports them.

If you are living common-law and claim the equivalent-to-married exemption, then you must report the family allowance payments in respect to the dependant upon whom you base the claim, even if your common-law spouse receives the family allowance.

In all other cases, such as single parent, divorced, widow or widower, the person who receives the family allowance reports it and claims the kids.

Unbelievable, isn't it? But remember, we elected the people who enacted this law.

INTEREST

Simply put, interest is taxable. But, again, read on.

There are three acceptable ways to report interest income for tax purposes. They can be confusing. The first method is the *cash* method.

If you use the cash method you simply include the interest income on your income tax return for the year in which you *received* it. For example, if you didn't receive any bond interest in a particular year, you don't have to include the interest on your return, even if the bonds or coupons could have been cashed and interest received. *However, remember that interest has to be reported at least every three years, whether you receive it or not, and the government has indicated that it intends to shorten this period.*

On the other hand, if you cashed coupons in a particular year covering a number of years, all of that interest would have to be reported on your return for the year in which you cashed them, unless some of it had been included in earlier years' returns under one of the other methods or the three-year rule.

The next method is the *receivable* method. Under this method you report interest on your return for the year in which it becomes receivable. For example, under the receivable method, bond interest which you *could* have received in a particular year would be reported on your return for that year even if you didn't actually receive it.

Then there's the *accrual* method of reporting interest income. Under this method you report interest as it is earned, regardless of when it becomes receivable or is actually received.

That's all pretty confusing, so let's look at an example. Suppose you bought a $1,000 bond on November 1, 19-0, with interest at 10%, payable each year on November 1. Suppose further that you don't cash in any coupons until November 1, 19-5.

Under the cash basis you would report $300 in 19-3 even though you received no interest in that year, because under the cash basis you have to report interest every three years whether you receive it or not. You would report nothing more until 19-5 when you would report $200 (even though you received $500 — remember $300 had already been reported in 19-3).

Under the receivable method you would report $100 each year from 19-1 to 19-5 inclusive.

Under the accrual method you would report $17 in 19-0 (the interest from Nov. 1 — Dec. 31), $100 in each of 19-1 to 19-4 inclusive, and $83 in 19-5.

So there are the three methods under which you can report interest income for tax purposes. There's more to keep in mind, though.

If you've been using the accrual method for reporting interest you're going to have to continue using the accrual method as long as you own those particular investments.

You can, however, switch from the cash method to the receivable or accrual method or from the receivable method to the accrual basis. If you do this, all of the interest earned to the end of the year in which you switch that was not previously reported for income tax purposes will have to be included on your return for that year.

You might want to switch to the accrual or receivable methods if your income is very low but you will be in a much higher bracket when the interest is actually received. Otherwise, there's usually little to be said for paying a tax sooner than you have to.

If you have Canada Savings Bonds, read carefully the instructions with the T1 guide for an explanation of the various methods of reporting interest. Be sure to read it *very* carefully.

The main point to remember is that there *are* three different ways to report interest for tax purposes. The cash method is the simplest, but one of the other two — the receivable or accrual method — might, in any particular set of circumstances, be more beneficial; but not likely.

Interest on joint accounts has to be treated carefully for income tax purposes. That's because interest income earned on joint accounts must be reported for income tax purposes in the same ratio as the money was contributed to the account. Remember, though, that interest earned on money you give or lend to your spouse or lend to your children remains taxable in your hands.

For example, if the only money in a joint account is from the earnings of one spouse, or from the earnings of that spouse plus what's been given or lent to the other spouse — or vice versa — all the interest would be taxable in the hands of the wage earner.

On the other hand, if both spouses were working and contributing to the joint account, the interest income would be prorated for tax purposes. If the contribution was even, the split would be fifty-fifty.

Let's take another example. Assume there's $15,000 in a joint account, $10,000 of which was built up from one spouse's earnings, and $5,000 from a small inheritance the other spouse received. In this case, 2/3 of the interest would be reported by one spouse and 1/3 by the other.

The T5 slip will be in both your names. If only one spouse is reporting the interest, that's who should file the T5 slip with his or her return.

If the interest is being divided between you, the T5 slip can be filed with either return, but each return should also have a note attached showing how you divided up the interest income.

DIVIDENDS

Dividends received from foreign companies are taxable in full. As in the case of all foreign income, the amount must be converted to Canadian dollars using the rate of exchange at the time the dividends were received. Foreign income tax withheld has to be included in income for Canadian income tax purposes, but a foreign income tax credit is usually available thereby avoiding double taxation. However, it's quite a different story when it comes to dividends from taxable Canadian corporations.

It's understandable if you're confused by the reporting of dividends from Canadian corporations for income tax purposes. You receive your T5 slip and immediately you're confronted by three different amounts. The first is the amount of dividends actually received from the corporation.

Then there's a higher figure called the "taxable amount." That's the one you report on your income tax return. By now you'll have noticed it's a lot higher than the actual dividend. But it *is* that higher amount you have to include in income. That may sound like you're getting cheated, but you're not.

The next figure you see on the T5 is called the "Federal Dividend Tax Credit." You reduce your federal income tax by this amount. It's not just a deduction from income, it's an actual reduction of tax. And because in all provinces, except Quebec, the provincial tax is a percentage of the federal tax, the dividend tax credit reduces your provincial income tax as well. Quebec has its own dividend tax credit.

The result is that by going through this complicated manoeuvre you end up paying less tax than if you simply included the actual amount of the dividend in income without the dividend tax credit. The extent to which you're better off depends on the amount of dividend income and your personal income tax bracket. But rest assured, you are not being cheated.

If your spouse received dividends from a Canadian corporation, you might be able to save a little bit of tax. As in the case of interest income, if your spouse has income from money obtained by gift or loan from you, you have to report the income for tax purposes. However, income earned on money which was earned or inherited by your spouse is taxable in your spouse's hands — not yours.

When that income consists of dividends from Canadian corporations, and there isn't too much of it, you sometimes lose a portion of your married exemption, but your spouse can't take full advantage of the dividend tax credit because he or she has little or no tax to pay. If you're in these circumstances, some relief might be available.

Where your spouse's dividends would decrease *your* married exemption, you have the option, if you want to, of including those dividends in *your* income. They would then qualify for the dividend tax credit on your return. Now, this isn't an advantage in every case, so always work it out both ways before making a final decision on which way to report your spouse's dividends from Canadian corporations.

If you do elect for this option, the same dividends should not be included in your spouse's income when claiming a deduction transfer from your spouse, nor should they be included in your spouse's income for purposes of determining the amount of your married exemption.

CAPITAL GAINS

Whole books have probably been written on the subject of the taxation of capital gains. It is a very complicated area of Canadian income tax law and if your capital affairs are at all complicated you should definitely seek professional advice. However, there are a couple of areas of capital gains taxation that could affect a lot of Canadians and which are generally not well understood. It is those, and only those, that we deal with here.

There's no capital gains tax on anything you sell for less than $1,000. Well, almost never. A lot of people don't realize that any time we sell anything at a profit, such as a painting, a piece of land, a car, a boat, a set of dishes, or any other asset, we are potentially liable for income tax on any capital gain.

The most common item that gives rise to a profit is, of course, a residence; and most of you know that if it's been your principal residence throughout the entire period of ownership, the gain is not taxed. Most of the other items mentioned are usually sold at a loss.

However, occasionally we do sell one of these items — such as a painting — at a profit. Well, the rules in the Income Tax Act state that for any particular item that might be subject to capital gains tax, you will be deemed to have paid at least $1,000 for it when you bought it. So as long as you don't get more than $1,000 when you sell it, there can be no capital gains tax.

Remember, though, that this particular rule doesn't apply to individual items that are normally sold as a set. So you can't get around paying capital gains tax on the sale of the set of silver by selling one piece at a time for less than $1,000 each. When items that are normally dealt with in a set are disposed of individually to the same person or persons, Revenue Canada will add all the individual sales together for the purpose of applying the $1,000 rule.

The government wants to share in our capital gains, but they're not so quick to share our capital losses. As explained above, if you or I sell a car, boat, cottage, antique or other household item and receive more than $1,000 for it, we could be subject to capital gains tax on any profit. Of course, a cottage which qualified as a principal residence would be exempt.

But it's pretty much a one-way street. If we lost money on the sale of the car, boat, cottage, antique or other household effect, absolutely nothing would be deductible for income tax purposes. The only exception to this rule is for a class of items referred to in the Income Tax Act as "listed personal property."

In the case of listed personal property, if you suffer a loss on the sale (and the $1,000 rule works in reverse here: you're going to be deemed to have *received* at least $1,000 for it), that loss is deductible *only* against gains from other listed personal property. Fat chance! ("Regular" capital losses can be carried back three years and carried forward indefinitely to be deducted from capital gains.)

If you had no gains from other listed personal property in the year, the loss can be carried back two years and forward seven years; but only against gains from other listed personal properties. In short, the government wants to share in *all* profits but only *some* losses — and darn few at that.

Oh yes, what are listed personal properties? They are: works of art; jewelry; rare books, manuscripts and folios; stamps; and coins.

Many taxpayers pay capital gains tax before they have to because they fail to take a deduction that's available when you've sold something at a profit which is subject to capital gains tax, but for which you have not been fully paid.

The most common example of this is where you sell real estate that doesn't qualify as a principal residence and you take back a mortgage for part of the selling price.

In these circumstances you can claim a reserve against the reported capital gain. How you calculate this reserve is explained in the Capital Gains Guide. In effect, it allows you to defer the payment of tax on a portion of the capital gain because you haven't yet been paid.

The amount of the reserve you deduct for one year has to be included in income in the next year, and then you deduct a new reserve, and so on. You'll probably not pay any less tax over the long haul than if you didn't claim a reserve, but you will pay it over a longer period, which is to your advantage.

However, it's not a complete reserve. For most properties you can only claim a reserve as if you'll be completely paid in five years, and then only to the extent you actually haven't been paid.

COMMODITY TRADING

Reporting gains and losses from commodity trading can be as nerve-racking as playing the commodities market itself. Those of you who speculate in commodities, whether it be gold, silver, platinum, or pork bellies, should be aware there are two different ways to report your gains and losses for income tax purposes.

One method is the "income" treatment, under which your *full* gain or loss would be taxable or deductible as the case might be. The second method is the "capital" treatment, under which your profits and losses would be treated like capital gains or losses, meaning of course that your losses would be deductible only against other capital gains.

It's important to note that interest incurred on money borrowed to use in commodity trading is deductible only if you are using the income method of reporting gains and losses.

Of course, I'm talking here about people who trade in commodities as a sideline. If you're in the business of trading in commodities then you have no choice. You have to use the income method.

But for those of you who have a choice, you should discuss it in detail with your accountant to determine which method of reporting your commodity gains and losses is apt to be better for you. There is no general rule which applies to all commodity players, and once you've chosen the income treatment you're stuck with it. You can never switch back to the capital method.

If your commodity gain or loss is substantial, get some professional advice.

RENTAL INCOME

Many people find the only way they can afford to own a house these days is to rent out a portion of it. Whether this is half a duplex, a basement apartment, an upstairs flat, or just a couple of rooms, you have to report your rental income for income tax purposes.

It isn't one-sided, though. You can also deduct any relevant expenses. Expenses which relate only to the rented portion can be claimed in full. Those that relate to the building as a whole — such as insurance, property taxes and mortgage interest — must be pro-rated between the rented portion and the part you live in.

One acceptable method of doing this, as far as Revenue Canada is concerned, is to use the ratio of square feet rented to total square feet. Or, for example, if you've rented out two rooms of an eight-room house, one-quarter of pro-ratable expenses would be deductible.

Although depreciation on part of the building is a perfectly legitimate expense in these circumstances, there are tax implications which are too detailed for me to deal with here. So before deducting any depreciation (which is referred to as capital cost allowance in income tax parlance) be sure to get professional tax advice. As a matter of fact, if you are in the rental business be sure to have professional advice. The tax implications go far beyond those mentioned here.

BUSINESS AND PROFESSIONAL INCOME

Business and professional income, net of expenses, is of course subject to income tax. However, as in the case of complicated capital and rental activities, the taxation of business and professional income is well beyond the scope of this book. In all of these circumstances you should definitely seek professional help.

SOME RECEIPTS AREN'T TAXED

There actually are some ways you can receive money that's not subject to income tax. The most common forms of receipts which are not taxed are: child tax credits; welfare payments; worker's compensation; and as already mentioned, war veterans' allowances and veterans' disability and dependent pensioners' payments.

You don't have to pay tax on gifts you receive or on money that you inherit. Lottery winnings aren't taxable either.

Of course, if you invest any of this money, the income you earn from the investments — such as interest, dividends, or capital gains — would be taxable.

Guaranteed income supplements and spouse's allowances are not themselves taxable to the person who receives them; but if a guaranteed income supplement or spouse's allowance is received by a dependant of yours, then you have to include such amounts in *their* income in determining how much of an exemption *you* are entitled to in respect of *them*. They also count as income for the child tax credit calculation and the federal sales tax credit calculation. The same applies to worker's compensation benefits.

The first $500 of scholarships, fellowships, bursaries, or prizes not connected with your work is not taxable. But only one $500 exemption is available each year. For instance, if you received two $750 scholarships in a year you would have to include $1,000 in income.

Chapter 22

Some Common Income Tax Deductions and Credits

As in the case of dealing with income for tax purposes, it is beyond the scope of this book to deal with all the technical aspects of all the various tax credits and deductions available. Many of them, such as personal exemptions, you are familiar with and information is readily available on the form itself and in the Tl Guide. Others, such as exploration and development expense and investment tax credits, need entire books of their own; if you're into these, get professional help.

So what this chapter is all about is to remind you of some aspects of the more common variety of income tax deductions and credits which you might otherwise overlook.

CHARITABLE DONATIONS

Even that little five-dollar receipt for sponsoring Johnny in the read-a-thon may be worth a couple of bucks.

A few years ago we used to have a standard deduction of $100 for medical expenses and charitable donations which you could claim without filing receipts. A lot of taxpayers did exactly that and fell into the habit of ignoring charitable receipts for small amounts. If you're one of these people, break the habit.

Every charitable donation, no matter how small, should be claimed. If you're giving a small amount, be sure to specifically request a receipt. Many organizations don't issue them for small amounts unless specifically requested to do so. Also, be sure to keep every receipt you get, no matter how small the amount. They soon begin to add up.

Another common mistake people make is to put cash in the collection plate at church. You'll not get a receipt for it, and, therefore, no tax credit. So always use envelopes at church. If you regularly attend more than one church, for example, at home, but also at the cottage or chalet, be sure to have envelopes for both.

Remember, too, that Revenue Canada allows either spouse to claim all the charitable donations made by both, regardless of whose name is on the receipt.

SOME THINGS YOU MAY NOT HAVE KNOWN ABOUT CLAIMING MEDICAL EXPENSES

There are some unusual wrinkles to claiming the tax credit for medical expenses. In the past, claims for medical expenses were fairly rare on income tax returns, mostly because the expenses had to be more than 3% of net income to be deductible. Of course, amounts covered by insurance don't count. Since 1988, though, expenses in excess of the lesser of 3% of net income and $1,500 will entitle a taxpayer to a credit.

There will be people who will miss credits because they don't fully understand the rules. For example, did you know that either spouse may claim all the medical expenses for both of them? You should always work out the claim both ways to be sure the person that's going to get the higher credit makes the claim.

When it comes to your dependants, you don't have a choice. The person who claims the dependant is the one who can claim the medical expenses. If you have a dependant you could have claimed, except that his or her income was too high, you can still claim the medical expense credit provided you add a large portion of the dependant's *income* to the *tax you owe*. This isn't always a great deal, so work it out, too, before making a decision. It's explained in your T1 Guide.

There are some unusual items that qualify as medical expenses for income tax purposes. Most people are aware that eye glasses, hearing aids and wheelchairs qualify as medical expenses for income tax purposes. But did you know that the cost of seeing-eye and hearing-ear dogs also qualifies? And did you know that their dog food is considered a medical expense? Not only that, but board, lodging and travelling expenses incurred to attend guide-dog school also qualify.

Hearing aid batteries are a qualifying expense. Also, TV closed-caption decoders qualify as a medical expense for income tax purposes. Modifications to a home to accommodate a wheelchair qualify.

If medical treatment is not available where you live, reasonable travel expenses, including meals and accommodation, qualify, provided you had to travel at least 80 kilometres to obtain the treatment. If you had to travel less than 80 kilometres, but at least 40 kilometres, then your transportation costs qualify — but not meals or accommodation. In either case, if you had to have a companion because you weren't able to travel alone, his or her costs also qualify. The need for a companion, though, has to be certified by a doctor. Even acupuncture qualifies as a medical expense, provided the fee was paid to a medical doctor. Witch doctors don't count.

You can claim amounts paid for one full-time attendant or for full-time care in a nursing home provided a doctor has certified the person receiving the care to be severely mentally or physically impaired. However, you may not claim these particular expenses if the extra personal exemption for a disabled person is claimed. So always work it out both ways to determine which is the better route to go.

Remember, too, that you can claim expenses for any twelve-month period ending in a taxation year. Therefore, all receipts should be retained. Even if you don't have enough to qualify you for a claim in one year or the next, by combining a twelve-month period within the two years you might be eligible for a claim.

Amounts paid to hospitals, doctors, nurses or dentists, or for other qualifying items outside Canada count. Convert the amounts to Canadian dollars at the exchange rates in effect at the time the expense was paid.

But remember too that medical expenses must actually be paid to qualify. If you simply owe the amount, that's not good enough. In addition, receipts must be filed for all expenses other than insurance premiums paid to private plans for medical coverage.

ALIMONY AND MAINTENANCE PAYMENTS

In order to claim a deduction for income tax purposes of alimony or maintenance payments, the payments must meet very specific conditions.

First of all, to claim alimony or maintenance deductions the payments must actually have been made. You cannot deduct alimony you owe but haven't paid yet. The payments must be on a periodic basis — monthly, weekly, yearly.

You cannot claim a lump sum settlement. The payments must be paid pursuant to a court order or written agreement, or if made before the order or agreement, they are acknowledged in the order or agreement. In short, there must be a binding, legal, written obligation to make the payments. Voluntary payments, or those pursuant to an oral agreement, simply aren't deductible unless later formalized. Finally, the payments must be made to your estranged spouse *or* to a third party clearly for the benefit of the spouse or children in the custody of the spouse.

In the year of separation or divorce — but only in the first year — you have a choice. You can claim either the payments made or the personal exemptions for your spouse and children, whichever is more beneficial to you. One exception is that you cannot claim an exemption for a child for whom your spouse has claimed the equivalent to a married exemption. In subsequent years you can claim only the actual alimony or maintenance paid — not the personal exemptions.

For any year in which you are making a claim for alimony or maintenance payments, you should attach a sheet of paper to your return showing the name and address of the person to whom the payments were made, and if the payments were made to a third party the name and address of the person on whose behalf the payments were made.

Although there's no legal requirement to do so, you'll likely save yourself a lot of bother if, in the first year you're claiming alimony or maintenance, in addition to the note I just mentioned, you also attach to your tax return a copy of the court order or agreement under which the payments are being made. Don't send your original. Have a copy made and send that.

The other side of the alimony coin, of course, is that if it's deductible by the person who pays it, then it's taxable to the person who receives it, or on whose behalf it has been paid.

So, if you received periodic alimony or maintenance payments under a court order or pursuant to a written agreement, or have had such payments — such as mortgage payments — made on your behalf to third parties, you have to include them in income.

On the other hand, if you receive a lump sum settlement on a marriage breakup, that's not taxable. So remember that for the next time.

DISABLED PEOPLE GET EXTRA TAX DEDUCTIONS

There's a special income tax credit available to disabled people. I suspect a lot of people who should be claiming this are not doing so. Any person who is mentally or physically impaired may be entitled to this special income tax credit. To qualify, the mental or physical impairment must have been such that it ''markedly restricted the person in the activities of daily living.'' The impairment must have lasted, or be expected to last, for a continuous period of at least twelve months.

The first time that this credit is being claimed, a special form must be filed with the regular income tax return. It's a form T2201, and it must be certified by a doctor. You can get this form at the District Taxation Office.

As mentioned in the section on medical expenses, you cannot claim this particular exemption if you claim the cost of a full-time attendant or nursing home fees as a medical expense. In these circumstances you should work out which is the more beneficial claim, and go that route.

On the other hand, though, if you qualify but don't need all the credit to eliminate *your* tax, your spouse or other supporting person can claim the unused part.

If you have any mental or physical impairment, or have a dependant with one, discuss with your doctor the merits of making a claim for this credit. Better to try it and get turned down than ignore it and miss out on a tax break you're entitled to.

NON-RESIDENT DEPENDANTS REQUIRE CAREFUL TAX TREATMENT

Claiming a non-resident dependant is not a straightforward matter.

For example, if you're claiming an exemption for a non-resident dependant, you need a special form. It's a TlE-NR, and it's available at your District Taxation Office. In addition to this special form, you should also be aware of the special income tax rules that apply to claiming non-resident dependants.

You cannot make a claim for parents, grandparents, sisters or brothers whom you might be supporting outside Canada. You could at one time, but for some time now you've been restricted to claiming your spouse, children, and grandchildren.

The amount you can claim is limited to the lesser of the actual money spent or the normal exemption for that person.

You also have to attach proof of payment of support with your return. This could be a receipt for a money order showing the amount, the date of payment, and the name and address of the recipient.

You can't claim anyone over 18 years of age unless they are infirm or in full-time attendance at school or university.

If you're claiming a non-resident grandchild you should attach a note explaining why the grandchild's parents were not able to support him or her.

Remember, too, that gifts made to non-residents don't qualify for a deduction. The spouse or child must actually be dependent on you for support in order to be claimed.

CLAIMING TUITION FEES IS A TRICKY BUSINESS

Claiming tuition fees is a tricky business. The first problem with claiming tuition fees for income tax purposes is that, to the extent possible, the student must claim them. Of course, in many cases it's the parents who actually pay the tuition fees. Many students don't have sufficient income to claim the fees, and even for those that do, the claim is made at marginal tax rates which are usually much lower than those of their parents.

Tuition fee credits which students don't need to reduce their income tax to zero can be passed on in part to their parents or other supporting persons. There's a fairly low limit, but every little bit counts.

Anyone claiming tuition fees must file an approved receipt issued by the particular educational institution to which the fees were paid.

Fees under $100 paid to an educational institution in Canada are not deductible. Generally speaking, fees paid to universities outside Canada are only deductible if you attended a degree course full-time for at least thirteen consecutive weeks.

If your employer pays any part of deductible fees, you have to include that amount in income, so you just break even.

The cost of board and lodging, books, student council fees and the like, even if included in an overall fee, is not deductible — only tuition.

CLAIMING THE EDUCATION INCOME TAX CREDIT

The education income tax credit is a small amount per month for each whole or part month in a taxation year during which a student was in full-time attendance at a college or university. Now this, like tuition fees, gives rise to a tax credit, not a deduction. It's small, but if you're eligible you may as well have it.

This credit, too, must first be claimed by the student to reduce his or her income tax to nil, after claiming all other deductions and credits. If the student doesn't need the full amount of the available credit to reduce tax payable to nil, the excess can be claimed by the person who claims that student as a dependant. However, this excess credit, when added to any tuition fee credit also being claimed by a parent, cannot exceed a fairly low limit per student. Check your T1 Guide to see how these transfers work.

The person claiming this education credit, either the student or the parent, has to file a special form with his or her tax return. It's form T2202 or T2202A. The appropriate form has to be obtained from, and certified by, the educational institution, which will give you the T2202 or T2202A, whichever is appropriate in the circumstances. This special form has to be signed by the student, even if it's someone else who's making the claim.

Remember it's quite possible that the student will be claiming the tuition fees, but a parent or other supporting individual will be claiming the education credit, or a part thereof.

In order for a student's attendance to qualify for the education tax credit, it must be in one of certain qualifying situations.

Normal university and college attendance, of course, qualify. So do courses of at least three consecutive weeks' duration, with at least ten hours' work in the program each week at a post-secondary level. Full-time attendance at a university outside Canada in a degree course at least 13 weeks long qualifies. (This is the same test which tuition fees must meet in order to be eligible for an income tax credit.)

There are certain job retraining and adult education courses which qualify, so if you're in doubt, ask at the educational institution — they should know. Remember, though, that no credit is available if you received a government adult training allowance in respect to the particular attendance. Nurses-in-training who receive free board and lodging or other allowances cannot claim the education tax credit.

Courses which relate to your job don't qualify if you earn wages or salary while taking such courses. Neither do courses for which you've been reimbursed.

Remember, if the course qualifies, the credit is available, even if the student lives at home.

AN INCOME TAX DEDUCTION MANY STUDENTS OVERLOOK

There's an income tax deduction many students overlook. It's moving expenses.

Students who move to take a job — even a summer job — or to start a business, can deduct some or all of their moving expenses, provided their new place of residence is at least 40 kilometres closer to their workplace than their old residence.

For example, a student from Toronto who took a summer job in Jasper could deduct the cost of moving out there against income earned from that job. Or, a graduating Winnipeg student who moved to, say, Moncton to work or start a business could also claim a deduction.

Back to the summer job in Jasper. If when that student returned home in the fall, he or she had scholarships, research grants or the like, the cost of coming back would also be deductible, but only up to the amount of such scholarships or research grants. Actually, this provision applies to any student who moves at least 40 kilometres to attend a university or college full-time. The cost of moving would be deductible against any taxable scholarships, bursaries, awards, etc., but not against anything else.

There are very strict limitations on what qualifies as moving expenses, and if you're claiming a deduction — student or otherwise — you're going to need a form T1-M, which you can get from your District Taxation Office. You should also get the pamphlet entitled "Moving Expenses." It'll explain it all to you.

MOVING EXPENSES — GENERALLY

Actually, any taxpayer might be able to claim some moving expenses. Provided, of course, you moved. Here's how it works.

If you moved within Canada to earn salary or wages (even with the same employer) or to start a business, and your new home is at least 40 kilometres closer to your new place of work than your old home, you might have some deductions coming to you.

A couple of things to remember, though. If you were working or carrying on a business before you moved, you must have ceased to work or carry on business at your old location. Also, you can't claim any expenses for which you were reimbursed by your old or new employer. And your deduction is limited to the amount of income you earn at the new location. However, if your deductible moving expenses are more than your first year's income at the new location, you can carry over the excess and deduct it against income earned at the new location in the following year.

As I mentioned earlier when talking about students, if you're claiming moving expenses you'll have to file a form T1-M, which you can get at your District Taxation Office. You should also get the pamphlet entitled "Moving Expenses" so you'll know exactly what's deductible and what isn't.

You don't need to file receipts, invoices and the like, but be sure to keep them in case Revenue Canada asks for them later.

PENSION INCOME TAX CREDIT

Another very confusing area of personal income tax is the pension income tax credit. This used to be a $1,000 deduction, but like so many other items is now a tax credit. But if you're eligible for it you should certainly be taking advantage of it.

The first thing to remember is there are three age groups involved.

If you are 65 or over, the first $1,000 of periodic payments from a pension plan, annuity payments from an RRSP, deferred profit sharing plan, or registered retirement income fund all qualify for the credit. Also, the income portion of certain other annuities will qualify.

If you are between 60 and 65 years of age, periodic payments from a pension plan qualify; but annuity payments qualify only if they were received because of the death of your spouse.

If you are under age 60, the same rules apply as to those between age 60 and 65, except that you cannot claim the credit if any amount has been rolled over from a pension plan to another pension plan or to an RRSP.

Remember, too, that Old Age Security and Canada Pension Plan payments *never* qualify for the pension credit, regardless of your age.

Check your T1 Guide carefully. If you qualify for the deduction but don't need it, your spouse might be able to use it.

THE CHILD TAX CREDIT

If you think the pension income tax credit is confusing, wait until you read about the child tax credit. One of the most confusing and exasperating income tax changes in recent years is the procedure which parents have to go through in order to claim the child tax credit.

The child tax credit is the amount per child which you are entitled to if your family income is below a certain level. But someone must file an income tax return to get it.

Now, only the person who is entitled to receive the family allowance for the child may claim the child tax credit. That's usually the mother. And even if she wouldn't ordinarily be filing an income tax return, she's going to have to in order to claim the child tax credit.

Remember, this has no effect on who claims an exemption for the child. That's going to be the parent with the higher income — often the father. And that's who reports the family allowance as income — the person who claims the exemption for the child, not necessarily the one who claims the child tax credit.

So, in most cases — although there are obviously exceptions to this general rule — the father will report the family allowance for tax purposes and claim the child as a dependant. But it's the mother who will file for and claim the child tax credit.

On the outside chance that you now know *who* can claim the child tax credit, here's *how* to claim it.

Remember, in the vast majority of cases it's the mother who claims the child tax credit. To do so she has to file a tax return containing a completed child tax credit schedule, even if she wouldn't otherwise be filing a tax return. All T1s have the appropriate schedule attached. Read it and the instructions carefully.

You will note the net income of *both* spouses has to be included on the schedule to determine if you're entitled to a credit and how much you're entitled to. If, at the end of the year, you were living with, but not married to, the other parent, that other parent's income must be included. Even if you think your total income might be too high to qualify you, do the calculation anyway. You might be pleasantly surprised.

Both parents have to sign the schedule, unless you're widowed, separated or divorced. In these cases only your signature is required.

Attach a copy of the TFA1 slip to the return on which the child tax credit is claimed, as well as to the return on which the family allowance was reported as income. The TFA1 slip comes with your January family allowance cheque.

Some of you receive a pre-payment of the child tax credit each year. Don't forget to deduct on the child tax credit schedule any amount of the credit you already received for the year. You can't get it twice.

CHILD CARE EXPENSES

If you had to incur child care expenses in order to earn income from employment or a business, to take an occupational training course for which you received a training allowance, or to carry on research or similar work for which you received a grant, you can deduct at least some of these expenses.

There are very strict limitations on the amounts that can be claimed, the types of payments that qualify, and the ages of the children involved. Also, the rules on which parent may claim the expenses remind you of the fine print in your insurance policy.

If you think you qualify, obtain the Child Care Expenses Tax Guide and read it very carefully.

INTEREST EXPENSES

Interest paid on borrowed money used to make investments or used in a business is deductible for income tax purposes. Interest on money borrowed for personal use (including the purchase of a home) is *not* deductible.

OTHER CARRYING COSTS

If you paid investment counsel fees (that is an amount paid to a person whose primary business is giving investment advice), they are deductible. Accounting fees paid to look after extensive investment income are also deductible under this heading. If you rented a safety deposit box to safeguard your securities, this cost is deductible.

WHAT COMMISSION SALESPEOPLE CAN CLAIM FOR TAX PURPOSES

There are specific income tax rules for commission salespeople. Here is a general rundown for you.

If you are an employee who received commission income, you can claim certain expenses, provided that you: were not reimbursed for them; did not receive a tax-free travel allowance; did have to carry on your duties *away* from your employer's place of business on a regular basis; and were expected to incur such expenses in the course of your employment duties. If you meet all these criteria, you can claim the following expenses provided they were connected with the earning of your commissions.

Automobile expenses, including operating costs and at least a portion of depreciation, are deductible. Of course, personal use can't be claimed, so it is important to keep a log of total and business mileage in order to support your claim. And driving to and from work is personal mileage — not deductible.

You can deduct 80% of business entertainment and meals, as well as all other promotion expenses. But be sure to keep receipts and records of the nature of the expense and who was entertained, so you can prove the expenses were incurred in the course of earning your commission income. Association dues, subscriptions and the like are also deductible if related directly to your income-earning activity.

Remember, though, your total expense claim can't exceed the amount of your commission income.

SALESPEOPLE AREN'T THE ONLY EMPLOYEES WHO MIGHT BE ABLE TO CLAIM TRAVEL COSTS

Commission salespeople aren't the only employees who might be able to claim travel costs. Other types of employment may give rise to deductions, too.

For example, if you work for a railway, bus, airline or trucking company, and have to pay the cost of your meals and lodging while away from home, you can claim a deduction. It's complicated and fairly restricted, but if you fall into this category you should check it out. Here's how. Call your District Taxation Office and get a copy of form TL2 and their circular called "Away From Home Expenses." These will explain the whole thing adequately.

Actually, any employees who have to regularly work away from their employer's place of business — such as maintenance and repair people, service reps, even auditors — and who have to pay all or part of their travelling expenses, can claim a deduction. In this case you need a form T2200. This particular form has to be certified by your employer, so don't leave getting it until the last minute.

Form T2200 is also available at your District Taxation Office. Although tax returns themselves are available at Post Offices, special forms like these are not. You'll have to get them at your District Taxation Office.

Chapter 23

After You File Your Return

Your income tax year doesn't necessarily become a closed book with the filing of your return. You may find a mistake. Or Revenue Canada may find one. Perhaps Revenue Canada will simply come looking for mistakes.

IF YOU FIND A MISTAKE

Sometimes, after you've mailed your income tax return, you'll find that it was wrong in some respect. If it's just an error in arithmetic, don't worry about it; Revenue Canada's computer will pick that up.

But if you've missed a deduction, put in a wrong amount, claimed something you shouldn't have, left off some income or received a new or amended T4 or T5 slip, here's what you should do.

First, though, here's what you should *not* do. Don't file another return!

If you haven't received your assessment notice, which is most often the case, write a letter explaining the change and enclosing any new T4 or T5 slips, or relevant receipts, and mail it to your Taxation Centre. Check your T1 Guide to determine your Taxation Centre.

If you have already received your assessment, write the same letter, but in this case, send it to the appropriate District Taxation Office. To determine which District Taxation Office you should send it to, look again in your T1 Guide.

In either case, be sure to include your name and address and your social insurance number.

The main thing to remember: Don't file another return. Just send the letter of explanation and any new slips or receipts.

YOUR RESPONSIBILITY

A few months after filing your income tax return you will receive an assessment notice for it. In some cases taxpayers will be shocked to discover they owe interest or penalties, or both, because of errors on the return or because it was filed late. They'll be especially shocked if somebody else prepared the return for them.

As far as Revenue Canada is concerned, the fact you had your return prepared by your accountant, lawyer or local gas station attendant is irrelevant. The mistakes are yours, and you have to pay.

When you sign your return, you certify the correctness of what's in it. When someone else prepares or mails it on your behalf, they are doing so as your agent, and you remain responsible for the information in the return and for getting it filed on time.

What can you do about it? Well, for last year's return, not an awful lot. You can try to recover any interest or penalty from the person who prepared the return. Some will reimburse you voluntarily. Unfortunately, when you run into resistance it might cost you far more than the amount involved to recover it.

But there are some things you can keep in mind for next year. First, be sure to provide all relevant information to your advisor. Second, review your return carefully before signing and mailing it. Third, mail it yourself — on time. Last, and most important, deal only with reputable, professional tax people.

WHAT TO DO ABOUT AN INCOME TAX ASSESSMENT

Okay, so you're responsible for your own income tax return. So what should you do if you receive an income tax assessment or re-assessment from Revenue Canada saying you owe more tax? Well, let's start with two things you most definitely should *not* do when you receive an assessment or re-assessment from Revenue Canada. The first is to ignore it. There's no point ignoring it because it will not go away. The second thing you should *not* do is to simply go ahead and pay the additional tax.

What you should do is this. First, read the notice carefully to be sure you understand what it's all about. If you don't fully understand it, get in touch with Revenue Canada and find out, clearly and specifically, why they are asking for more money.

Then examine the situation objectively. If Revenue Canada is right, and you've made a mistake on your return, pay up. On the other hand, if Revenue Canada is wrong, write them and explain why — but don't let it drop there. I'll explain why in a moment. If there is some doubt as to who is right or wrong you should get some professional advice, but don't leave this too long either.

Regardless of how you intend to deal with it, remember this above all else: you have ninety days from the date of the re-assessment to file a formal notice of objection, which is the only way to preserve your rights to argue the re-assessment beyond that time.

It's usually a pretty good idea to file a notice of objection if you haven't got the matter settled within the first sixty days.

THE DIFFERENCE BETWEEN EVASION AND AVOIDANCE

There's quite a difference between tax avoidance and tax evasion and it's very important to keep the distinction in mind, especially when preparing your income tax return — the time of year when people's income tax sensitivity is highest. This sensitivity, coupled with the general displeasure with our tax system, may cause some people to teeter on that very thin line between income tax avoidance and income tax evasion.

Tax avoidance is the arranging of one's affairs so as to legitimately minimize the amount of income tax payable. A simple example of tax avoidance is putting money into an RRSP so as to lower your taxable income, and having the RRSP make an investment that could have been made outside the RRSP.

That's tax avoidance. It's perfectly legal and moral, even if some politicians don't like other people doing it.

Tax evasion, on the other hand, is deliberately doing, or not doing, something with the intent to deceive Revenue Canada, so that the tax payable is less than it should be under the law. The classic evasions, of course, are failing to report income, claiming expenses which weren't incurred or which are clearly not deductible, and other deliberate misrepresentation of facts, such as claiming non-existent dependants.

Tax evasion is illegal and immoral. Don't try it. You won't like it. You are almost certain to get caught and fined. You could even go to jail.

HOW REVENUE CANADA FINDS TAX EVADERS

Revenue Canada is very good at nailing income tax evaders, and we should all be happy they are, because if everybody paid their fair share of income taxes, theoretically at least, rates would be lower. Here are some of the ways Revenue Canada smokes out evaders.

Informers. Yes, someone is apt to rat on you and Revenue Canada will follow it up. Even though Revenue Canada doesn't offer rewards it still gets lots of leads, and the informers are assured their names will not be disclosed.

Pronounced and unusual changes in a taxpayer's style of living, inconsistent with the amount of income he or she is reporting, is another clue for Revenue Canada auditors to follow.

Then, of course, there's simple cross-checking of returns. If taxpayer A claims a deduction for wages paid to taxpayer B, taxpayer B better have those wages on his return or somebody is in trouble. As a matter of fact, my guess is that evasion is most often spotted from information gleaned by tax assessors or tax auditors in the course of their normal review of tax returns or during the audit of other taxpayers.

DEALING WITH AN INCOME TAX AUDITOR

If you're one of the unfortunates whose turn has come up to have your income tax affairs audited, there are a few things that you should keep in mind. Here they are, in no particular order of priority.

Be sure the auditor has proper identification. Refuse to show anything to a person, or let them into your premises, until they produce identification with which you are satisfied. If you have any doubts, make a note of the information the auditor presents to you and check it out with the District Taxation Office.

Don't think, just because you're being audited, that Revenue Canada considers you a criminal or cheat, or both. The overwhelming odds are that your return was simply selected at random and the audit is going to be routine in every respect.

Cooperate fully. The powers of Revenue Canada are such that they can get their hands on almost any document you have anyway, so you may as well be decent about it. However, do not accept discourteous treatment or obvious harassment. It's rare, but if this does happen, don't argue with the auditor — simply report the matter to your local tax director.

Finally, remember that the income tax auditor will make adjustments in your favour just as readily as he or she will ask for more tax if the circumstances warrant it.

Chapter 24

Tax Shelters

It should be made abundantly clear right now that the income tax shelters referred to in this chapter are the likes of films, natural resource deals, real estate shelters, and leasing deals limited only by the bounds of the promoters' imagination. This chapter's comments do not apply to registered retirement savings plans or to other so-called "statutory" plans, such as employee pension plans, which are beyond the scope of this book.

In almost all cases these retirement-oriented tax shelters should be taken advantage of to the maximum extent. But like all things connected with income tax, you must make sure that you are completely familiar with the provisions as they apply to you. The general application may be fine, but in your particular circumstances there may be some exception. So always get professional advice and guidance.

Tax shelters come and tax shelters go, depending for the most part on the whims of successive Finance Ministers. About the only thing consistent about the various tax shelters that have come and gone in recent years is the wake of unhappy people left behind — people who lost money, even after the tax break.

Therein lies the secret of investing in tax shelters. If the particular deal — whether it be a real estate development, a movie, television show, or an oilwell — needs the tax break to make it viable, then don't go for it. On the other hand, if the tax break makes an otherwise reasonable return on the investment better, then it makes some sense. There's precious little to be said for getting a fifty-cent tax refund because you lost a buck.

Never invest in a tax shelter without first obtaining professional advice regarding both the tax implications and the investment attributes of the deal. Always be sure you get your own independent advice; don't rely on the promoter's advisors.

One question to which you should always obtain an acceptable, reasonable answer before investing in a tax shelter that's being offered to the public is: why are the industry people (the insiders) not investing in this; why is it being offered to the public?

No one was around trying to get me to invest in the movie *Rainman*, but I had lots of opportunity to invest in *The Day That the Sheep Stood Still*.

Another problem with tax shelters that rely on the tax break to provide a reasonable rate of return is that tax laws change, and sometimes with retroactive effect. Still another problem is that as a rule tax shelter investments are often very hard to dispose of. In many instances the tax break is only available to the first investor. In others, the very existence of the tax shelter causes a glut on the market.

Still another problem with tax shelters is that so much money is spent on hype and promotion that the deal always ends up being a lot more expensive than it's really worth.

One piece of advice says it all when it comes to so-called tax shelters: never let the tax tail wag the investment dog.

PART THREE

The Market

Chapter 25

Introduction to Investment

You have just completed Parts One and Two of this book, parts devoted primarily to personal money management. Now you're about to begin Part Three, which concentrates on investments. Before concluding that Part Three isn't relevant to you because you don't view yourself as an investor — or even a potential investor — there are some considerations to take into account. For example, anyone who owns real estate, including the home you live in, is an investor, and if you found the chapter "Investing in Real Estate" interesting, there is more of the same type of information in the pages following (except that it refers to the money markets). As a matter of fact, the next chapter, "Investment Clubs," outlines a very easy and relatively safe way for inexperienced people to get started in the stock market.

Another reason to familiarize yourself with Part Three is that even if you don't have money invested directly in the money market you may still be affected by what the market does. If you have an RRSP, a pension plan or an insurance policy, the odds are that some portion of the assets of the institution with which you have your policies or plans is invested in the market, and how the market performs will affect either the value or the cost of your plan or policy, perhaps both. Part Three will help you understand how the market works and, in turn, influences your financial affairs, even if indirectly.

Last, and certainly not least, perhaps you *should* have some money invested in the market. Part Three will help you make that decision. Should you decide to become a market player, you will have a much better chance of protecting your capital and enhancing your investment income if you read on. Even if you decide not to invest in the market, you'll have a greater understanding of the economic forces operating around us every day.

Chapter 26

Investment Clubs

WHAT, WHY, AND HOW

Groups of interested individuals often get together in order to pool their funds and invest in the stock market. That's your basic investment club.

People form these investment clubs for a variety of reasons. Perhaps the members don't have enough money available individually to invest themselves.

Since it's necessary to have at least hundreds, if not thousands, of dollars available to take advantage of the yields offered by some securities (as well as to reduce brokerage fees), club members may decide to combine their money with that of friends in order simply to be able to play the game. It's also a good way to invest in a diversified portfolio without having a lot of cash. As individuals, club members may not be able to build up enough cash to purchase shares in more than one company or industry. As a group there may not be a problem spreading their risk around a bit.

Perhaps they simply want to gain experience in the stock market without risking a great deal of their own money. By investing a small amount periodically they can discuss investments with a group of other interested people and in this way learn how to evaluate investment opportunities.

Perhaps the individuals involved may not have had much experience in handling money. For example, a housewife whose husband handles all the family finances would, as a member of an investment club, learn about making monetary decisions. This would help stand her in good stead if she was suddenly put in the position of having to manage the family finances by herself.

An investment club is also a good way to develop an awareness of our economy and the many forces that affect it. In today's unsettled economic times it is comforting to at least be aware something is happening even if you don't fully understand what's going on.

Finally, an individual may want to make some money. This point should not be played down. By investing carefully it is possible to make money in an investment club, either by holding securities that earn income or by trading them to realize capital gains. After all, joining an investment club could be an expensive lesson if the only thing gained was experience.

Whatever the reason for forming it, the concept of an investment club is basically simple. Each member of the club contributes a lump sum amount at the beginning, regular amounts on a periodic basis, or a combination of the two. As enough cash is built up, the investment committee, which could consist of one member, the entire club, or anything in between, studies the market in order to find the securities that best fit the club's objectives and philosophy. When the securities are chosen, the committee, or its delegate, contacts a broker who will complete the transaction. As income is received, or capital gains or losses realized, the transactions are recorded. Each year annual returns are filed with Revenue Canada reporting the income or losses of the members. Of course, the income or loss is allocated to the members and paid out or absorbed according to the club rules.

That sounds pretty straightforward. But before you run out and form a club, a number of important points should be carefully considered.

INCOME TAX

There are a number of specific income tax rules that apply to investment clubs. Professional advice should always be sought before embarking on this type of venture, and once in operation you should always keep up-to-date on income tax changes.

MAKE CLUB RULES

As investors, you should carefully consider what the ground rules will be for the operation of the club. If you're going to have one person making the investment decisions, he or she should report on each trade made; or if a committee is struck to perform this function, it should have a set voting procedure to avoid squabbles.

It's essential that the amount and timing of cash contributions be decided in advance. Otherwise control is lost over the amount of new investment that can be made on a regular basis.

Along the same lines, you have to decide whether any income earned in the club can be withdrawn or must be re-invested.

Perhaps the most important ground rule of all is to decide how new members are to be admitted and how members who want to leave can get their money out.

PHILOSOPHY

Next comes the question of the club's philosophy. This is probably the most difficult area to decide since each member will have his or her own opinion. However, it is essential that each member of the club have the same investment goals and risk/return levels. Conflicts will inevitably arise if some members want to buy stocks on margin or borrow from the bank while others want to reduce their risk and simply invest money contributed or earned in the club. Also, some may want to invest in high-risk, speculative securities in order to make a quick capital gain while others may be content to buy blue-chip securities in order to protect their capital and at the same time earn some income.

If these issues are not considered and resolved before the club is formed and money is contributed, you can be sure they will come up in the near future — and when their own money is at stake, your erstwhile friends may not be so easy to get along with.

VALUING THE INTEREST

The question of the value of an interest in an investment club usually comes into prominence at two points in time: first, when a new member is admitted, and next when an existing member wants to get out. In each case the fair market value of the club's assets has to be arrived at.

Although this calculation can be done anytime, it's easiest to do at the end of a natural reporting period, such as the end of the month.

Financial statements should be prepared regularly. If members contribute on a weekly or monthly basis and the amounts vary, then statements should be prepared monthly to take into account fluctuations in the value of securities held. If each member contributes the same amount each period and no one joins or leaves the club, then quarterly or yearly statements may suffice. How often statements are prepared really depends on the level of activity and the personal desires of the members.

The following steps are necessary to arrive at a value for each member's interest in the club:

- Record the initial cash input by each member.
- Determine the proportionate share of the initial contribution paid by each member.
- Invest that money in securities.
- Add new contributions by each individual to their respective share of the total initial contribution.
- Invest these new contributions.
- Record income or losses realized.
- Record any amounts paid out to members.
- At the end of the accounting period calculate the market value of the net assets held in the club.
- Determine each member's share of this value based on his or her share of the value at the end of the prior period plus cash contributions since, less any amounts withdrawn.

This calculation determines the value of the holding of each individual member. It may sound complicated, but in order to take into account different proportionate shares in the club, changes in the value of the securities held, withdrawals, and varying contributions over the period, this calculation is necessary to arrive at a fair market value for each member's share.

Before an individual can buy into or withdraw from the club, a calculation such as the one above has to be made. On joining the club the individual would make a cash contribution and the proportion that this cash contribution is of the new market value of the club would be his or her proportionate share in the value of the club. A member may feel that he or she should receive a higher interest in the club to take into account the fact that some of the securities held may have unrecognized capital gains with an underlying tax liability to each member, which should be adjusted for. This is another club rule for you to decide. Rather than adjusting for it, you may feel that this is an appropriate initiation fee. On the other hand, if there is an unrealized capital loss, the existing members may feel that new members should pay more if they will be able to claim their proportion of the losses on their personal tax returns in the year the securities are sold. The same line of reasoning can be made for possible adjustments due to accrued interest or declared but unpaid dividends at the date someone leaves or joins. This point is, the club as a whole must decide these issues ahead of time.

The situation is a little different when club assets have to be disposed of to pay off a member who is leaving. Should the departing member be allocated a proportion (calculated prior to the redemption of the share) of any capital gain realized on the liquidation of the club assets in order to share the tax burden? Since the departing member caused the problem in the first place you may feel he or she should help pay for it. If you decide that the member should help pay for it, then he or she will get an appropriate share of any capital gain. If, on the other hand, a capital loss is realized on the liquidation of assets, that share should probably be allocated as well.

Another way to deal with shares in an investment club is by buying and selling between individuals. In this way the club itself is not affected. The new member simply takes over the old member's proportionate share in the club. Any gain or loss to the vendor on the sale is not calculated based on his or her share of the market value. It is based on the cost base of the investment at the time of the sale.

Another important ground rule is the determination of the method of allocating income among members. This rule basically falls out of the determination of the value of each member's interest in the club. Income or losses can be allocated at the end of each accounting period based on each member's proportionate share in the current value of the club. For example, if someone's share of the club is 10% he or she would be allocated 10% of all interest, 10% of all dividends and 10% of all capital gains or losses.

As you can see, the ground rules for an investment club are not simple. However, a workable system must be pounded out. Since the success of the club depends on it, it's well worth the extra care involved.

MORE PHILOSOPHY

Other important philosophical issues must be dealt with before an investment club begins operating, issues which will have a definite impact on the eventual success of the club, from both an economic and a human relations point of view.

These issues are often the most difficult to resolve. Because they relate to personal values and objectives, most are not easily quantified, measured or reduced to hard and fast, written rules of operation. On the other hand, there are some which are quantifiable, but usually the quantity determined to be right has to be arbitrarily set.

To avoid some of the possible conflicts which may otherwise come up during the lifetime of the club, it is important that the majority of these issues, too, be resolved before the actual operations of the club begin. In this way, if disagreements arise, any members who wish to leave can do so without creating some of the problems discussed earlier.

One of the first issues to be resolved is the atmosphere under which the club will be operating. If it's primarily going to be a social club, where people are involved because they have a general interest in investments but also want to meet with their friends on a regular basis, then some of the investment decisions may not be as carefully thought out as they should be. But then, that may not be essential to these people. If, on the other hand, the club will be operated primarily as a business, the investment decisions may be sound but there may not be enough socializing to satisfy some members.

In order for a club to be successful in the long run, it is necessary for the members to assess themselves, as well as the rest of the group, to find out if there is a match. It isn't necessary that everyone think exactly the same. In fact, it may be best if they don't. Those people who are keenly interested in the business aspect can form the core of the investment committee and ensure that good, sound decisions are reached. Those who joined because of the good times as well as an interest in investment can arrange the meetings, look after administration and keep morale high. The danger lies in the extremes — all work or all play — since these may lead to early conflicts or dissatisfaction.

Once the atmosphere has been established, you have to decide how much money is to be contributed and when. The choices range from one large sum to small amounts regularly, or a combination of the two. The decision, to a certain extent, will be based on where the club lies between a purely social club and a business club. If the club is all social and general interest, then the contributions may be kept low to reduce the amount of money at risk. If it is all business then the amount may be high in order to build up a large amount of capital as quickly as possible. It isn't necessary that each member contribute the same amount, but it does make the bookkeeping easier.

One of the most important decisions to be faced by your group is the determination of your investment goals. Somehow you have to decide whether you are going to invest for the short or long term and what level of risk you're willing to accept. This is where the fun begins. In order to invest for short-term gains you will look for the quick capital gain to be made on special information or sound reasoning, or you will look for the securities paying higher than normal income yields. In either case, this type of activity normally carries with it a higher degree of risk, especially if your group is inexperienced. By looking at long-term investments, for either capital appreciation or income yields, you don't necessarily eliminate your risk. Many stocks, even over the long run, prove to be losers. By investing in blue-chip securities you can reduce the amount of risk involved, but this may also reduce the members' degree of interest in the club.

Whichever decision is made, long or short term, it is important that you do your homework before investing. Talk to your stockbroker, read the financial press, listen to economic forecasts and do anything else you can think of to find out more about your potential investments before you pay out the cash.

Speaking of cash, you must decide whether or not you're going to borrow money to invest. Again, this decision will be based on the amount of risk your group is willing to assume. In a period of rising prices, leverage (using other people's money) will increase your gains above those which you normally would have enjoyed. However, in a period of falling prices, leverage will also increase your losses above the level you would otherwise have experienced. In addition, with today's volatile interest rates, you would have to ensure there is always enough cash on hand in the club to meet the monthly interest charges. As a result, someone always has to watch the cash flow carefully in order to avoid missing an interest payment.

One other point which should be discussed at the start is the size of the club. Some may want to keep it to a group of close friends, say, 10, while others may want to let it get up to 30 or 40 in order to build up the cash base from which to invest. This decision should take into account the extra bookkeeping and paperwork involved. You could also run into the problem of where to hold the meetings. In addition, when new people are added, you would have to ensure that they have the same goals and objectives as the original group. Otherwise, these new members could overrule your previous decisions as to ground rules and philosophy.

The numbers question becomes increasingly important once you begin to approach people who are not close friends. At that time you should contact your provincial securities commission to see whether or not you will be considered to be making a public issue of securities. As you can see, big is not necessarily best, especially since your share of the income will remain the same in terms of absolute dollars.

The resolution of these issues will not guarantee the eventual success of your club. However, by dealing with them early, you will at least have cleared the air of questions on how the club will operate. You can then concentrate on fulfilling your objective for forming the club.

Chapter 27

Investing in Securities

You don't have to be a Rockefeller or Conrad Black to invest in the stock market. As you will see as you read on, there is a place in the market for investors of all sizes and attitudes. Indeed, as pointed out in Chapter 25, the market affects the financial affairs of most of us even if we don't own stocks or bonds directly. This is so because nearly every institution that we deal with — banks, trust companies, insurance companies, and their plans and policies — rely in large part on investments for income, in the form of either capital gains or dividends. Even education and health care costs are affected by the market because colleges, universities and hospitals all rely in part on investment income to meet their costs. If their investment income is down, our costs — either taxes or fees — go up.

As a matter of fact, you don't invest in the stock market at all. When you buy a share or a bond you're investing in the corporation or organization that issued the share or bond. The "market" is just the store at which you bought it, and where you sell it later.

Of course we've all heard of people being burned "in the market," and there's no denying that happens. But few endeavours are completely safe. A good friend of mine broke her hip going to church.

An understanding of how the market itself affects the value of your investment (which this part of the book will give you), combined with a healthy dose of common sense, will go a long way toward helping you make money by investing in securities.

The word "securities" is used here to mean stocks and bonds traded on the stock markets. Although in recent years investment attitudes have favoured everything from real estate to precious metals and art, you should always consider the stock market as a place to invest.

Remember that it isn't important what "the market" is doing — what counts is what *your* investments are doing. As one investment house aptly put it in its advertisements a few years ago: "Asking how the stock market is doing is like asking what the weather is like in North America."

Carefully chosen securities offer as much protection of capital as do most real estate investment opportunities readily available to the general public. You must always remember that there are many, many corporations and individuals who are actively involved in the business of investing in real estate. They usually take up the vast majority of large, direct real estate investment opportunities. So those available to the general public are usually high-risk ventures which, from an investment standpoint, are probably not as safe as blue-chip stocks.

Because most of us have seen real estate in certain high-growth areas continue to increase in value by leaps and bounds, we tend to look upon all real estate as a perfectly safe investment. This is simply not the case. You can lose money investing in real estate — especially, as already mentioned, if you sink your money into the left-overs that the professional real estate investors consider to be too high-risk to fund completely themselves.

Continuity of a reasonable income from investments in many securities is an advantage not always available from investments in real estate. For example, the Bank of Montreal has paid dividends on its common shares every year since 1828. The Bank of Nova Scotia has paid dividends on its common shares every year since 1833. A reasonable annual rate of return is obtainable by investing in top-quality securities. On the other hand, vacant cottage lots will not produce annual income, income which might be more important to you than future capital gains.

Considering the preferential income tax treatment given to income from Canadian securities (particularly dividends), the insidious and seemingly never-ending increases in property taxes, and the rent control mentality of many governments, it's not always easy to find an after-tax return from rental real estate comparable to that available from top-quality stocks and bonds.

Although bonds don't provide much of a hedge against inflation, good-quality shares often do. Those who feel that real estate is the only reasonable hedge against inflation might ask their brokers to provide them with a list of stocks whose values have more than kept pace with inflation. Yes, they do exist.

A major advantage attached to investments in securities is the ability to invest as much or as little as one pleases. There is literally no upper limit, and you can invest as little as a few hundred dollars in stocks or bonds.

Then there is the almost instant marketability of all or a part of your securities to meet emergencies or planned major expenditures. This marketability feature affords excellent flexibility in being able to adjust your holdings in accordance with changed investment objectives, fluctuating market conditions vis-à-vis particular securities, or their underlying attractiveness.

Investments in securities are easy to manage and publicly traded securities can be realistically valued immediately, except in very unusual circumstances, by referring to the financial press. Contrast this feature of investments in publicly traded securities with the difficulty, cost and range of results of real estate appraisals.

It must be emphasized now that these comments are not in any way intended to detract from the many, and very real, attractive features of real estate as an investment, but rather are meant to call attention to the advantages of investment in securities — advantages which are often overlooked or not given adequate consideration by many investors. Real estate investments are dealt with in Chapter 16. Meanwhile, back to some more advantages of investing in publicly traded stocks and bonds.

There is always the possibility of investment growth in the form of the receipt of rights which can be sold to realize a pure profit or exercised to obtain additional shares at a reduced cost. Then there is the additional possibility of shares being split. This usually results in growth of the holder's original investment.

Finally, there exists the chance that one corporation may want to acquire control of another, a situation normally accompanied by a favourable price being offered to the shareholders of the corporation which is being taken over. From time to time there are epidemics of takeovers and attempted takeovers, admittedly to the chagrin of some, but nonetheless to the advantage of many shareholders.

In addition to the foregoing, many investors gain a great deal of satisfaction from their active participation in a corporation's growth. The fact remains, too, that investment in stocks and debt of corporations is desperately needed in order to continue adequate development of our country and its resources.

There's a lot to be said for investing in securities. From a nationalistic point of view, a constant problem is that our country needs more investment. From a business standpoint, there is always a shortage of investment funds. Finally, from a strictly selfish standpoint, there is the continuing opportunity to make money in the stock market. To repeat, it doesn't really matter how "the market" is doing — what's important is how *your* stocks and bonds are doing.

The next few chapters are designed to help you better understand just how the stock market works. They will also point out and explain some of the most important elements you should be familiar with before committing funds to the market. You should refer now to the Glossary found in the back of this book. Some of these terms, particularly those from the legal and accounting worlds, have general meanings apart from, and often different than, their specialized meanings within the investment business. So it is important to read through the glossary now and refer back to it whenever you run across a word the meaning of which is not known to you, or of which you're not certain.

Chapter 28

Types of Market Players

THE THREE TYPES

Once you're convinced that the stock market is worth a try, the next thing you have to decide, even before contacting a broker, is what kind of market player you're going to be. There are three distinct classifications of market players. They are the investor, the speculator and the gambler. The reason you have to classify yourself is to determine the type of investments which will form the bulk of your activity.

Following is an examination of the characteristics of each of the three types of market players.

The Real Investor

Time is an important factor to the real investor. Generally speaking, the real investor adopts a longer-term view of things than the speculator, who in turn takes a longer-term view of things than does the gambler. The hallmark of the investor is patience. The real investor invests capital to produce a regular income as well as a capital gain over a period of years. The main concern of the real investor is safety of capital followed closely by regularity of income. Good credit risks only are selected, with the favourite purchase being a security of a company with a good record, a good reputation and a solid, promising future. When the real investor buys an industrial issue it's an established company with a good history. The real investor demands evidence of earning power and asset values and looks for a reasonable margin of safety in both.

The real investor never buys securities at random, doesn't invest with borrowed money (unless assured of a higher return than the cost of borrowing on an after-tax basis) and works toward definite investment objectives by following a long-term, well-thought-out investment plan.

The Speculator

The speculator is a different breed altogether. The speculator is impatient and adopts a much shorter view than the investor. The speculator is continually on the lookout for securities which are undervalued in relation to short-term prospects. Speculators take calculated risks and seek rewards in the form of quick capital gains rather than regular income or long-term appreciation. Speculators are quite prepared to accept capital losses when they guess wrongly.

But it should be recognized that the speculator is not necessarily to be branded a non-desirable. Speculators perform two very useful services. They tend to level out what would otherwise be great swings in prices by buying when prices are depressed and selling when prices are rising. They are also a source of risk capital. Intelligent speculation may quite properly form part of the investment program of some investors.

The main point is to understand the difference between investing and speculating and to know which you are doing. It could be disastrous to think you are investing when in fact you are speculating.

The Gambler

A completely different kind of cat, the gambler bets on the unknown by acting on hunches and tips rather than on carefully studied data. The gambler's trademark is buying long shots in the hope of making a killing — quick or otherwise.

Gamblers normally appear on the scene after the stock market has enjoyed a period of rising prices and volume. They hear about people making money in the market and want to get a piece of this — to them — easy money. Gamblers, though, are usually not prepared to go to the trouble of getting the facts about their "investments." Normally they know only what they hear, and usually what they hear are rumours and tips passed on by people as poorly informed as they are. It's possible to conceive of a gambler acting on a rumour he or she had started. I'd love to be there when it happens.

Other characteristics of the gambler include: operating on limited capital; generally prospering only while the market is buoyant; being caught totally unprepared when the inevitable downturn comes; selling at a loss; and blaming others for his or her troubles.

Gamblers should stick to buying lottery tickets, going to the track, and taking the occasional trip to Las Vegas or Atlantic City. At least then they'll have the pleasure of looking up their numbers, watching the horses run, or seeing some good shows.

INVESTMENT vs SPECULATION

Remember that the distinction between investment and speculation is clearly one of quality rather than one of form. Either bonds or shares might be suitable as either investments or speculations. The definition becomes a function of determining the quality of a security before purchasing it by investigating the relevant facts. Later on some advice will be given as to how to go about this.

All the securities available form a broad spectrum ranging from top-quality, high-grade investments all the way down to outright gambles. There is no clear-cut dividing line anywhere on this spectrum between investment and speculative securities — just degrees of each type. There are some general rules of thumb, though.

Government and municipal bonds are seldom, if ever, speculative. If they are not in default, and have no unfavourable history of defaults of interest or principal, they are usually considered to be of investment quality.

When it comes to corporate bonds, a number of tests have been devised to measure their investment calibre and, as mentioned, these will be dealt with later. Suffice for now to say that such tests are largely measures of safety of principal and certainty of income. In short, the hallmarks of investment-quality corporation bonds are consistent earning power and adequate underlying assets.

There have also been a number of tests devised for measuring the investment quality of stocks. Stocks are considered of investment quality rather than speculative if they have a trend of strong earnings, have paid regular dividends for a number of years, and have all the appearances of carrying on these traditions.

We have to examine investment objectives in a little more depth before moving on to other detailed aspects of investing in securities.

Chapter 29

Investment Objectives

SETTING GOALS

Unless you have specific goals in mind, it is very difficult to build a successful and appropriate portfolio.

Of course, investment objectives vary from person to person. One person may be mostly interested in protecting capital, another in earning income to live on. Someone else might be primarily concerned with capital growth, perhaps to live on the income therefrom in retirement. The point is you must decide what your objectives are before you even pick a broker.

Security of Capital

Individuals who are dependent on investments for all or most of their income need a high level of safety and price stability. The same holds true for people who are, in effect, setting up a fund to meet some future need, such as children's education, future care of a disabled dependant, or retirement.

Maximum safety is found in securities such as Canada Savings Bonds, government treasury bills and some high-quality preference shares. Blue-chip common stocks may well have a place in this type of portfolio, but probably not if short-term price stability is a major criterion.

Income

It is well known that the higher the yield the greater the risk. When income is the main objective — or ranks equally with security of capital, which is often the case — a balanced porfolio is usually preferable.

This could be a portfolio consisting primarily of short-term government bonds, high-quality preferred shares and blue-chip common stocks with a good dividend record.

Capital Gain

When growth of capital in the form of appreciation in the value of a portfolio is the main objective, then common shares are the way to go. This is usually the objective of the investor who has enough annual income to meet current living costs, but wants capital to grow to meet future needs, such as retirement or children's education. Also, investors who would prefer to pay tax later on a capital gain rather than now on interest or dividends should look for growth situations. The longer you can put off paying a tax, the less it costs in real terms; furthermore, your tax rate may be lower during retirement than when working full-time. But not just any old common shares will do. A happy medium must be struck. What has to be found is that elusive investment known as the growth company.

In this context a growth company is one whose common shares have maintained an above-average rate of growth over a period of five years or more and are likely to continue to do so. The increase in price must be the result of permanent factors such as good profits, increasing asset value, adequate working capital and above-average return on equity. Anything else is not growth investment, it's speculation.

Growth companies usually are characterized by a high rate of earnings on capital invested, a high level of retention and reinvestment of earnings as opposed to a high dividend payment (although some growth companies do pay nominal dividends), capable and dynamic management, and an above-average opportunity for increased earnings, such as a technological competitive edge.

A real growth company should have an above-average rate of earnings on its invested capital over at least a five-year period. It should also appear reasonable to expect that the company will be able to maintain a similar or better rate on additional invested capital. The real test is increasing unit and dollar sales over a reasonable number of years combined with a firm control of costs.

Characteristically, real growth companies finance a major part of expansion out of retained earnings. The company with above-average sales and earnings which are all paid out in dividends, or a company that increases capital through outside financing as quickly as earnings expand, is not a real growth company, but it's probably an excellent choice for the investor who is looking for a mix of income and some growth. Growth companies have a conservative dividend policy.

Another characteristic of the real growth company is competent and dynamic — even aggressive — management. Growth companies tend to spend a lot of money on research and development. As a matter of fact, a detailed study by the Stanford Research Institute of the relative post-war growth of 400 corporations revealed that high-growth companies were predominantly research- and development-oriented. That, of course, is not surprising.

But it's also not enough. Emphasis must also be placed on merchandising, advertising, public relations, cost control, product management and personnel management and development, as well as on product research and development.

The opportunity for earnings growth is often greater in young, expanding industries. The opportunity may exist in the form of key patent or copyright ownership. Sometimes it's in the form of management which consistently recognizes and capitalizes on new opportunities before their competitors do.

Caveat Emptor

Never is the adage "let the buyer beware" more appropriate than in the purchase of growth stocks. Ideally a growth stock should be purchased in the early stages of its growth cycle. Because growth stocks tend to have low yields, you must guard against paying prices which have already taken into account most of the expected growth.

It's impossible to have the ultimate in capital security, income, and growth potential all at the same time. Your investment portfolio must be designed to attach the right degree of importance to each objective based on your particular circumstances.

Having decided what type of investor you are and what your investment objectives will be, the next steps are to open an account and to choose a broker.

Chapter 30

Operating an Account

If you're going to invest in Canadian securities by playing the stock market you should open an account with a broker who is subject to the regulations of the various stock exchanges and the Investment Dealers Association of Canada.

For your safety, these regulations require investment dealers to: maintain adequate capital in their businesses; carry extensive insurance; maintain proper accounting control and supervision over employees; and be subject to independent audits. Furthermore, the Investment Dealers Association and the various stock exchanges have established a national contingency fund. Payments from this fund may be authorized to help investors who suffer losses from the financial failure of a member.

All accounts are handled by professionally trained and licensed representatives who buy and sell on your behalf. The representative's services will be available on a personal, confidential basis, and although not an investment counsellor per se, your representative can help you with your investment decisions.

We should pause for a moment here to consider a relatively new development in Canada. In the early '80s the rules for buying and selling stocks were changed to allow brokers to negotiate the amount of commission charged to clients rather than having to stick to a prescribed rate schedule. This change resulted in the establishment of no-frills brokerage houses which simply execute your order and, because they offer no other services whatsoever, are able to charge a lower commission than the conventional, established firms which have large research departments, underwriting facilities, and brokers who offer advice to clients when asked.

The question, of course, is: Should investors place their orders where the commission is lowest, or should they deal with the firms offering the broader range of services, even if it costs them more to do so?

Unless you're the type of investor who knows exactly what to buy, when to buy, and when to sell, you will probably be better off with the larger, non-discount broker. The higher commission, for most market players, will be more than offset by the availability of information about investments; access to blocks of stock and new issues; the more efficient execution of trades; stability of the firm; and most important of all, the knowledge your broker has about you. Your broker should be looked upon no differently than your doctor, lawyer, accountant, or any other professional advisor. Your broker should be completely familiar with your investment goals, your resources, and the type of investments that you will be comfortable with.

When an account is opened, in addition to the usual information such as name, address, occupation, and bank references, the broker will want to know about your financial circumstances, your investment objectives, and details of any securities you already own.

The most common type of account opened is a cash account. This means that you pay in full for securities bought, or deliver securities sold, by the settlement date (usually the fifth day after the date of the transaction).

Another type of account is the margin account, which works generally as follows. Stocks, but no penny stocks, may be purchased on margin, meaning that cash equal to at least 50% of the purchase price is put up by you, with the balance being borrowed from the broker. Of course, interest must be paid on this loan. Also, if the value of the stock declines, you will have to put up more cash because the amount of the loan cannot exceed 50% of the market value of the relevant stock. As a matter of fact, depending on the circumstances, sometimes the percentage is higher than 50%. So check it out.

After an account has been opened with a broker, orders can be placed either in writing or orally. Brokers are usually happy to provide up-to-the-minute bid and ask quotations for their clients on any publicly traded stock or bond.

When an order is executed, your broker will mail you a written confirmation — usually on the same day. You then have evidence in writing of exactly what has been bought or sold, the price paid or received, the commission charges (or accrued interest where applicable), and the net cost or proceeds.

If you bought a security, the cost and charges will be debited against any funds you may have on deposit with the broker, otherwise you will have to pay the broker by the fifth business day after the transaction.

If you sold a security, you would have to deliver the shares sold, in negotiable form, no later than the fifth business day after the transaction — unless, of course, the shares were already held for safekeeping by the broker. Also, if you made a sale, the broker will either send you a cheque or keep the funds on deposit for you. It's entirely up to you. Interest is earned by you on funds left on deposit with your broker, but check out the rate and any minimum balance requirements to be sure you can't do better elsewhere. Of course, if you plan to make some purchases soon you might want to leave the funds on deposit with the broker for the sake of convenience, regardless of the interest rate.

If the security sold is registered in your name, you must sign your name on the back of the certificate in exactly the same way as it appears on the front, date it, and have your signature witnessed. If it is jointly held, all joint holders must endorse it.

If you have certificates which were previously duly endorsed, they are already negotiable; in effect they are bearer certificates. Bearer certificates need not be endorsed; they are negotiable by delivery.

Securities purchased will also be in either registered or bearer form. Now, there's quite an important distinction between having registered or bearer securities.

The names and addresses of the owners of securities in registered form are kept on record by the security issuer, who will mail any interest, dividends, and shareholder or bondholder information to the registered owners. Should you change your address while owning a registered security you should notify the transfer agent, whose name is usually shown on the certificate, so that mail may be correctly directed. A registered security may be registered in the owner's name, in a nominee's name or in "street" form (i.e., in the broker's name). For convenience in handling, many securities are registered in nominee or street form.

A bearer security is negotiable in the same way as money. The holder of a bearer security — that is, the person in possession of it — is presumed to be the owner. Accordingly, if bearer securities are stolen or lost, it's relatively easy for a thief to turn them into cash. Bearer bonds have numbered and dated interest coupons attached and arranged in convenient order for clipping. As each coupon becomes due it should be clipped and cashed at any chartered bank or your broker's office.

Interest or dividends on securities the broker holds on your behalf will be sent directly to you by the issuer's transfer agent if the securities are registered in your name. If they are not registered in your name be sure to check your monthly broker statements carefully to ensure your account has been credited by the broker with any amounts you are entitled to.

At the end of each month your broker will send you a statement of transactions during the month, showing any credit or debit balance outstanding on securities transacted or held on your behalf. The confirmation slips and monthly statements provide a valuable check to ensure that your records agree with your broker's. Any discrepancies should be called to the broker's attention immediately.

It is also a good idea to retain all confirmations and statements for tax and investment management purposes. Most brokers will provide you with year-end summaries, but it's best to maintain your own separate check.

However, you're not yet ready to call a broker. Read on.

Chapter 31

Choosing and Dealing with a Broker

GIVE IT SOME THOUGHT

Many investors give less time and thought to selecting a broker than they do to buying a newspaper. Although most people who play the market are by nature somewhat cynical (particularly if they have been in it longer than six months), it's surprising how many naively believe that most of the thousands of men and women who sell stocks are more or less equal in their knowledge, honesty, and ability to separate the wheat from the chaff in the contradictory information and hearsay that abound in the stock market.

They are not.

Many are outstanding. Some, while honest, are so inept they should be in other businesses. The majority, however, as in any other profession, are capable. And, in fact, the average broker today is better trained and better motivated than the average broker of twenty-five or thirty years ago, when many of them were attracted to the business by visions of quick killings amid the excesses of a speculative market.

The sad truth is many investors who have had bad experiences in the market can justifiably attribute their losses, in part, to relying on brokers who were more interested in making a commission than helping their clients. Although, in fairness, you must always remember that brokers make their money buying and selling securities, not by advising you what to do. But you can still make good and bad choices of brokers.

Unfortunately, there are no guaranteed guidelines to help you select the right broker. The choice is extremely subjective and made even more complicated by the fact that there is no simple way to evaluate a broker's handling of your account. Nonetheless, the decision as to who is handling your portfolio should, like all investment decisions, be reassessed from time to time, if for no other reason than as a precaution to ensure that your needs are still being met.

In selecting a broker, the first thing you should do is ask yourself honestly what it is you want out of the market, always remembering that your level of investment return will depend largely on the degree of risk you're willing to take. Determine how much of your time you are willing to spend analyzing investments; and don't expect a lot of attention from a broker if your total portfolio is worth a couple of thousand dollars. Some firms discourage their sales personnel from taking on accounts that will deal in what is to them nuisance-size orders. Others, however, take the attitude that all accounts are worthwhile because they grow over time.

If your age and income indicate that a conservative portfolio consisting of bonds, preferred shares and blue-chip stocks for income is in order, then you will probably be best off dealing with one of the really big brokerage houses. They are best suited to provide you with large allotments of the low-risk, new issues that are suitable for your type of portfolio. But even then you must find an individual within the firm who is willing to provide you with information pertinent to your particular needs and to advise you on portfolio changes, if necessary.

If your portfolio is large and broadly diversified, and you want conservatism, then you will want to deal with a firm that offers a portfolio review service.

It comes down to picking a firm that can and will provide you with the services that are most suited to your investment philosophy, and choosing an individual within that firm who can and will give you the personal service and guidance consistent with your objectives.

Many investors simply accept their broker's recommendations without question, failing to realize that many brokers don't actually analyze the securities they sell, but rather are just passing on information they've been handed. The really good broker will do more than quote a few platitudes from a promotional blurb. A good broker will give you detailed information which will enable you to determine whether a particular investment meets your particular needs.

Look at the reputation of the brokerage firm and ask to see the type of information it produces for its clients. You'll want to know if its recommendations are sent to all investors at the same time. You don't want information a week after the firm's largest clients have had it.

Although the final decision on a purchase or sale is yours, you may still rely heavily on the broker for advice, so it's imperative that you determine how a specific recommendation was arrived at. Be sure your broker is prepared to spend the necessary time talking to you. It is *your* money that's at risk.

Although the firm's research capability and method of distributing information to clients like you are key considerations, always remember that the individual broker you deal with is more important to you than his or her firm's reputation as a whole.

A good broker should be willing to take the time necessary to tailor an investment program to fit your individual needs. Ask the broker what a typical client's investment activity is: that is, the amount of money invested, how often they buy and sell, and the types of securities they deal in. If it's way out of line with your circumstances you probably should look elsewhere.

You should always have a face-to-face meeting with any brokers you are considering. Actually, some brokerage houses insist on such meetings to determine what is a suitable investment level for the client and whether the client can afford them. If the broker doesn't insist on it, be sure you do.

If you have never opened an account with a broker, be prepared to answer a lot of questions about your net worth and other financial information. A broker is almost certain to check out your bank references and will probably refuse to execute your first order until you have been thoroughly checked out.

Having checked each other out, the next move is to establish some guidelines with your broker. This is a key step, but overlooked by most investors, sometimes with costly consequences.

AVOIDING BROKER PROBLEMS

An incredible tradition of honesty and fair play has prevailed over the years in dealings between brokers and clients. In an age when almost every transaction requires a signature, certified cheque or cash, the informal broker–client telephone call is an almost unbelievable way of doing business. Nearly all the tens of millions of dollars in security trading done daily is at least started by a telephone call.

But to you, as admirable as this trusting approach may be, it's worth less than last week's market quotations if you suddenly discover your broker has misunderstood, mismanaged or misled you about your account. And it does happen.

The odds on your ending up with a dishonest person out of the thousands of licensed securities brokers and dealers are very slim. But the mishandling of your account or a serious misunderstanding is a possibility, especially in a system so dependent on telephone conversations. You will likely never have to sue your broker for messing up your account, but knowing how to handle a misunderstanding with your broker is still extremely important.

If you aren't happy with what your broker is doing or not doing, your first move should be to contact someone higher up in the firm involved. In almost all brokerage houses, sales staff are under the supervision of a manager who oversees transactions and the handling of portfolios. Such a person, or an officer of the firm, should be asked to look into your complaint. In almost all cases this is where the complaint stops. In most cases the firm will be inclined to take your word on what happened and the chances of your getting a settlement without much difficulty are good.

If your claim is not satisfied by the broker, your next step should be to contact the Investment Dealers Association of Canada and the stock exchange where the transaction took place. Both the I.D.A., whose membership consists of investment houses, and the stock exchanges have considerable regulatory and disciplinary powers over member firms — including the right to levy fines and to suspend or expel individuals or firms.

Upon receipt of your complaint, which you should submit in writing if you get to this stage, these bodies will conduct an investigation. If they find in your favour, the broker will be under considerable pressure to settle with you quickly, particularly since disciplinary action may be taken against the individual or the firm, or both.

If you still aren't satisfied, contact the appropriate provincial securities commission. These commissions are charged with regulation of the underwriting, distribution and sale of securities, based on policies that are fairly uniform across Canada. Under the authority of provincial law, securities commissions can undertake prosecutions for violations of security regulations. Bear in mind that the commissions have no power to compel a firm to return your money; they can, however, suspend a firm's registration or impose severe penalties for misrepresentation, fraud or intentional omission of material facts concerning a stock.

At this level it's important to remember that an investigation begins with your written statement, which should be signed and include all relevant facts, such as the date of the transaction, details of the security involved and its price, as well as any special circumstances about the transaction. Try to recall as accurately as you can all communications you had with the broker, and the date and the approximate time any telephone calls were made. List the names of all individuals in the brokerage firm you had contact with both during and after the transaction in question. If you have any record of the deal — including scribbled notes — attach copies of them to your letter. This way your complaint will have the effect of a written affidavit.

Usually, a commission will begin investigating on an informal basis, sending its investigators to interview you, the broker and any others involved. If a formal investigation is called for, the commission can subpoena records and witnesses.

After the investigation of your complaint by the securities commission, a hearing, which could last anywhere from a couple of hours to days depending on the complexity of the matter, may be held. At its conclusion, the broker, if found to be at fault, may be reprimanded, suspended or expelled from the securities industry. But, if not, and you are determined to pursue the case, your next recourse would be to file a civil suit. Time to get a lawyer.

On a simple complaint — say a disagreement between you and your broker over the number of shares purchased — the investigation would probably take very little time. More complex cases involving possible fraud or misrepresentation could take months.

The most frequent complaints concern simple misunderstandings, but they often pose the toughest problems for investigators. If, say, you asked your broker to buy 100 shares of a stock and he or she purchased 500, the only evidence is your word against the broker's, and you often can't do much about the complaint. Of course, if it happens with more than one client, then the broker's credibility begins to suffer.

Legally, your oral order to a broker constitutes an enforceable contract. The only exception involves the purchase of new shares covered by a prospectus. In this case you can withdraw an order within 48 hours after receipt of the prospectus. Though binding, the contract is, of course, subject to proof. In a dispute based on a telephone call, proof will likely depend on the relative credibility of the witnesses — which of course are you and the broker.

Even in a case where your broker is disputing what you said, you will probably win if you have taken the trouble to jot down a few notes detailing the telephone call at the time you made it. While not evidence in the strictest sense of the word, a memo including the date, time and details of the order would lend support to your recollection of an oral order. People can pretty well judge the veracity of an individual, and if you've got a good memory of your side of the story or notes confirming it, you will likely be in the driver's seat.

Another alternative following a purchase dispute is simply not to pay. If you have a genuine grievance, brokerage firms will rarely resort to a court proceeding in order to collect your account. The cost to the firm in time, expense and public relations is usually prohibitive. If, however, the value of the stock in question has dropped considerably following your disputed purchase, be prepared. A firm may decide to sell the stock and sue you for the difference between the original purchase price and their loss. In most cases involving small amounts, the firm will simply write off the loss — and you as well.

The market is full of habitual complainers, and if your refusal to pay is really based on sour grapes after taking a loss, don't expect to get away with it. The brokerage industry is well aware that the world is full of people on both sides who might be stretching facts a bit to get things to work out in their favour. If you make a practice of not paying losses, you could end up blacklisted. Though no actual list is said to exist, the industry does take steps to protect itself from chronic offenders. It is rumoured the Toronto Stock Exchange occasionally sends member houses names of people who may have had questionable dealings with a member firm. Other firms which have had dealings with the individual are asked to contact the exchange. Such notices, said to appear on average about once a month, are posted in the order and clearance departments of member houses.

So checks and balances do exist on both sides to weed out brokers and investors who don't belong in the securities field. Like most grievance procedures, however, those existing for the benefit of the investor are best if they are never needed. One way to avoid disputes is to clarify the ground rules your broker acts under and to review them every now and then. Let your broker know that you are aware of your rights. Above all, keep your broker informed about your financial circumstances and investment objectives.

When initiating a transaction, be sure your broker completely understands your order. Take the time to question any strange terms your broker uses when your order is read back to you on the telephone.

If your broker isn't in the habit of reading back your orders, get another broker.

Your best defense is knowledge. There is no way you should let someone else blindly run your financial affairs for you. If you're interested in shares of companies in a particular industry, you should learn as much as you can about four or five companies in that or similar industries. Take the trouble to obtain the annual reports and read them. See what the market price movements of the particular companies have been. Without this research, you will wind up trying to evaluate the broker instead of the stocks.

However you arrange your dealings with your broker, remember that reliability doesn't automatically mean profit. If you intend to play the market you will have to take risks that should be made on the basis of *your* knowledge, not your broker's *opinion*.

Finally, bear in mind the next time you call your broker just how imperfect the telephone alone is as a communications link. Make notes — and keep them. Your broker probably does.

DO'S AND DON'TS

Here are some basic ways to reduce the risk of misunderstanding between you and your broker.

Do's

1. Deal only with securities houses which meet the standards of the Investment Dealers Association or one of the major stock exchanges.
2. Select a broker who operates an office near you, has a sales representative with whom you are able to establish a close working relationship and who provides the type of services you are especially interested in (e.g. research, new issue underwriting, mutual funds, etc.).
3. Require, as part of the terms for opening a discretionary account, that you receive from the broker on a frequent and regular basis a written report of the status of your account. (A discretionary account is one whereby the broker can buy and sell on your account without first obtaining your permission for the specific transactions.)
4. Tell your broker when and where you are most reachable. Your broker should know whether you prefer to be called at the office. If there is a number where you can always be reached, you should consider giving it to your broker.
5. Make decisions — whether yes or no. Always hesitating to act on recommendations will work against you. Your broker probably has hundreds of clients to service; if you always hedge you're very apt to be put at the end of the list.

Don'ts

1. Don't deal in securities sold under high pressure, whether in the form of a telephone call or letter. Request the person offering securities to mail you written information about the company, its operations, net profit, management, financial position and future prospects. If you do not understand the written information, consult someone who does.
2. Don't deal with a person who guarantees what the price of a stock is going to be in the future or offers to buy it back from you at cost if it doesn't go up in value.
3. Don't deal with a representative of a securities firm which is unknown to you until you have had time to carefully check the company's reputation.
4. Don't invest on rumours. So-called inside information is quickly discounted by the market — usually long before you hear it. This probably is the basis for the adage "sell on good news, buy on bad news."

SOURCES OF INFORMATION

It seems ridiculous to have to say it, but many people who consider themselves to be competent investors totally ignore the main ingredient required in order to make sensible investment decisions. That ingredient is information.

If you obtain as much information as you possibly can about a company before committing funds to the purchase of its securities, you will be considerably more secure in your choices than those who blindly plunge in and take a chance.

There is no shortage of information available. Canadian securities legislation is based on the principle of full and true disclosure of information pertaining to issuers of securities, and annual and interim financial reports of those who are subject to its rules. In addition, Canada is blessed with a fine financial press, not to mention the many American publications available.

There are really three information routes available. The first is to rely entirely on investment counsellors or brokers. If you have neither the time nor the inclination to do your own investigations, this is the way to go. The second method is to be your own researcher. The third route, and probably the most satisfying — and perhaps the best — is a combination of the first two.

The Canadian business and financial press is varied and informative. It ranges from daily financial publications, through weekly business newspapers to monthly business magazines.

Examples of popular financial publications are *The Globe and Mail Report on Business*, *Financial Times of Canada*, *The Financial Post*, and *Canadian Business*. And there are others.

In addition, many Canadian investment houses and the major Canadian financial institutions issue regular reports dealing with current business, economic and political trends, and items of general interest. Look for them at your bank and trust company branch. The investment houses also frequently publish special industry and company reports.

As you would expect, there are numerous U.S. financial publications which are of interest to Canadian investors. Two truly outstanding American financial publications are the daily *Wall Street Journal* and the weekly *Barrons*. Two of the more relevant American financial magazines are *Fortune* and *Forbes*. The British publications *The Economist* and *The Financial Times of London* are also excellent sources of financial and economic information.

For those who want to delve even deeper into financial and business information, there are many Canadian government publications available. There's almost no end to the information — useful and useless — which is available from Statistics Canada. Its data gathering and publishing is a whole industry unto itself, from which you can obtain information on the trends and activity in practically any industry in Canada — whether they're expanding, orders placed, retail sales, manufacturing activity, inventory levels, bankruptcies, and on and on.

Last, but certainly not least, the Toronto, Montreal and Vancouver stock exchanges publish excellent monthly bulletins (available at very little cost) outlining information about the Canadian securities markets.

Chapter 32

Common Shares

WHAT ARE COMMON SHARES?

The common shares of public companies are by far the most popular investment vehicle among people who play the market. It seems incredible, then, that many investors are completely unaware that a common share is anything other than something which they bought and hope to sell at a profit sometime in the future. A common share is much more than that.

First and foremost, common shares represent the residual ownership of an incorporated business. After creditors are paid and preferred shares redeemed, the common shareholders are entitled to all the remaining assets of the corporation, regardless of the par value or actual cost of the common share.

Moreover, common shares are normally voting shares. Indeed, it's a rare set of circumstances in which common shareholders do not have voting control of a corporation. Ownership of even one common share will normally entitle you to a vote at the shareholders' meetings.

In addition, many common share issues pay regular dividends, thereby forming an integral part of many investors' income packages. And, of course, common shares are the investment looked to by most investors for capital growth.

Ownership of common stock is usually evidenced by registered, transferable, engraved printed sheets called share certificates. A share certificate is the actual legal document giving legal ownership of the shares described on it. The reason for intricately engraving share certificates on high-grade paper is to make forgery of them more difficult.

If you are the registered owner of common shares — meaning that your name is in the share register of the corporation as the holder of the particular certificates — your name will appear on the share certificate along with the number of shares that certificate represents. On the other hand, certificates are often in "street" form.

A street certificate is made out in the name of an investment dealer or broker and endorsed on the back by that company or person. This means the shares are freely negotiable and acceptable for delivery anywhere in the country. They change hands many times with no actual change in registration being made in the corporation's share register.

If you are merely trading in common shares to make gains, it's of little concern whether or not the certificates are in street form. However, if you intend to hold dividend-paying shares for a long time, or want to receive company annual reports, etc., directly, you should have the shares registered in your name, or in the name of a nominee, because all dividend cheques, reports and other shareholder data are sent to the registered owner, which, of course, is the name appearing on the certificate and in the shareholders' register.

But, of course, whether your certificates are being held in street form or registered form, you'll want to be sure they're kept in a safe place to avoid theft or forgery. Most investors either keep their securities in a safety deposit box or have them held in safekeeping by their broker, bank or trust company. Share certificates should not be left lying around the house, office or work bench. This is particularly so if the certificates are in street form. Certificates in street form are perfectly negotiable with no need to forge anything on them, so if they're lost or stolen you may well be completely out of luck in any attempt to recover your loss.

If you own a dividend-paying stock in street form, the dividends will be paid to the dealer or broker whose name appears on the certificate. You need only get in touch with the dealer or broker concerned in order to collect your dividend. Indeed, in most cases your broker will automatically look after this for you and either credit your account or send you a cheque. Also, your broker will normally issue to you the information slip reporting interest and dividend income for tax purposes showing the amount and type of income received on your behalf.

DIVIDENDS

It must always be remembered that the declaration and payment of dividends on common shares is not automatic nor is it some inalienable right. The board of directors of the corporation must first decide whether a dividend will be paid at all. Then they decide the amount and when the actual payment will be made. Payments may be quarterly, semi-annual, annual, or follow no fixed pattern at all. Special dividends are sometimes declared.

If shareholders are not happy with the board's dividend policy — or lack thereof — their options are to sell the shares or vote against re-election of the recalcitrant directors.

Ex-Dividend; Cum-Dividend

When a corporation has a lot of shareholders it usually advertises the declaration of a dividend in the financial press. There are two key dates in connection with a dividend declaration. The first is the date "of record." The second is the payment date.

When a stock is actively traded, the record of shareholders' names changes virtually every minute the stock exchange is open. Therefore, the corporation must pick a time at which the shareholders who are to receive the dividend are determined. The shareholders whose names appear on the corporation's records as of the close of business on the date chosen are the ones who will receive the dividend. The date chosen is called the "record date."

The usual pattern is to name a record date a week or two subsequent to the date the dividend is declared. For example, a corporation might declare a dividend on May 25 payable to shareholders of record as of the close of business on June 8. The record date would be June 8. The payment date of the dividend would be two weeks to a month later — to allow time for the preparation of cheques. In this case, the payment date might be June 29.

You can readily see there will be some shareholders whose purchases and sales will straddle these dates. In order to determine whether it is the buyer or seller who is entitled to the dividend, the stock exchange will name an "ex-dividend date." On and after this date, the shares are sold "ex-dividend," which means the *seller* retains the right to the dividend and the buyer will not get it. The ex-dividend date is usually four business days before the dividend record date.

In the above example, then, anyone buying the stock on or after June 4 would likely not receive the dividend. That fact will be reflected in the price paid for the shares.

"Cum-dividend" is, of course, the reverse. In the above example, purchasers of the stock between May 25 and June 4 would know *they'll* be receiving the dividend — not the seller — and will pay a correspondingly higher price for the shares.

Stock Dividends

Sometimes dividends are paid in the form of additional shares rather than in cash. This is called a stock dividend. Corporations will sometimes do this when they have sufficient earnings to warrant a dividend payment but want to preserve cash, say, for expansion.

Theoretically, the recipient of a stock dividend can turn it into cash by selling his or her "new" shares.

Regular and Extra Dividends

Many public corporations that pay common share dividends designate a specified amount which will be paid each year in the absence of evil times befalling the corporation. Such dividends are usually called "regular" dividends. In particularly good times these corporations might then pay an additional dividend at the end of the fiscal year. The financial press usually refers to these payments as "extra" dividends. The term "extra" is a precaution to investors and potential investors that they shouldn't assume the extra dividend will be paid the following year.

It is usual to include extra dividends in the calculation of yield for common stock. However, if in doubt, the conservative approach is to calculate the yield based on regular dividends only. In any event, when reading the financial press, always check the legend and symbols to determine whether the indicated dividend is regular or extra. If it isn't stated clearly, a further enquiry is in order before making an investment in the expectation of a future dividend, when the corporation may have no intention of repeating its payment.

Dividend Re-investment Plans

Some public companies have introduced an option for the shareholders called a dividend re-investment plan. For the shareholders who so elect, the corporation, instead of paying cash dividends to the shareholders, uses the funds to purchase additional shares of its own stock on behalf of the shareholders, which in effect turns the dividend into a stock dividend. In most cases these purchases are made on the open market by a trustee who periodically keeps the shareholders informed of their status under the plan.

The advantage to the shareholders of dividend re-investment plans is the provision of an automatic savings plan allowing them to re-invest small amounts of cash in shares in circumstances under which they could not otherwise do so, because individually the amounts would be too small to purchase full shares, and fractions of shares can't be bought in the market. By combining their dividends, though, the shareholders make sufficient funds available to the trustees to buy in bulk, thereby realizing considerable savings on commissions in comparison to what the individual shareholders would have to pay to buy odd lots — if indeed they could. Furthermore, the trustees have no problem allocating fractions of shares to participants and keeping track of them.

Some corporations have plans permitting participants to also contribute cash to the plans which in turn is used by the trustee to purchase even more shares. Again, the attraction is economy of scale. There are usually limits placed on the amounts of cash that can be contributed to the plan by shareholders. These limits are often relatively low. Otherwise shareholders could use the re-investment plans as their brokers.

SPLITS

When a corporation's earnings grow and dividends increase, the market price of its shares rises considerably. The higher the price of shares, the more restricted their marketability becomes because small investors can't afford to buy a lot of high-priced stock, and bigger investors are sometimes loath to put all their eggs in one basket.

There are a number of reasons why corporations like to have a wide distribution of their shares. The more shareholders a company has, the easier it is to raise additional capital through the sale of new securities. Also, employees who own shares tend to be more highly motivated than those who do not. Not to be overlooked is the simple fact that the shareholders are more likely to buy the corporation's products or use its services. Accordingly, when the directors of a corporation feel the price of their shares has reached a level that's inhibiting their wide distribution, they "split" the shares. This is accomplished by submitting a by-law to a shareholders' vote which would permit a subdivision of the shares. This can be done at the annual meeting or at a special general meeting called for that particular purpose.

Once shareholder approval is obtained, the actual share split is strictly a mechanical procedure that doesn't change the actual capital of the corporation. For example, shares with a market value of $100 might be split five for one, resulting in the market value dropping to $20 per share. The existing shareholders are in exactly the same position as before the split, except they now have five shares worth $20 each instead of one share worth $100.

The logistics are as follows. In the case of stated par value shares, the old share certificates are called in and new ones issued for the larger number of shares. In the case of no par value stock, an announcement is made in the financial press (and, obviously, directly to the existing shareholders), and certificates for the additional shares created by the split are mailed out to the shareholders.

There are no income tax implications to a share split and there is no reason why a shareholder should resist a split: the total value of his or her holdings remains the same, as does his or her pro rata interest in the corporation. In fact, shareholders should welcome a split because their shares will immediately be more marketable.

CONSOLIDATION OF SHARES

I've just described the mechanics and effect of a stock split. The reverse situation, sometimes called a consolidation, occurs occasionally.

The mechanics are similar to a stock split but the result, of course, is the opposite. On a consolidation, for example, four shares worth 25 cents each might be replaced with one share worth one dollar.

As in the case of splits, the shareholder's total investment and pro rata interest in the company remain the same, there is no change in the corporation's capitalization, and there is no income tax effect.

Consolidations usually take place in low-priced junior mining and oil and gas exploration companies. They raise the market price of the shares and place the corporation (mainly because of investor psychology) in a better position to raise additional capital through the sale of new shares. It's sort of like daylight savings time; nothing really changes but everyone thinks it has and feels better about it.

RIGHTS

A "right" is the term given to the privilege granted by a corporation to its existing shareholders enabling them, if they wish, to acquire additional shares directly from the corporation itself. This is simply a method of raising additional capital for the corporation while allowing the existing shareholders to avoid dilution of their shareholdings without the necessity of incurring commission expenses or the additional cost resulting from an increase in market prices caused by new demands for stock. As a matter of fact, the offering price for the new shares is normally a bit lower than the current market price of the old shares, with the result that the rights themselves have a value.

The privilege attached to the rights is in direct proportion to the number of shares already owned. For example, the "right" may be the opportunity to purchase one share for each ten shares owned. As mentioned, the price of the one new share would likely be a bit less than the current market value.

Because the rights themselves have a value, a market for them usually develops quickly, enabling any shareholders who don't want to exercise their rights to make some money by selling them. Obviously, additional rights can be purchased by existing shareholders, and non-shareholders can get into the act by acquiring rights on the open market. If the corporation issuing the rights is listed on a stock exchange, the rights themselves will automatically be listed when the usual red tape has been cleared away.

Remember that rights normally have a very short life. They usually have to be exercised within a month or so, after which they expire and become worthless.

The logistics of a rights issue are identical to the payment of a dividend. The corporation's shareholders register is closed as of the close of business on a particular date and shareholders of record at that time receive rights in the form of certificates.

As in the case of dividends, shares go "exrights" four business days before the record date. Purchasers of shares after the ex-rights date will not be entitled to the relevant rights — that privilege stays with the seller. Between the time of the announcement that rights will be issued and the ex-rights date, the shares are described as "cum rights" and the purchaser will be entitled to receive the rights.

Although they are usually transferable it is completely within a corporation's power to issue rights which can be exercised only by existing shareholders. But this is rare.

A non-shareholder buying transferable rights on the open market is able to exercise them under the same conditions as the original rights holder.

The price of rights tends to rise and fall as the price of the relevant common stock rises and falls, but not always in lock-step. The theoretical value of rights is affected by buying and selling costs and the ever-present influences of supply and demand.

WARRANTS

Rights and warrants are not exactly the same, although they do have some similarities.

A warrant, like a right, is really an option to buy capital stock and is traded on the stock market. However, in contrast to a right, which usually has a very limited life, warrants often have terms extending for years. And, whereas rights are initially issued to existing shareholders before finding their way into the marketplace, warrants are often attached to bond, debenture and preferred share issues. They are detachable (either immediately or after a relatively short period of time) and then trade on their own.

The main attraction of both rights and warrants is that they, in effect, permit investment in the issuing company at considerably lower levels of absolute dollars than investing in the actual shares. It follows that this limits potential losses and a conservative investor might prefer the rights or warrants route in an uncertain situation.

INCOME TAX

The income tax treatment of investment income and capital gains and losses is constantly being changed by the government. You should keep up-to-date on the current law, as recommended earlier, by obtaining the readily available, and easily readable, summaries provided free by most firms of chartered accountants and most financial institutions, such as banks, trust companies, brokerage firms and insurance companies.

FACTORS AFFECTING COMMON SHARE PRICES

Now, let's turn to some of the factors affecting common share prices. Actually, common share prices are probably the best example of a free market operation because they rise and fall in direct response to supply and demand. It is necessary, then, to understand what determines the level of demand.

Any such analysis runs the risk of being over-simplified because the subject is tremendously complex. But there are five fundamental forces which probably wield the greatest influence and these are easily understood. They are:

1. profit and dividend outlook
2. investors' resources

3. tax outlook
4. economic outlook
5. technical market factors

Each deserves examination in greater detail.

PROFIT AND DIVIDEND OUTLOOK

This market force itself has a number of facets, any one of which can significantly affect the market price of common shares. For example, consider the effect on the stock market of the federal government's announcement in the mid-1970s that the anti-inflation rules would include restrictions on the payment of dividends. Right after the announcement the general price level of common stocks on Canadian stock exchanges declined.

Conversely, two years later, when the federal government announced that controls would be phased out, there followed a general rise in stock prices which had to be due, at least in part, to that particular announcement. But these circumstances were unusual in that they affected the market outlook as a whole. Usually, the profit and dividend outlook is considered in the context of a particular stock.

One facet of this outlook that will drive up a stock's price, as has been witnessed many times in the past, is the possibility of a takeover bid, merger or other such major development. Although you might think a crystal ball is necessary to ferret out these situations, this is really not the case. Experienced investment analysts can often identify public companies that are ripe for a takeover.

The most usual consideration which investors rely on, though, is the company's earnings outlook. In short, this is an informed guess as to when and to what degree a company is going to have a significant improvement in its earnings or dividend pay-outs — or both.

This type of prediction has to be made in the light of three interrelated factors: the economy, the industry, and the particular company itself.

More important, the prediction has to be made and acted upon before the majority of other investors reach the same conclusion. Otherwise, the expected favourable conditions will already be reflected in the market price of the stock. This is what is meant by the expression "already discounted by the market."

The price/earnings ratio and yield of a particular stock, in relation to other stocks in similar circumstances, are two rules of thumb by which an investor can tell whether the market price is high or low in relation to anticipated company earnings. For example, assume two companies in the same industry — say company A and company B — seem to be equally sound financially and both well managed. If company A's price/earnings ratio is higher than company B's, then company B's stock might be a better buy in terms of future growth. Similarly, if the yield on company B's stock (the dividend divided by your cost per share) is higher than company A's, you'll get a better return on your money by investing in company B. Either of these situations suggests that company B's market price might be low or company A's high. But be sure there isn't some other reason for the difference. The easiest way to find out is to ask your broker for an explanation.

INVESTORS' RESOURCES

An obvious factor affecting the demand for common shares — or any investment for that matter — is the amount of money that the general investing public has to invest. This includes the funds that find their way into common stocks through financial institutions such as mutual funds, trust companies and insurance companies.

The more discretionary income there is available, the more demand there is apt to be for common shares. For example, a sustained period of low rates of inflation should have a positive general effect on stock prices. So would a cut in tax rates. This leads naturally into the next fundamental factor.

TAX OUTLOOK

Many income tax regulations have a direct effect on stock prices. The sweetening of the dividend tax credit would make investment in the stock market a more attractive option and would cause an increase in stock prices. An announcement of an intention to eliminate the capital gains tax on common shares would undoubtedly increase demand, and, therefore, prices.

It is apparent, then, that a budget speech is an event which might well have a profound effect on stock prices. Look back on the devastating effect on the prices of natural resource stocks when the federal and provincial governments almost taxed them out of existence in the early 1970s.

ECONOMIC OUTLOOK

When people think the economy will be in good shape in the foreseeable future, they invest more in common stocks in order to share in the expected economic growth. If the past is any indication, this will result in an increase in value of publicly traded common shares. On the other hand, during times of economic pessimism or uncertainty, investors have a tendency to put their money in high-yield debt securities or high-quality preferreds, or just leave it in savings accounts or short-term paper — all to the detriment of the demand for common shares with the predictable bad effect on their general price level. This is what happened in the early 1980s.

The general economic outlook can actually have more far-reaching effects, which in turn affect the demand for common share investments. Quite apart from and in addition to the direct effect just described, the general economic outlook also influences the overall demand by corporations and all levels of government for capital as well as the actual supply of capital that is available for all types of investments, from institutions as well as individuals. Again, in optimistic times the effect on common share prices is positive; in times of pessimism the effect is bad.

Some of the barometers which sophisticated investors use to gauge the economic outlook are: interest rate trends; the rate of inflation; unemployment levels; wage settlements; general labour unrest; the value of the dollar; the federal government's monetary policy; general profit trends; and the probable effects of recent or anticipated government budgets — most generally the federal budget, but astute investors are also aware of the impact on stock prices particular provincial budget provisions might have. Significant changes in provincial natural resource taxation is one example that comes readily to mind. For example, if Alberta or Ontario raises its royalty charge on oil and mining operations, this would undoubtedly have an adverse effect on the shares of resource companies operating in those provinces, unless investors were confident the increased cost of operation could be readily passed on to consumers.

TECHNICAL MARKET FACTORS

Last, but by no means least, of the five fundamental factors affecting the demand for, and therefore the price of, common shares is what the professional investors term "technical" market factors. In plain language, the term means nothing more than the effect of investor psychology; in short, the reaction by investors to the other four fundamental factors. But it deserves closer examination.

No informed analyst who knows anything about the October 1987 market crash doubts the effect of investor psychology on the market prices of common shares, or any other investment for that matter.

As a matter of fact, there are many analysts who believe the psychological factor is so important that they practically ignore attempts to predict future earnings for a particular stock and instead plot the stock's price performance on charts and base their price predictions on the patterns this shows. This is called in the trade a ''technical'' analysis, in contrast to ''fundamental'' analysis, which is based on earnings trends. Anyone who doubts the validity of technical analysis — and there are many who do — might pause to consider the many times when a stock's price swings radically in the absence of a fundamental change in the company's earnings outlook, takeover vulnerability, major announcement or any other rational reason therefor.

The basic theory underlying technical analysis is that the future trend of a stock's price is predictable from its past range of prices in relation to the volume of trading. Technical analysts believe their charts allow them to predict when a heavy demand or sudden supply is imminent. To take a very simple illustration, it's likely that news of a favourable or unfavourable development which is apt to affect a company's share price tends to spread in waves from one group of investors or potential investors to another. The whole investment world doesn't hear about it at the same time or react to it in the same way.

If it's a favourable development, first one group of people will hear about it and will buy the stock, driving its price up on a heavy volume of trading. Then there will be a lull and the stock will sell off a bit on a low and declining volume as the wave moves on and some profit taking occurs. After a while a new group of people will get the news and buy the stock, again driving up the price on heavy volume. Then another lull and so on until the effect of the news eventually peters out. Of course, if it's an unfavourable development the effect on demand and price would be the opposite, but the wave patterns would still be there.

A technical analyst, spotting this type of pattern on a chart, assumes there is something going on that's affecting investor psychology and that money can be made trading that stock.

Remember, though, there are innumerable and various formations on charts which the technical analyst uses to make interpretations.

It's a pretty risky business. You must always remember the demand and supply factors the technicians are watching for are actually the result of one or more of the *other* fundamental factors translated into investor psychology. The point is, if these trends can be spotted well in advance of the crowd, it should be possible to make some money in the market.

Technical analysis is, therefore, an additional tool which might assist in fine-tuning the timing of purchases and sales. There's little doubt it is helpful to consider the potential demand for a stock in addition to the fundamental earnings picture. In this context facts are important only insofar as what people think about them.

Investors in common shares must always remember that the main characteristics distinguishing common shares from bonds or preferred shares is that common shares tend to be subject to wide price swings.

For example, in any twelve-month period wide price ranges are apt to be experienced by even traditional highly regarded common shares. Watch IBM for example.

It's trite to say that anyone who can predict such swings with accuracy will be able to make a great deal of money. Of course, such predictions are impossible to achieve consistently. But the other end of the stick is to buy and sell blindly, strictly on instinct (or lack thereof), without giving consideration to the major facts which affect share prices. These were dealt with above, but some underlying aspects of these factors are always particularly relevant and deserve some additional comment.

BULLS, BEARS AND PIGS

There is a stock market adage that says "the bears get some, the bulls get some, and the pigs get none." Like most adages, there is a great deal of truth in this one. Just to refresh your memory: the bull is an investor who feels there is inherent value in a particular stock or a particular segment of the market, and buys on that basis; the bear is the opposite. The bear feels a particular stock or segment is overpriced and wants out — but the bear is still an astute, informed investor. The pig, on the other hand, is the gambler who wants as quick and as huge a profit as can possibly be made and who buys and sells irrationally with the predictable result that over the long run, pigs lose money.

However, the existence of the gambler in the market (and there are some observers who insist there are more gamblers than true investors or speculators) has an enormous impact on excessive rises and declines in common share prices.

The difference between the gambler and the investor is that the gambler doesn't have the patience to wait for inherent value to be reflected in stock prices. If the stock doesn't go up quickly, the gambler unloads, regardless of the underlying values of the stock.

EMOTION

Even real investors sometimes let their emotions overrule their logic.

There aren't many veteran investors who have not at some time in their investment lives made one or both of the following common emotional errors: when earnings are on the up-swing, assume that the rise will continue and pay too much for the stock; or, in a year when earnings fall, panic and sell at a low point, then watch the stock recover nicely over the next few months.

Both these scenarios have an exaggerated effect on market prices. The main point is not to panic because of a market swing caused largely by investor psychology. On the bright side, wide swings in prices offer opportunities to make money. Be a bull, then a bear — but never a pig.

WORLD EVENTS

It is difficult to understand why some world happenings affect common share prices, but they surely do. Strikes, U.S. presidential elections, war threats, peace offerings, OPEC decisions, assassinations, and countless other events and non-events all send the stock market into a frenzy.

Investors must remember that, as Bernard Baruch put it more than half a century ago, the stock market is the thermometer, not the fever. There are so many factors affecting common share prices that the real investor must always consider the long term and not be stampeded by favourable or unfavourable news with only short-term implications.

LONG-TERM FACTORS

Economic trends, quality of management, technological advances, new discoveries, strike vulnerability, new products, raw material supplies, transportation, distribution, government intervention, and population shifts are all important factors affecting the inherent value of a stock on a long-term basis. Factors such as these should be given far more weight by the investor than investor psychology or world events having short-term implications. For the speculator, of course, the reverse is true.

Decisions to buy or sell common shares should be made on the basis of sound business judgment. In addition to the factors listed in the preceding paragraph, consideration should also be given to current yield and price-earnings ratio, the financial condition of the corporation, the capitalization of the corporation, and the marketability of the shares.

FACTORS TO CONSIDER BEFORE INVESTING

The Canadian Securities Institute wisely and correctly suggests five main factors to be reviewed when deciding whether to invest in common shares of a particular company. They are:

1. the nature and characteristics of the industry
2. the past performance of the industry
3. the future of the industry
4. the position of the company in the industry
5. the relative performance of the company compared to other companies in the industry

Nature of Industry

It's important to understand the nature and characteristics of the industry in which you're investing in order to match your investment objectives with the probable behaviour of common share prices. For example, retired people (whose investment objectives are income and protection of capital) would not want to invest heavily in an industry which is subject to wide, cyclical fluctuations in stock prices, such as the construction and building supplies industry.

On the other hand, a young investor looking for substantial growth in a portfolio would likely stay away from an industry characterized by higher income and slower growth, such as public utilities.

There are a number of main industry classifications in which a person can invest through the ownership of publicly traded common shares in this country. For example:

1. the automobile and allied industries
2. banking and finance
3. chemicals and allied industries
4. computer services
5. construction and building supplies
6. electronics
7. entertainment and leisure
8. food and beverages

9. forest products
10. heavy machinery and equipment
11. light manufacturing
12. insurance
13. iron and steel
14. mining
15. oil and gas
16. printing, publishing and broadcasting
17. public utilities
18. real estate
19. textiles
20. transportation

An additional category is the public investment or holding company through which indirect investments can be made in some or all of the above industries.

Knowledge of the characteristics of an industry aids in evaluating problems or opportunities likely to be encountered by a particular company and which might have a significant effect on share prices. For example, the general level of interest rates greatly affects the construction and building supplies industry. The state of technological advance can make or break a company in the field of electronics. The value of the Canadian dollar has a tremendous effect on the prices of shares in the forest products industry.

There is a wealth of information available about industry sectors. The larger brokerage houses will always be pleased to provide you with data on particular industries. Most industry sectors have their own organizations — such as the Canadian Manufacturers' Association, Mining Association of Canada, Canadian Textile Institute, Canadian Bankers' Association, and the Housing and Urban Development Association of Canada, just to name a few — which will also be pleased to help you learn about their particular industries. In addition, most public companies will be delighted to help you learn, not just about their own company, but their particular industry as well, by sending you reading material.

Past Performance

Although most relevant when considering well-established companies with a long record of earnings, the past performance of an industry can often offer important clues to its future potential or that of a particular company.

The key is to spot a trend, either favourable or unfavourable, and then try to establish the underlying reasons behind the trend. This information can be used to determine the direction the industry is apt to follow. These conclusions are then used as a backdrop against which knowledge of particular companies within the industry is considered. If you spot a trend early enough, you are in a position to make money by buying shares during a favourable trend and to maximize your gain by getting out early when things are beginning to look bad.

Industry Outlook

As important as past performance is, it would be unwise in the extreme to make an investment without giving great consideration to the future. Some factors which might have a drastic effect on a particular industry are:

1. government intervention and legislation
2. technological advances
3. new products
4. population shifts

The Company Itself

Having satisfied yourself that the outlook for a particular industry is bright, attention should then be turned to the factors which pertain to the particular company whose shares you're considering buying or selling.

In addition to its financial position, capitalization and management, the company's place in the industry and its relative performance vis-à-vis competitors must be evaluated. In doing this always remember it is often necessary to study more than one industry. Many companies today are so diversified that they span many industry classifications.

When comparing the relative performances of two or more companies — after considering their financial position, capitalization and management — there are other major areas to consider, such as sales, profit trends, tax rates, return on equity, cash flow, dividend record, price-earnings ratio, and marketability.

Objectives

Overriding everything, though, is your own investment objective.

Be sure what you buy is consistent with your goal. There are three possible major objectives:

1. security of capital
2. income
3. growth

Of course, in many instances an investor will try to achieve more than one objective. This can usually be accomplished. Right now you might want to re-read Chapter 29, where investment objectives are discussed in detail.

SPECULATING

Now a word for the speculator. Some people may assume that share speculation is inherently bad. Not so. The rookie speculator should, though, follow these rules:

1. Recognize the difference between speculating and investing, and don't confuse one with the other.
2. Speculate only with money you can afford to lose.
3. Deal only with reputable investment houses.
4. Judge each issue on its own merits.
5. Always ignore tips and rumours.

Chapter 33

Preferred Shares

WHY PREFERRED SHARES?

Like other forms of investment vehicles, the preferred share evolved to meet the needs of the issuer on the one hand and the desires of investors on the other. For example, the preferred share is attractive to investors who are interested in a security providing less uncertainty than common shares but who also prefer an equity (share) position to holding debt, even though preferred shares often act more like bonds than shares in responding to shifts in interest rates.

From the issuer's standpoint there are any number of reasons why the preferred share route might be preferable to a debt issue or the issue of additional common shares. An obvious disadvantage of issuing additional common shares is the dilution of existing shareholdings. In other cases market conditions might be unfavourable for the issue of new common stock.

Once the decision has been made not to go the common share route, the reasons for a preferred share issue rather than a debt issue come into play and are more varied. For example, the corporation's assets may already be fully pledged so that it has no room for an additional mortgage bond issue, or the corporation may be in a type of business that has few pledgeable assets, such as a finance company. On the other hand, the market may simply be temporarily unreceptive to new debt issues, or perhaps the issuing corporation hasn't yet established a sufficiently high credit rating to sell unsecured debentures.

Sometimes the issuing corporation's board of directors makes an outright unilateral decision to issue preferred shares rather than additional debt or common shares regardless of what the outside market forces might seem to dictate. The board of directors might simply want to balance the corporation's capital structure, or it might want to avoid fixed interest obligations on new debt. Furthermore, issuing preferred shares rather than debt often avoids a fixed maturity date. A board of directors will sometimes postpone payment of a preferred dividend but will go to almost any length to avoid missing an interest payment or a maturity date. Indeed, the effect on the public of missing or postponing a deferred dividend is nothing compared to the trauma of a missed interest or redemption date.

The preceding comment notwithstanding, investors shouldn't automatically assume a sinister motive when preferred shares are issued rather than common shares or debt. On the other hand, the prudent investor will restrict his or her investment in preferred shares to those high-quality issues which have earnings available for dividend payments well in excess of the minimum requirements insisted on by informed investment analysts. Later on we discuss ways of evaluating the quality of a particular preferred share issue. For now, back to a description of the actual position of preferred shareholders.

The preferred shareholder is a hybrid occupying a position between a common shareholder and a creditor. If the corporation falls upon evil times the preferred shareholder is in a better position than a common shareholder but is not as well protected as a debt holder.

As their name implies, preferred shares carry with them certain preferences which are not available to the common shareholders. These preferences can, and will, vary from corporation to corporation and even from one issue to another of the same corporation. (A corporation can, and often does, issue more than one class of preferred shares.) The point to keep in mind is to determine exactly what the preferences are and how they should affect your investment decision.

The most common preference given on preferred shares is a prior claim on the assets of a corporation ahead of the common shareholders in the event the corporation is wound up. In these circumstances creditors rank first, preferred shareholders next, and the common shareholders get what's left — if anything. The other side of the coin, though, is that the preferred shareholder gives up any claim on corporation earnings beyond the stated dividend, whereas once creditors and preferred dividends are satisfied the common shareholders can theoretically pay the balance of earnings to themselves as dividends.

Preferred shares normally have a par value and the preference as to asset distribution is usually that amount, in the event of an involuntary liquidation, and par plus a small premium where the liquidation is voluntary. It's probably fair to say, though, that situations where this particular preference is of importance are apt to be situations which you should avoid.

Preferred shares usually carry a fixed dividend rate expressed as a percentage of the par value. Like all dividends, these too have to be declared by the board of directors and can only be paid from current or past earnings. However, another common preference is that no dividends can be paid to common shareholders if dividends are not paid to preferred shareholders.

In recent years floating rate preferred shares have developed. The main difference between these and the so-called straight preferreds is that the dividend varies with current interest rates, often based on a key indicator such as the 90-day treasury bill rate.

Many preferred share issues carry a provision entitling preferred shareholders to elect one or more directors to the board to represent their interests if dividends are in arrears or have been omitted. In some cases the preferred shares become fully voting when dividends have not been paid. These provisions usually apply only after a stipulated number of consecutive dividends have been missed — for example, two or three.

Let's now take a close look at the variety of types of preferred share issues which exist. Although the number of preferred share features is limited only by the bounds of the issuers' imaginations, there is a very definite limit to the number of variations which investors will buy. Accordingly, the vast majority of preferred share issues carry with them one or more of a few fairly well-established characteristics.

VOTES

Preferred shares are generally non-voting. But they can be voting and they often carry with them provisions which cause them to become voting in certain circumstances — the most common of which is, as already mentioned, when dividends are in arrears. It is a rare situation, though, when control of a public company is affected by votes of preferred shareholders.

However, preferred shareholders are usually granted a vote on matters affecting the underlying quality of their security. Examples would be an increase in the amount of preferred stock authorized or the creation or increase of funded debt.

CUMULATIVE AND NON-CUMULATIVE

A cumulative preferred share is one for which a record is kept of any dividends that have not been paid and on which the accrued amount of such dividends must be paid before payment of any dividends to the common shareholders or before any preferred shares can be redeemed by the issuing corporation.

Of course, a non-cumulative preferred share is one for which the shareholder is entitled only to dividends which are actually specifically declared. If a dividend on a non-cumulative preferred share is passed, it's gone forever and doesn't accrue.

Although in theory some cumulative preferred shares with dividend arrears might be worthwhile speculative investments, there isn't exactly a bull market for such issues.

PARTICIPATING AND NON-PARTICIPATING

Participating preferred shares carry with them rights to participate in the issuing corporation's earnings over and above their stated dividend rate. For example, an issue of participating preferred shares might share equally with the common shares in any dividends paid over, say, \$2.00 per share on the common.

Sometimes the participation is limited. For example, the participating preferred share might be entitled to a specified cumulative dividend of \$1.00 per year, after which each common share is entitled to a dividend of \$1.00 in a particular year, then both classes share dividends equally until an additional \$1.00 is paid on each in that particular year, after which the preferred shares would no longer be entitled to further dividends in that year.

Again, the obvious: a non-participating preferred share would be limited to the specified dividend regardless of the level of dividends paid to the common shareholder.

CALLABLE OR REDEEMABLE

Callable or redeemable preferred shares are redeemable at the option of the issuing corporation during a specified period of time for a specified price. The call price is never less than par and it is quite common for the issuer to pay a small premium upon calling in the shares as compensation to the investor for giving up the investment. In addition, any unpaid accrued dividends would be included in the amounts received by the preferred shareholders upon giving up their shares in these circumstances.

RETRACTABLE

In a manner of speaking, retractable preferreds are the opposite of callable or redeemable preferred shares. The holder of retractable preferred shares has the right to tender his or her shares to the issuer for redemption, again at a specified price and time. So you, the investor, will know when you will give up your shares. On the other hand, redeemable securities are redeemed at the option of the issuer. You really have no choice in the matter.

CONVERTIBLE

A conversion feature gives the shareholder the right of converting preferred shares into another security — usually common shares — of the issuer. Again, this must usually happen during a specified time period and on specified terms.

Convertibility is probably the feature most sought after by preferred share investors.

QUALITY OF PREFERRED SHARES

There are five key questions to be considered when attempting to judge the investment quality of a particular preferred share issue.

The first question is: do the issuing corporation's earnings provide ample coverage for the payment of preferred dividends and meeting any relevant redemption or retraction provisions?

The next question is: has the issuing corporation established a good record of dividend payments?

Third: is there an adequate cushion of common share capital beneath the preferred shares?

Fourth: was the security sponsored and underwritten by a reputable investment dealer?

Finally: are there any special income tax disadvantages inherent in the particular issue?

Remembering that investments are made in preferred shares by investors whose goal is income and security rather than potential capital gains, you see that "yes" — or, at least, "probably" — has to be the answer to all of the first four questions and "no" the answer to the fifth question before a particular issue would qualify as a high-quality investment. Let's now examine some of the rules of thumb used by many financial analysts in answering the first four questions. The fifth answer can be obtained by asking the issuer or your broker.

For these and other such tests mentioned in this book, always remember there are no foolproof methods of testing the quality of an investment. The tests suggested are some of the types most commonly used by investment analysts. But, to repeat, when it comes to evaluating investments, nothing is foolproof.

Now that you have the warning that excessive use of these tests may be dangerous to your wealth, we should quickly add that they are extremely useful if not relied on in the extreme.

To do these tests you will need a copy of the company's most recent annual report. Annual reports are easily obtained by writing or calling the company itself. Some financial publications have services through which they supply copies of many public companies' annual reports. Finally, your broker will almost always be able to supply them to you. As a matter of fact, your broker should be pleased to perform these tests for you. If not, find a broker who will.

ADEQUACY OF DIVIDEND COVERAGE

The first test suggested was a determination of whether the issuing corporation's earnings provide adequate coverage for preferred dividend requirements. Because preferred shareholders are in a weaker position than creditors, the minimum requirements for a preferred investment must be higher than those for bonds or debentures.

These are two usual methods of calculating dividend coverage of preferred shares: the simple method and the prior charges method. The simple method is used where the corporation has no funded debt outstanding. As the name implies, it is a fairly simple formula consisting of *net earnings before extraordinary items* divided by *annual preferred dividend requirements*.

In corporations where there is a large proportion of debt relative to preferred share capital outstanding, the simple method can be misleading.

For example, in these circumstances the simple method might show the preferred dividend coverage to be many times greater than the interest coverage on long-term debt. This could lead to the ridiculous conclusion that the preferred share is of a higher investment quality than the bond.

This would hardly be the case, because during a financial squeeze the corporation would always pass on declaring a dividend rather than miss an interest payment. In such circumstances, the prior charges method — although slightly complicated — is a truer picture of the margin of safety.

PRIOR CHARGES METHOD

This procedure requires the application of a formula, which is where the complication comes in. However, as mentioned earlier, your broker should be delighted to do this calculation for you, and it is a calculation that might best be left up to your broker. But for those of you who want to give it a go, here's how.

The formula for the prior charges method can be expressed as *total income after operating expenses* divided by *interest and preferred dividends before tax*. It is the denominator of that formula, when the formula is expressed as a fraction, that provides the complication. Because preferred dividends are paid after income taxes and the calculation is made on a before-tax basis, this requires the preferred dividend figure to be adjusted by the appropriate rate of income tax that the corporation usually pays.

To be precise about this, two mathematical steps are required. You first solve the following equation:

$$\frac{\text{income tax}}{\text{net earnings before extraordinary items} + \text{income tax}} = \text{tax rate}$$

Then:

$$\text{actual preferred dividends} \times \frac{100}{100 - \text{tax rate}} = \text{preferred dividends before tax}$$

It is the *preferred dividends before tax* figure so obtained that is added to *interest* in the denominator referred to earlier. As suggested, if you find this too complicated, ask your broker to do it for you.

This brings us naturally to the question of what is adequate coverage, once you've calculated it.

ADEQUATE DIVIDEND COVERAGE

Of course, adequate dividend coverage can't be defined precisely, if for no other reason than the fact that it varies from industry to industry and even from corporation to corporation.

For large corporations which are prominent in their respective industries, the Canadian Securities Institute suggests the following minimum coverage: Public Utilities — 2½ times under the simple method and 1½ times under the prior charges method; Industrials — 4 times under the simple method and 2 times under the prior charges method. Preferred investments in cyclical industries — e.g. textiles — should be watched carefully if the coverage is near the minimum.

Remember, too, that this is only one of the key suggested tests, and the foregoing minimums are a rule of thumb only, but a good one.

DIVIDEND PAYMENT RECORD

The second main test is whether the corporation has established a good record of dividend payments. The easiest and most reliable source of this information is the annual report or your broker. No special knowledge or formulas are required to assess this information. The corporation's record is good, bad, or something in between.

EQUITY BACKING

The third test is equity backing. In a good quality situation, the equity per preferred share would not be less than the par value of the shares, and ideally there should be a solid cushion behind each share issue over at least a five-year period. For a top quality rating the equity per preferred share should be on a rising trend.

DEALER SPONSORSHIP

Underwriting by a reputable investment dealer indicates that a thorough investigation of the merits of the proposed preferred issue was carried out and that experts in the field (the dealers) are satisfied the issue is worthy of inclusion in at least some investors' portfolios. It's up to you and your advisors to determine whether it should be in yours.

In reaching your preferred share investment decisions, you should not rely solely on the key questions dealt with above. There are definitely other factors which must be taken into consideration. Indeed, in any individual's circumstances one or more of the following factors may turn out to be more critical than the so-called key tests.

ELIGIBILITY FOR INSURANCE INVESTMENTS

Some investors place a lot of emphasis on whether the issue is an eligible investment for life insurance companies without recourse to the so-called basket clause. If it is, this is usually an indication it is a reasonably solid investment.

The basket clause is a provision in the *Canadian and British Insurance Companies Act* which allows a life insurance company to invest up to a particular percentage of the book value of its total assets in investments not otherwise qualifying under the principal conditions of the Act. At the time of writing, to qualify outside the basket clause, full preferred dividends would have to have been paid for each of the five years immediately preceding the date of the insurance company making the investment.

PROTECTION

The protection built into the preferred share issue should be examined and evaluated. For example, sometimes consent of two-thirds of the preferred shares outstanding is required before the issuing corporation would be allowed to sell or transfer substantial property. A similar consent might be required before the issuer could consolidate or merge with another company whose securities would rank prior to or with the existing stock.

It's not unusual for a protective clause to restrict the creation of other preferred shares senior or equal to the existing issues to situations in which prior approval of the current preferred shareholders has been obtained or certain specified financial conditions have been met.

Amendments to provisions of a class of preferred shares normally require the consent of a stated percentage of the outstanding preferred shares.

A very common protective provision is one designed to ensure that the issuer's working capital is not seriously depleted by the payment of dividends on common shares.

Ask your broker to explain in plain English what the protective provisions of a particular issue are.

MARKETABILITY

Marketability may be the most important consideration for many investors. Key considerations are whether the shares are listed on a stock exchange and whether they are widely traded. Even if they are traded publicly — either listed or over the counter — that is of small consolation if they are so thinly traded that there is effectively no buyer when you want or have to sell.

FUNDING

The very existence, and terms thereof, of any sinking fund (funds systematically set aside to redeem shares or pay off debt) could be an important consideration for some investors. However, if most other considerations suggest a good-quality issue, not too many potential investors would back off simply because there is no sinking fund.

MARKET PRICE vs CALL PRICE

Another area of possible concern is the relationship between the market price of an issue and its call price. You should hesitate if the market price is higher than the call or redemption price, unless there's a good explanation, such as an unusually high dividend with a long time to go before redemption can be triggered. Naturally, conversion terms or retractable features must be examined in relation to the market price.

THE ISSUER

Most important of all, of course, is a general evaluation of the issuing corporation itself, its financial health, its trend of earnings, and to the extent feasible, its market position and its management capabilities. This is a tall order and the vast majority of investors must rely on expert analysis by experienced investment counsellors and dealers. But the information is available and the careful investor makes every reasonable effort to obtain as much information as possible.

Making investments without attempting to gain as much relevant information as possible is really speculation. As already mentioned, speculation has its place, but it's critical that you are not speculating when you think you are, or should be, investing. There's a vast difference.

THE MAIN POINT

Preferred shares are designed to meet particular needs of issuers and are of interest to certain types of investors. Be sure you have a good fit. They are not suitable if you are looking primarily for capital growth, but are usually attractive to the person who wants a relatively safe equity position providing a reasonable level of income.

You should always examine and understand the characteristics of the particular issue being considered. It's rare for any two issues to be identical.

You should evaluate the issuing corporation to the best of your ability or obtain the opinion of experienced, professional investment dealers or counsellors — preferably both.

You should also pay particular attention to the protective features of the issue in addition to the so-called key tests for evaluating an issue. You must satisfy yourself regarding the factors, such as marketability, which may be of particular importance to you.

Because there is no contractual promise to pay off the preferred shares, and most corporations would miss a dividend before missing an interest payment, preferred shares carry more risk than bonds and debentures. The best bet is to restrict preferred investments to those whose dividends are well covered by earnings and assets.

On the positive side, their preferences as to dividends and claims on assets make them safer investments than many common shares — but remember, the growth potential isn't as great as with common shares.

Higher-quality preferred shares are a reasonable income investment with a significant degree of safety. But remember, there is always some risk involved, no matter how small. It is always possible for a company to fail so utterly that even the preferred shareholders get little or nothing back.

Chapter 34

Bonds and Debentures

WHAT ARE THEY?

A bond simply represents a loan made to the corporation or government body that issued it.

There are differences between bonds and debentures on the one hand, and shares or stocks of a company on the other. A stock represents an actual interest in the ownership of a corporation whereas a bond, as already mentioned, is evidence of a debt. A debenture is a type of bond, but the term is usually used in reference to municipal or unsecured bonds.

The issuer promises to repay the face amount of the bond (which is not necessarily what you paid for it) on its maturity date, and in the meantime, in most cases, to pay interest on it. In terms of investment objectives, high-quality bonds and debentures usually provide greater certainty of income than common or preferred shares. On the other hand, there is usually less certain prospect for capital growth with bonds than with common shares, and in times of rising interest rates the marketability of bonds is poor. However, bonds purchased at deep discounts or carrying with them warrants or conversion features often do provide an opportunity for capital appreciation.

Issuers of bonds sometimes reserve the right to pay them off before maturity, which they would do should interest rates drop. This is usually accomplished by the issue of a callable or redeemable bond. The issuer normally agrees to give a reasonable notice — say, 30 or 60 days — to the bondholder that the bond is going to be redeemed. If you are making an investment in particular bonds and you want to ensure it remains a long-term investment, then be sure the bonds are not subject to an early redemption.

The amount which the issuer of a bond agrees to pay on maturity is shown on the face of the bond itself and is referred to as its denomination, par, or face value. The smallest corporate bond denomination is usually $500. Denominations of $1,000, $5,000, $10,000, $25,000 and even $100,000 are common. The intended market will indicate the denomination. Bonds designed for a broad retail market will be issued in small denominations (for example, Canada Savings Bonds have been issued in denominations of $100 to accommodate the small investor) while those designed for institutional investors might be available in denominations reaching into millions of dollars.

In addition to the denomination, the face of the bond will also state the rate of interest payable. Remember, though, that the interest rate is applied to the face amount of the bond, not to the amount you pay for the bond.

The price paid for a bond will depend not only on its denomination but also on its stated interest rate, the general level of interest rates at the time it is purchased, and the length of time to maturity. Prices of outstanding bonds tend to fall as general interest rates rise and go up when interest rates go down. For example, if you are holding a $1,000 bond with an interest rate of 6% at a time when the interest rate for term deposits is 12%, no one would pay you $1,000 for that bond. They would only pay the amount that would give them a return of 12%. This brings us to bond yields — the figures that really count.

Bond yield is the true rate of return received on the amount of money invested, which is the price paid — not the bond's denomination. For example, if a $100 bond with a 7% interest rate is purchased for $99 and that bond matures in a year, your yield will be 8%. The 8% consists of $7 interest and $1 ''gain'' on principal. Now, assume you had to pay $101 for the same bond. Your yield now drops to 6% — $7 interest less a $1 ''loss'' of principal. Obviously there would be a wider variation in yield if the term is lengthened and the bond is purchased at a higher discount or premium. A 7%, $100 bond due in ten years and purchased for $94 would yield an annual rate of about 7.9%. Fortunately, although bond yield calculations are complicated, you need not worry about doing them because any investment dealer will have bond yield tables readily available.

Of course, yield is not the only consideration in making your decision whether to invest in a particular bond. The investment quality of the bond or debenture should also be considered. Indeed, this aspect will also have some bearing on the yield available for the simple reason that the higher the quality the lesser the discount or greater the premium.

VARIOUS TYPES OF ISSUERS

There are four major classes of bond issuers: the federal government, the provinces, municipalities and, of course, corporations. We'll now turn to the qualitative considerations of each type.

So far as the quality of Government of Canada bonds is concerned, if the federal government ever defaults on its bonds, it's hard to imagine the total chaos that would be existent throughout the entire Canadian investment community. Most investments would be in jeopardy. So the quality of Government of Canada bonds is of the highest order.

There are three main considerations in judging the quality of a particular provincial bond issue. You should consider how much the province already owes, and how much it will owe after the particular issue, on a per capita basis in comparison to other provinces. The next consideration is just how well off the province is in terms of natural resources, agricultural production and industrial development. Finally, consider the stability and soundness of the provincial government, historically and potentially as well as currently. The best guide to the value of this type of security is the advice of an experienced investment dealer who specializes in the field. On balance, provincial bonds are considered to be pretty reliable investments in terms of safety of capital, usually second only to Government of Canada bonds.

With some bad experiences having been reported in the United States, many people became a bit reluctant to invest in municipal debentures. To date in Canada, investment dealers and institutional investors (pension funds, insurance companies, etc.) tend to consider municipal debentures in much the same category as Government of Canada and provincial bonds. They look upon them as very high-grade investments as regards safety of capital.

Investment dealers and institutions do have a checklist for rating the quality of municipal bonds. They consider such items as population growth, industrial growth, condition and quality of municipal services, ratio of annual debt charges to total revenue, tax levies, tax collection record, assessed value for tax purposes per capita, debt per capita, and the integrity and experience of elected municipal politicians and senior civil servants. As in the case of provincial bonds, the best way to get an accurate reading on the quality of municipal debentures is through the advice of an experienced specialist in that field.

Each year Canadian corporations issue billions of dollars worth of bonds and debentures, normally to acquire fixed assets, retire existing debt or expand their businesses.

With the passage of time, different types of corporate debt securities (always remember that a bond or debenture is nothing more or less than evidence of debt which is owed by the issuer to the holder) are designed to help bring the needs of the corporate borrower in line with the desires of the investor-lender. In colloquial terms it's a case of different strokes for different folks. In any event, investors who are interested in the bond market should be familiar with the different types of debt securities and their various characteristics. Following is an analysis of the most common types.

MORTGAGE BONDS

Any mortgage is a legal document evidencing that the borrower (the mortgagor) has pledged fixed assets, such as land, buildings and equipment, as security for a loan and entitling the lender (the mortgagee) to take ownership of the properties pledged if the borrower fails to pay the interest or repay the principal when due. There is no basic difference between the legal effect of a mortgage and a mortgage bond. The only difference is in the actual form of the document.

The mortgage bond, like other forms of corporate debt securities, evolved to fill a particular need. When the borrowing requirements of corporations became too large to be financed by one source, and many hundreds — indeed many thousands — of lenders became involved, it became impractical for a corporation to issue separate mortgages securing portions of its properties to each lender, and the mortgage bond was born. What happens is that one blanket mortgage is deposited with a trustee, usually a trust company, and that trustee acts on behalf of all the investor-lenders in protecting their interests under the terms of the blanket mortgage. The total amount of the loan is divided into appropriate denominations and each investor receives a bond as evidence of his or her pro rata claim under the terms of the blanket mortgage.

This brings us to the various sub-types of mortgage bonds.

First Mortgage Bonds

As the name implies, first mortgage bonds are the senior securities of a corporation for the simple reason that they constitute a first charge on the corporation's assets and earnings. Of course, it would be necessary to study the terms of the issue to determine specifically which properties are covered by the mortgage. Anyone who has tried this will quickly recognize the difficulty of understanding the legalese in which the terms are drafted. They rival the *Income Tax Act* for sheer incomprehensibility. This is another instance where your best bet is to rely on the advice of a specialist in the field.

When the legalese is stripped away, you usually find that most first mortgage bonds carry a first and specific charge against the corporation's fixed assets and a floating charge (a general claim on assets without attachment to specific items) on all other assets. First mortgage bonds are generally regarded as the best security a corporation can issue. This is particularly true if the mortgage contains an "after-acquired clause." This is a stipulation that the mortgage applies to all fixed assets of the corporation, whether owned now or acquired later. Its desirability from the investor's standpoint is obvious.

In short, first mortgage bonds have a prior claim over other classes of debt security, which, depending on the quality of the corporation itself, makes them a high-quality investment.

For the record, it should be mentioned that in some circumstances a corporation may, with the consent of existing first mortgage bondholders, issue what are referred to as prior lien bonds. The effect of such a move is that the first mortgage bondholders allow the prior lien bondholders to share a specific claim on the corporation's assets.

Second or General Mortgage Bonds

As you would logically expect, second mortgage bonds — often referred to as general mortgage bonds — rank after first mortgage bonds in any claim on assets or earnings of the borrowing corporation, meaning that the claims of the first mortgage bondholders must be settled in full before there is anything left for the second or general bondholders. Because the situation results in the second mortgage bonds being of a somewhat lower quality from an investment protection standpoint, they usually sell at a price that gives a higher yield than first mortgage bonds.

Actually, in many circumstances the asset coverage on first mortgage bonds is so good that the quality of a second or general bond issue is equal to the senior bonds. For example, sometimes a corporation with an existing first mortgage issue will float an issue of general mortgage bonds secured by its own unpledged assets and those of its subsidiaries. Although the new issue would be junior to the first mortgage bonds as far as the parent company's assets are concerned, the new issue would have a prior claim on the assets of the subsidiaries. In fact, it was just this type of issue which gave birth to the term "general mortgage bond." As the title of mortgage bond issues can be at best confusing and at worst misleading, it is advisable to check the terms of the issue if the priority of the claim to assets is of particular interest or concern to you. It is better still to obtain the advice of a knowledgeable expert.

DEBENTURES

As mentioned earlier, debentures represent direct debt obligations of the issuer, but they are not secured by the pledge of assets. In fact, their only security is the general credit of their issuer. Holders of debentures have no prior claim on assets as against other general creditors. Should you come across the term "secured debentures," it is not a complete contradiction in terms. This term is applied to debentures which are partly secured by particular assets, but not sufficiently covered to constitute a full mortgage.

The absence of an underlying pledge of assets doesn't necessarily mean the debenture is of a lesser quality than a bond. What you must look at is the reason a debenture rather than a bond is being issued. It could be one of a number of perfectly acceptable reasons and it is important to ascertain which one applies in the particular circumstances.

For example, a well-established, large, successful corporation may have such a good credit rating that it is able to borrow money on favourable terms without having to pledge any of its assets at all. A corporation might be large, successful and perfectly solvent but not have sufficient assets to pledge due to the nature of its business, which is frequently the case with commercial or mercantile operations, whose only significant assets are those in which they trade and therefore cannot easily pledge. To cite an extreme example, Eaton's could not be expected to pledge its inventory.Nor would it be reasonable to expect the Bank of Montreal to pledge its deposits. You would not likely assign a lower quality rating to debentures vis-à-vis bonds in either of these circumstances.

On the other hand, a corporation with a heavy investment in fixed assets might be going the debenture route because all its assets are already pledged as a result of earlier bond issues and mortgages. In these circumstances, unless there were compensating factors such as a top credit rating and excellent long-term prospects for the company, you should consider the debenture to be a cut below a bond and either pass up the opportunity or seek a higher return to offset the higher risk.

''Subordinated debentures'' are, as the name clearly implies, debentures which are junior to some other security of the issuer. Once again, the possibility exists that this type of issue is not top quality, and the advantages of obtaining expert investment advice before putting up money for a subordinated debenture are obvious.

INCOME BONDS OR DEBENTURES

Generally speaking, income bonds or debentures are bonds or debentures in the ordinary sense except that interest is not payable on them unless the issuer has earned profits sufficient to cover the interest thereon.

In this connection ''profit'' is usually defined by the terms of the issue and may not be the generally accepted definition of the word, so be sure to check it out carefully.

Furthermore, the term ''income bond or debenture'' has a specific meaning under the *Income Tax Act,* and special income tax treatment may apply. Accordingly, this is one type of investment that is clearly suitable only for the very sophisticated investor and should never be undertaken without the benefit of expert investment and income tax advice.

SINKING FUND BONDS

These are not securities issued by steamship companies or oilwell diggers — not necessarily, that is.

A sinking fund is a sum of money or pool of investments earmarked to provide resources for the redemption or retirement of a bond issue. A sinking fund reserve is the portion of earnings earmarked for the purpose of establishing and expanding the sinking fund. It is a means of providing for the ultimate payment of the debt on a piecemeal basis each year throughout the term of the particular debt rather than by re-financing it all when it comes due.

Usually a trust company is appointed as a trustee to administer the fund. On a fixed date each year the borrower provides the required amount (which might include bonds of the particular issue concerned, which the issuer reacquired) to the trustee who will invest and hold it in trust for the ultimate redemption of the issue. The borrowing corporation will no longer have any control over those particular funds.

Bond issues which carry sinking fund provisions usually indicate this fact in their title. The significance to you as an investor is assurance that money is being set aside which can be used only to redeem your securities.

COLLATERAL TRUST BONDS

A collateral trust bond is secured, not by a pledge of fixed assets, but by a physical pledge of other securities. For example, a corporation issuing a collateral trust bond might pledge as security bonds or shares of other corporations. It's a situation similar to an individual pledging securities to a bank to secure a personal loan.

You might think the quality of this type of bond is lower than a mortgage bond, but that's a dangerous generalization. Sometimes the pledged securities are of such a high quality themselves that the collateral trust bond is just as secure.

Occasionally, to provide an even greater than normal security for a mortgage bond, collateral in the form of other securities is also pledged.

This type of issue is usually referred to as a "mortgage and collateral trust bond."

EXTENDIBLE BONDS AND DEBENTURES

These issues usually have a relatively short maturity term, say, five years, but carry with them the option for the investor to exchange them for a longer-term debt, say, 20 years, at the same or a slightly higher rate of interest.

You will normally have to make your decision during an election period of about six months, usually beginning from one year to six months before the original maturity date. If you take no action your bonds will automatically mature on schedule. The advantage to the investor is that you will have more time to make your decision as to how long you wish to commit your funds, but will have your money working for you in the meantime.

RETRACTABLE BONDS AND DEBENTURES

As you may have already guessed, these issues are the exact opposite of extendible bonds or debentures. These are issued for a long term, say, 20 years, but you have the option of turning in the bond for redemption earlier, say, after 10 years. As in the case of extendible bonds, the election period usually lasts for six months and begins from one year to six months before the retraction period expires. Once again, if you do not elect, the bond matures on the original maturity date — in this case, 10 years later.

The quality of a bond is not affected by these special features — although the rate of interest would be — and you are still going to have to look at the underlying security and credit rating of the issuer to satisfy yourself completely. Extendible and retractable issues are appropriate vehicles for the investor who wants an investment which is not purely short-term, but also wants to retain flexibility in avoiding a very long term.

Extendible and retractable bonds and debentures are sometimes issued by governments as well as by corporations.

SERIAL BONDS AND DEBENTURES

With these types of issues some of the principal comes due and is paid off each year on a predetermined basis. Individual investors don't usually buy into the short maturities of a serial issue. They are usually of interest (no pun intended) to institutional investors looking for short-term situations.

As the burden of debt decreases and the interest cost is correspondingly reduced each year, the quality of the remaining longer-term outstanding bonds tends to improve.

CONVERTIBLE BONDS AND DEBENTURES

Convertible bonds or debentures carry with them a right allowing them to be exchanged for common shares of the issuer under specified terms.

A convertible issue combines some of the advantages of both debt and share ownership. Because they have a fixed interest rate and a definite maturity date, they possess the advantages of bonds and debentures. On the other hand, they offer possibilities of obtaining capital appreciation through the option to convert them into common shares at a predetermined price over a stated period of time.

From the issuer's standpoint the conversion feature makes an issue more saleable at a lower borrowing cost while at the same time raising equity capital indirectly on more favourable terms than through the direct sale of common shares.

Although the heading above refers to both bonds and debentures, issues of convertible bonds are really quite rare. The investor looking to combine safety and certainty of income of a corporate debt instrument with the prospects of future capital growth will likely have to settle for a convertible debenture.

This is because it is easier to arrange a convertible issue which is not secured by specific assets.

Often, the conversion price increases with the passing of time. This encourages earlier conversion and reflects the fact that most companies' net worth grows with the passage of time. Always remember, though, that it makes no sense whatever to invest in a convertible debenture if the conversion price is higher than the present and probable future price of the underlying share.

Convertible issues require a little more babysitting than most investments because their prices are more volatile and decisions whether or not to convert must be made. You also don't want to miss any time deadlines.

In addition to the investment quality of the debenture itself, the price level of the underlying common shares also affects the price of the debenture. Normally, when the underlying stock is well below the conversion price, the convertible debenture behaves like any other bond or debenture by responding to the general level of interest rates and the quality of the security. When the underlying stock is near to the conversion price the debenture usually sells at a premium, and when it rises above the conversion price the debenture should rise correspondingly in price.

To take a simple example, assume a $100 debenture allowing you to convert to ten common shares. Assume further that the interest rate of the debenture is comparable to that obtainable from alternate sources. When the common shares are trading around $10 each there will probably be a premium of a dollar or two attached to the debenture so that you could sell it for, say, $102. If the common shares were trading at $12 each, the debenture is obviously worth close to $120 — the value of the common shares into which it can be converted. On the other hand, if the common shares are trading at $9, the conversion feature has no value.

DEBENTURES WITH WARRANTS

A warrant is a certificate giving the holder the right to purchase stock (normally one common share) at a specified price over a stated period of time. Warrants are sometimes attached to debentures to make them (the debentures) more saleable and, of course, may themselves be bought and sold on stock exchanges or over the counter.

Warrants are a very attractive investment vehicle. If the warrant allows you to purchase the relevant common shares at a price below the going market price, you have two favourable options available to you. You can either purchase the shares at a bargain, or if you don't want to hold common shares in that particular company, sell the warrants themselves at a profit.

Buying and selling warrants will often allow you to make as much profit at much less risk than dealing in common shares. For example, if a stock costing $25 goes up to $30 you would have to risk $5,000 to make $1,000 (200 shares x $25). If there were warrants available allowing the purchase of that stock at $25, they would rise in price by about $5 each as well.

So if you bought those warrants at, say, $10 and sold them at $15, you could make $1,000 by risking only $2,000 (200 warrants x $10).

ZERO COUPON BONDS

As the name implies, this type of bond pays no interest at all over its life. They are sold at deep discounts on the basis that all of the yield will be available in one lump sum at the time the bond matures. For example, at a time when the going interest rate was, say, 10.5%, a fifteen-year $1,000 bond could be bought for around $200.

There are all kinds of problems associated with zero coupon bonds. They are very sensitive to inflation rates. The income tax provisions affecting them are brutal — you would have to pay tax on an assumed interest income each year even though no actual income is received. Finally, there is often a stiff commission involved in their purchase. My personal view is that zero coupon bonds are suitable only for RRSPs (because the income tax aspect is of no concern until the money is actually removed from the plan) and even then only when you are absolutely certain you won't need the cash until the bond matures.

STRIPPED BONDS

Stripped bonds sound like something we shouldn't be talking about in a book meant for all members of the family, but really they are just bonds which have had all the interest coupons clipped off them.

Because the bond will not be paying any interest — that will go to the holder of the coupons — you can buy the bond for a very deep discount. The point is that the only way you can get any money back is to sell it to someone else, or hold it until maturity and receive the face value.

The problem with these two alternatives is that there may not be a buyer around when you want to sell the bond; and if you hold it until maturity you're going to have to pay tax in the interim on money you haven't received yet. As with zero coupon bonds, Revenue Canada considers the difference between what you pay for the stripped bond and the amount it will be worth on redemption to be compound interest earned over the period between purchase and maturity. Again you would be paying tax on money you haven't yet received.

As with zero coupon bonds, because there really is no difference between them, stripped bonds, in my view, are suitable only for RRSPs and then only when you are certain you won't need the money prior to maturity.

JUNK BONDS

Once again the name says it all. Junk bonds are just that — junk. They are bonds with clearly insufficient assets backing them up issued by a debt-ridden company (usually in a highly leveraged takeover situation). They carry an abnormally high interest rate.

Provided the issuer survives, you can do quite well with them. On the other hand, if the issuer doesn't survive, you lose your money.

Junk bonds are suitable only for the gambler or the speculator who has lots of money to spare. They are never of investment quality.

INVESTMENT QUALITY OF BONDS AND DEBENTURES

Judging the investment quality of a corporate bond or debenture is difficult. Many investment analysts use five main rules of thumb (in the form of questions to be answered) to assist in making such an evaluation. As you review these now you'll see they are quite similar to the rules of thumb for evaluating preferred share issues.

Interest Coverage

Do the corporation's earnings provide sufficient coverage for the payment of interest and the repayment of principal?

The Canadian Securities Institute offers the following formula to use as a test:

$$\frac{\text{total income after operating expenses}}{\text{total interest requirements in latest fiscal year}}$$

Although quick to point out that adequate coverage can't be defined precisely, the C.S.I. does suggest the following minimum standards for interest coverage:

> **Public Utilities** Current year's interest should be covered at least two times by the average annual earnings available in the last seven-year period.
> **Industrials** Current year's interest should be covered at least three times by the average annual earnings available in the last seven-year period.

When it comes to repayment of principal, you must consider the level of interest coverage and the ability to meet sinking fund requirements — especially what emergency measures might be available to the corporation, such as eliminating a dividend on common shares. However, another consideration in this connection is the next rule of thumb.

Asset Coverage

The next question is: Do the assets pledged offer sufficient security? You might get a plausible answer by dividing total long-term debt by net tangible assets. (Generally speaking, net tangible assets are total assets less intangible assets, current liabilities, deferred income taxes, other credits and minority interests.)

Minimum standards suggested are:

> **Public Utilities** $1,500 of net tangible assets per $1,000 of outstanding debt.
> **Industrials** $2,000 of net tangible assets per $1,000 of outstanding debt.

However, remember that most balance sheets do not reflect the increase in price levels since assets were purchased. Assets arc usually shown at cost.

Debit/Equity Ratio

Probably the best known of the five tests, the debt/equity ratio answers the question: is there a large enough cushion of equity capital beneath the bond or debenture issue?

As a minimum, a corporation's long-term debt should not exceed the current market value of all the corporation's outstanding classes of stock.

This is a very good rule of thumb, particularly in circumstances where the results of the asset coverage test may not be satisfactory.

Another advantage of this test is that it reflects a decline in the earnings of a corporation because this fact itself would cause a decline in the market value of the corporation's stock.

Dealer Sponsorship Test

In many cases this is the only test which individual investors ever apply — simply answering the question: was the security sponsored and underwritten by an established, reputable investment dealer? A "no" answer here is cause for pause, while a "yes" answer is a good indication that the security has been thoroughly investigated and found to be soundly constructed. It is reasonable to expect the issuer will be able to meet its obligations in respect to both principal and interest.

Eligibility for Life Companies

The last question: is the security eligible for investment by a life insurance company without recourse to the basket clause? This requires some explanation.

The types of securities in which life insurance companies may invest are classified by the *Canadian and British Insurance Companies Act*. Eligibility under this Act is a favourable factor in determining investment quality as long as eligibility is not achieved under the Act's basket clause. The basket clause allows up to a particular percentage of the book value of a life insurer's total assets to be invested in investments which would not otherwise qualify under the principal conditions of the Act.

Other Factors

In addition to the five foregoing tests (note that a "yes" answer is desirable for each question; a "no" is bad news) there are other factors which should be taken into consideration when evaluating the quality of a particular debt security. These include the trend of earnings over the past seven to ten years; interest coverage in the year of lowest earnings; the nature of the corporation's industry in light of both the industry and general economic outlook; and sinking fund and other protective provisions.

Protective Provisions

This is the term applied to the features of a particular security designed to protect the interests of the investors. Such provisions include prohibition of prior liens; restrictions on additional borrowing; sinking fund provisions; and requirements that dividends not result in the reduction of the corporation's working capital below a stated amount.

Caveat

The C.S.I. is careful to caution users of their rules of thumb that mechanical standards are far from foolproof when it comes to rating securities. There exist qualifying factors which are not measurable by statistical means, the most important of which is the quality of the corporation's management. Another example is the progress, or the lack thereof, of the natural business cycle and the effects of general economic swings.

Objective

Never lose sight of the real objective of investors who buy bonds and debentures. They are looking for certainty of income. The best way to achieve this objective is to ensure that there is an adequate margin of safety in the particular security.

CANADA SAVINGS BONDS

Canada Savings Bonds, in effect, give you an interest income on cash in your wallet. This is so because they can be turned into cash at any time simply by presenting them to your bank.

As for security, nothing is better. If the Government of Canada defaults, it is hard to conceive of any investment being any good.

In determining whether the rate of return is adequate, you should compare it to what is available on daily-interest savings accounts, not term deposits or other investments which are less liquid than Canada Savings Bonds.

Canada Savings Bonds are an excellent investment to make while you're learning more about investments generally.

Chapter 35

Annuities

VARIOUS KINDS

Webster defines an annuity as "an amount payable yearly or at other regular intervals." If only it were so simple! When you go to buy an annuity, you are suddenly confronted with an array of products that truly boggles the mind. Too often people make a bad choice rather than suffer the embarrassment of admitting they don't understand all the terms and buzz-words which characterize various annuity options.

This chapter examines some of the more common options available and what they normally mean. Even this approach is fraught with danger because there are dozens and dozens of insurance and trust companies offering annuities for sale in the country, and they don't all call the options the same thing. But as cowardice is seldom rewarded, here goes.

Immediate Annuity

With any annuity the income payments received may be monthly, quarterly, semi-annual or annual. They have to be at least annual. Theoretically, the payments could be received weekly or daily, but any payment period less than monthly is rare, if indeed any exist at all.

If the annuity is an immediate annuity, the payments begin immediately — well, almost immediately. The point is they aren't deferred for any significant period of time. For example, if an immediate annuity is purchased on July 23, payments would likely begin no later than September 1, and possibly even as early as August 1.

The amount of the income you will receive is determined by the amount paid for the annuity, the period of time over which payments will be received by you and prevailing interest rates at the time of purchasing the annuity.

Deferred Annuity

Just the opposite of the immediate annuity, payments out of a deferred annuity will not begin until some specified date in the future. They might begin on a date determined by a particular number of years, such as 5, 10 or 15 years after purchase. Or they might begin on a date determined by the purchaser's age, such as at age 50, 60 or 65.

Once the annuity starts to pay, the payments again can be monthly, quarterly, semi-annual or annual, and their amount will be determined by the premium paid for the annuity plus a stipulated rate of return thereon throughout the deferral period.

Life-Only

Under this type of annuity the purchaser receives payments only as long as he or she lives. Because the annuity holder's beneficiaries will receive nothing from the annuity after the annuitant dies, the return on this type of annuity is usually higher than on any other.

But it's shooting dice. The purchaser is really betting against the issuer and the stakes are high. If you live longer than the mortality tables suggest, a gain will be made at the expense of the issuer. On the other hand, if you die the day after buying the annuity it's a total loss.

It's a rare set of circumstances in which a life-only annuity is appropriate, but the fact that a market still exists for them is testimony that some investors go that route. Probably the same ones who visit Las Vegas regularly.

Life With Guaranteed Period

If you'rc looking for income for life but want to hedge your bets against the total downside risk inherent in the life-only annuity, the life annuity with a guaranteed period is the way to go.

Under this type of annuity, payments will be made as long as you live, but should you expire before the guaranteed period does (which can be many years, depending on a number of circumstances), the annuity payments will continue to be made to your beneficiary for the unexpired portions of the term.

Annuity Certain

With an annuity certain, payments will be made for a specific number of years — normally, five, ten or fifteen — regardless of how long the purchaser lives. Suppose you buy an annuity certain for a ten-year period. At the end of the ten years the payments stop. If you die before the ten years are up, payments will continue to be made to your beneficiary throughout the balance of the ten-year period.

Joint and Survivor Annuity

Under a joint and survivor annuity, payments will be made for the balance of your life and will continue to be made to your beneficiary for the rest of his or her life. Of course, if your designated beneficiary dies before you, the annuity payments will end upon your death.

Impaired Life Annuity

Often overlooked in financial planning, the impaired life annuity should be considered in appropriate circumstances. If for some reason a person's life expectancy is significantly shorter than normal, upon receipt of adequate medical evidence an insurance company may provide considerably larger life annuity payments than in ordinary circumstances, because the issuer can reasonably expect to pay them for a much shorter time period. This is the reverse effect of being "rated" for insurance purposes.

Life Annuity Specially Guaranteed

Still another hybrid. The option offered by a life annuity with a special guarantee is that should you have the misfortune to die before receiving annuity payments equal to the purchase price of the annuity, the difference will be paid to your beneficiary either as a lump sum or in periodic installments.

Variable Annuity

The variable annuity option is really one which can be tied to any of the above. The annuity ultimately chosen can, if you wish, be tied into a variable factor — such as prime rates of interest or a stock or mortgage fund — which will increase or decrease the annuity payments according to the performance of the fund or rate to which it is tied. In the absence of choosing such an option, you would know exactly how much your annuity payments would be.

DIFFICULT CHOICE

Considering that the foregoing is not a complete list of available options, and that many of them can be combined to create still more choices, it is obvious that the selection of an annuity must be made with great care and always in the light of your own particular circumstances. There is no general rule. However, if you want to consider extremes, just to put the matter in perspective, a middle-aged, perfectly healthy individual would most likely be better off in the long run with an annuity for life; whereas a Hollywood stuntman would be well advised always to insist on a guaranteed term of fifteen years.

Shop carefully, consider all alternatives and be absolutely certain that you understand all the terms, and their implications, of the type of annuity you finally settle on.

Chapter 36

Treasury Bills

Back in March 1980, the Bank of Canada began basing its bank rate (which, of course, ultimately dictates the interest rates for all Canadian financial institutions) on the average rate established in the weekly tender of 91-day treasury bills issued by the federal government. Instead of the Bank of Canada making announcements from time to time as to what the rate would be, since March 13, 1980, the rate is set at one-quarter of one percentage point above the treasury bill average rate. The new bank rate is announced at 2:00 p.m. Eastern Time, each Thursday.

In 1980 Canadians suddenly became aware that there were these mysterious things called treasury bills and that every Thursday they were auctioned off, probably in some well-guarded vault with walls six feet thick and money all over the floor, amid the racket of auctioneers' gavels and frantically shouted bids from hordes of hysterical financiers. Even now, many Canadians still think that's the way it is.

Well, it's a shame to blow away the mystique, but the fact is Government of Canada treasury bills are nothing more or less than simple negotiable bearer promissory notes issued by the federal government to obtain working capital. And the auction is held at the Bank of Canada building in Ottawa. Not only is there no money on the floor, there are no gavels and no auctioneers, and the bidders aren't even there.

Here's what really happens. First, a bit about the treasury bills themselves. They are, as already mentioned, promissory notes issued in denominations of $1,000, $5,000, $25,000, $100,000 and $1,000,000. There are two types of treasury bills issued weekly, one with a term of 91 days and the other with a term of 182 days. Treasury bills with a term of one year are issued every four weeks.

The bills themselves do not carry a specific rate of interest. Rather, they are sold at a discount with the yield to the purchaser determined by the difference between the price paid and the par value which will be received upon maturity.

To take a very simple example, assume a bidder acquires a $1,000, 91-day treasury bill for $970 on, say, July 17. On October 15 the bill can be redeemed for $1,000. So $30 has been made in 91 days on an investment of $970. That's an annual return of 12.4%.

If the 12.4% represented the average rate established in the weekly tender of treasury bills on July 17, that afternoon the Bank of Canada would set its bank rate at about 12.75%.

The amounts and the maturity dates of the bills to be offered are announced a week in advance and the Bank of Canada, acting as an agent for the federal government, calls for tenders.

The chartered banks, about a dozen or so of the largest investment dealers in the country, and the Bank of Canada itself regularly submit tenders at the weekly auction. However, any bank or investment dealer on the list of "primary distributors" (a list, it is understood, containing about 100 names) is eligible to bid.

The potential buyers submit their bids, normally by sealed tender, to the Bank of Canada in Ottawa. This cannot be done until noon, Eastern Time, on the day of the auction. Representatives of the Department of Finance and the Bank of Canada receive the bids. Some bidders tender a single amount and others tender bids covering a range of prices.

The highest bidder receives all of the bills it bid for at that price, then the second highest, and so on until the entire issue has been sold.

Although a potential buyer can submit more than one bid, the buyer's top bid is considered first. It is possible that a bidder could have all bids accepted and acquire several bills with the same maturity, each at a different price. If the amount of bids at the lowest successful price exceeds the total of the issue remaining, that remainder is allotted on a pro rata basis among the participants who submitted bids at that price. Settlement, both payment and delivery, must be completed by 3:00 p.m. the following day.

The Minister of Finance always reserves the right to accept or reject any tender in whole or in part. Furthermore, in addition to bidding for bills it wants to buy, the Bank of Canada may, if it wants, tender a reserve bid for the entire issue. Although on the one hand this allows the government effectively to continue control of the central bank's interest rate, it also guarantees a market for the entire issue and prevents any group from forcing a significant reduction in the price of the bills either by boycotting the issue or forming a syndicate to submit low bids.

It must never be overlooked, though, that this procedure provides the federal government with an effective mechanism by which to exert an enormous effect on all interest rates — in short, to control them. This is particularly so when the Bank of Canada's rate is tied to the weekly auction, but even in the absence of that, the weekly treasury bill auction has been, is, and will likely continue to be the single most important influence on all short-term interest rates.

So we now know treasury bills are usually acquired by the chartered banks and large investment dealers. But then what happens to them?

Well, in the case of the chartered banks, most of them are simply kept until they are redeemed upon maturity. This is so because they constitute a very important part of a chartered bank's legally required reserves, although some banks make some of their acquired bills available on the secondary market.

Investment dealers, on the other hand, buy the bills primarily to sell on the secondary market to investors having excess cash to invest for a short term. Such investors include commercial and financial institutions, municipal and provincial governments, foreign investors, other dealers, corporations, individuals, and the Bank of Canada itself. As a matter of fact, unsuccessful bidders at the weekly auction usually enter this secondary market immediately in order to meet their particular requirements. This second phase of the weekly auction is usually more lively and interesting than the original auction.

Apart from the chartered banks, large corporations are probably the most active investors in treasury bills. They acquire their bills in the secondary market from the investment dealers and find them to be particularly attractive short-term investments. Not only can they be acquired in amounts suiting any particular treasurer's needs, but maturity dates (ranging from a day or two up to a year) dovetailing nicely with any date on which a particular corporation needs its cash back are normally available. Furthermore, treasury bills are as close to a risk-free investment as can be found. And they are totally liquid.

That is another reason why they are so important to the Canadian money market. They provide a ready and relatively easy means for the free movement of money from places in which it is not needed for the time being, to places where it can be put to work effectively.

But it is only the really big individual investor who is able to invest directly in treasury bills. As mentioned earlier, individuals are not involved in the weekly auction. Therefore they have to make their treasury bill investments by dealing with a broker in the secondary market described above. Normally brokers and banks prefer to deal in units of $50,000 or more. They will, of course, drop below this level, but at the lower levels the yield to the investor is not necessarily better than what's available with other types of investments. So it can be seen that the only direct significance of treasury bills to the vast majority of Canadians is the fact that it is the treasury bill rate which sets the level for most other interest rates in the country. But that fact alone is sufficiently important to warrant an understanding of how treasury bills work.

The yields on new treasury bills, of course, vary from week to week and are extremely sensitive to all changing credit conditions. However, an investor's yield is set at the time of purchase because although it is bought at a discount, maturity at full face value is assured. Accordingly, the sensitivity does not result in uncertainty.

There is no doubt as to the importance of treasury bills in the total Canadian money market, and although they became household words only in the 1980s (because of the Bank of Canada's interest rate being tied to them), they've been around for a long time.

Canadian treasury bills, payable in sterling, were sold on the London market and in continental Europe in the early 1900s. Beginning in 1914, they were sold to Canadian chartered banks, but there was no secondary market. Then in the mid-1920s the issuance of treasury bills was discontinued. In March 1934, they again appeared on the domestic scene and sale by auction was introduced.

Although regular bi-weekly auctions began in 1937, there was very little secondary market activity; the bills were acquired almost exclusively by the chartered banks. This began to change in the early to mid-1950s when deliberate steps were taken by monetary officials to establish a purely Canadian money market, including an increase in the amount of treasury bills outstanding and the introduction of a weekly auction.

In 1954 chartered bank day-to-day loans to investment dealers were introduced, with one of the effects being to provide investment dealers with an alternate source of funds for financing, among other investments, inventories of federal treasury bills. At the same time the demand for treasury bills was increased further by a revision to the *Bank Act* which permitted banks to invest more funds in the short-term money market. Naturally, treasury bills were the most attractive form of doing so.

Then in 1955 the chartered banks agreed to maintain a secondary reserve of 7% of their statutory deposits, and treasury bills qualified for this reserve.

In recent years the yield-spread between treasury bills and other short-term investments narrowed considerably, with the predictable result that a strong secondary market for the bills has developed to the point where they are now the cornerstone of the Canadian short-term money market. The yield on treasury bills is now higher than on most other short-term investments. But trying to assess whether treasury bill yields have increased or other yields have decreased is akin to attempting to resolve the age-old chicken and egg controversy.

Chapter 37

Options

This chapter does not deal with stock options in the sense of those which are offered to employees by corporations, but rather the options which can be traded on the major stock exchanges by buying and selling options issued by TransCanada Options Inc. on the shares of certain corporations.

Dealing in options is a way to "invest" in high-priced shares without having to put up amounts of money equal to the value of the underlying shares. However, it is also a way to get completely wiped out very quickly.

Basically, options work this way. Brace yourself to learn a few technical terms here; options have their own jargon. A call option is a contract allowing you to purchase a given number of shares in a company within a set period of time at a given price. The shares in question are called the underlying security; the price at which you are allowed to buy them is the exercise price or premium. Option contracts are usually for 100 shares, so multiply all prices by 100. Once issued, options trade on the market just as stocks and bonds do, until they expire.

Equipped with that basic information, you can now read the options listings in your daily newspaper.

Suppose you see this listing:

Option	Volume	Last	Close
X Ltd. Jul 27½	10	3¼	28⅜

The option is to buy 100 common shares of X Ltd. at a price of $27.50 each before the end of July. Ten option contracts (each for 100 shares) were traded on the previous day and the last option traded sold at a price of $3.25 per share, or a total of $325 for one option contract. The "close" column refers to the previous day's closing price of the underlying security — $28⅜.

Obviously, investors are expecting X Ltd. stock to rise; they are willing to pay $3.25 for the chance to buy a share at $27.50, which brings the total price they would pay (if they exercised their options) to $30.75 plus commissions. They could buy X Ltd. shares more cheaply than that on the open market at $28 ⅜. So why buy options? The simple answer is that if X Ltd. shares go even higher — say, to $33 — they will make some money because their total purchase price is only $30.75.

On the other hand, if the shares fall to, say, $25, no one in his or her right mind will want to exercise the option. But even if an investor misses a chance to sell the option and has to let it expire, the total loss is still only $325 — the price paid for the original contract — instead of $2,837.50 − $2,500 = $337.50 (or much more if the stock's value went down even further). In other words, for a relatively small capital input you get a chance to make a large profit (but not as large as if actual shares had been bought at $28⅜).

Don't think you now know enough to rush off and place a large options order with your broker. If you do, the first thing he or she will do is give you a copy of the prospectus of the TransCanada Options Inc., then tell you to go away for at least two days and read the prospectus, plus some other material you will be given. It will really take you two weeks to read it.

Your reading will open up a whole new — and confusing — world. First you will be introduced to the concept of the clearing corporation. In one sense, the clearing corporation is simply the options exchange. But it also plays a far greater role. In order to understand this, you will have to digest some more jargon. Essentially, the clearing corporation is the intermediary between holders and writers of options.

Holders are the people we discussed above — the buyers of option contracts. But they have to buy their options from somebody; that is where the writer comes in. A writer is an individual who undertakes to sell a given number of shares at a set price within a set period (the duration of an options contract is usually three, six or nine months). In return for this promise — that is, in return for writing the option — the writer is paid a premium, the amount of which is essentially determined by the market.

This is where the clearing corporation comes in. It acts as the middleman between writer and buyer. And, what is much more important, once the option has been issued, the clearing corporation assumes final responsibility for the contract.

It works this way. Suppose you have 100 shares of X Ltd. which you bought at $47 and which are now sitting at $45. You would like a little extra money but don't want to take a capital loss by selling the shares.

So you tell your broker that you are willing to write an option to sell your shares at $50 any time within the next six months, and that for this you would like a premium of $2.50 a share. Your broker notifies the clearing corporation, which then finds a buyer who is willing to buy the option at that price. You immediately receive $250 ($2.50 each for 100 shares), but you still have your shares.

If the holder (or other holders who buy the option on the market) do not exercise the option, you have nothing to worry about. You have your shares plus $250. If, on the other hand, it is exercised, you have $250 plus a capital gain of $3 a share. But suppose that X Ltd.'s stock has suddenly become the hottest thing in the market and you think it's going to go way up. You've changed your mind and you don't want to sell your shares at $50. What to do?

Simple. You buy another option to pick up 100 shares of X Ltd. at $50, thus offsetting your earlier commitment to sell your own shares; your broker notifies the clearing corporation that you have thereby made a closing purchase transaction. Now, when the holder of the option you originally wrote arrives to exercise it, the clearing corporation (and not you) is responsible for seeing that he or she gets shares. You are in the clear.

In this particular example, you have been a *covered writer* — a writer who actually owns the shares you are contracting to sell. If you are a conservative investor you probably will be happiest being a covered writer. If you have a more daring streak, you may wish to be a naked writer — that is, to write the option without actually owning the shares. The risk here is, of course, that if the option is exercised you will be caught having to buy the shares on the open market for more than the option holder is going to pay for them, which makes the whole deal a lot more speculative. It's all perfectly legal, just risky. You would only do this if you are willing (and able) to gamble that the price of the underlying stock is going to fall.

If you want to be a holder rather than either kind of writer, that generally is still more speculative. The risk, of course, is that your option will expire before the underlying stock price gets where you expected it to. Remember that an option is a wasting asset — it will vanish completely at the end of its term. Remember also that as the expiry date nears, the market price of options generally declines. If your timing is bad you can lose your shirt.

Options strategies are numerous. If you're interested, your broker can provide information about rising and falling market strategies, variable protection, "straddles" and a host of other approaches. But those probably should be attempted only by fairly sophisticated investors. For most, a few basic strategies are sufficient. It is essential to bear some key points in mind:

1. The options market is very risky. You can minimize the risk, but you can't eliminate it.
2. Timing is everything. It's not enough to guess right about the price trend of a stock; you have to guess right about when that trend will develop.
3. The Canadian options market, though growing, is still small. This means that buyers or sellers may not always be there when you want to unload or buy an option. And you almost certainly will want to sell it, if you are a holder. Only a small percentage of options are ever actually exercised. Options are not, by themselves, investments. If you were really interested in the stock you probably would buy it in the first instance. Most holders make their money by trading, just as in the stock market.
4. There is a very limited number of listed companies eligible for the options market.

Many astute financial advisors suggest the best way to deal in options is never to be a buyer of options and restrict your selling to covered writing (as described above).

On the other hand, if you want to speculate you can make a lot more money with less invested by trading options rather than by trading the actual stock.

Chapter 38

Diversification

WHY DIVERSIFY?

The second most difficult problem investors face — second only to actually picking the right investments — is deciding what proportion of their total funds should be committed to particular types of securities, or any other investment for that matter. Spreading investments among various types of securities is normally referred to as diversification. The difficulties of diversification are matched only by the importance thereof, because diversification of holdings is the only way to reconcile the incompatible objectives of safety of capital, maximum income, and growth.

An investment policy is not sound unless diversification is an integral part. This is because any investment in publicly traded securities always carries with it an element of risk, and it is clearly good strategy to spread that risk over a number of different securities. If investments are distributed over a number of securities and one of them performs badly, only some of the investors' capital is affected. Furthermore, in a diversified holding, the odds are that some securities will do better than expected. This will offset losses incurred by those in the portfolio which do not perform as well as expected — and the odds are there will be some of those, too.

There are two headings under which diversification should be discussed, risk reduction and investment convenience.

RISK REDUCTION

For most investors, reduction in risk is the compelling reason for diversifying their holdings. There are essentially four ways to reduce risk through diversification.

The first is to limit the amount of money you put into any one investment. When confronted with an investment opportunity that looks particularly attractive, the temptation to plunge in completely is often overwhelming — but it is a temptation that must be resisted. Regardless of how good a particular issue looks, it is normally wise to spread your capital among a number of issues of different quality or rank. In this way diversification strengthens your overall position without making any great sacrifice of income, marketability or possible capital growth. If your main objective is income, your capital risk is greatly reduced through diversification.

The second way to reduce risk through diversification is to distribute funds among particular issues of similar quality in a number of corporations of similar rank engaged in the same kind of activity. For example, the bonds of a number of public utilities, governments, and Crown corporations could be purchased in preference to putting all your cash into the bonds of one utility. If diversified, you don't depend on the fortunes of one entity.

The third method of reducing risk through diversification is to invest in corporations that are engaged in different types of businesses. The advantage of this type of diversification comes from the external conditions which often influence an entire industry. For example, while a general recession affects most industries to some extent, there is no doubt it affects some more severely than others. Public utilities and food and beverage industries tend to continue to hold their own, relatively speaking, during a recession. On the other hand, a recession usually has a more drastic effect on the lumber, construction, real estate and heavy manufacturing industries. And there is everything in between. The advantages of diversification are fairly obvious in these circumstances.

Consider, too, that holdings in a number of industries operating in various parts of the country — or in various parts of the world, for that matter — will provide even greater protection through ownership in a cross-section of businesses augmented by geographical diversification.

Another form of diversification falling into this category is to devote a portion of your funds to providing straight income, while using the rest to seek capital appreciation by investing in growth stocks.

Although risk reduction may be the prime objective, the principle of diversification will allow you to invest in securities which themselves carry an element of risk without sacrificing the safety of your entire bundle, while at the same time possibly increasing your total investment income.

The fourth method of reducing risk through diversification, and one favoured by a great number of investors, is investing in holding or investment companies.

The classic holding company scenario features a corporation with a very high capitalization that purchases shares of a number of operating companies in various industries that may or may not be related. The holding company is non-operating in the normal sense, but the really big ones usually participate, indirectly and in varying degrees, in the management of companies in which they invest through the provision of managerial talent and technology.

Another method of diversifying this way is to buy shares in a mutual fund. Mutual funds will be discussed in greater detail a little further on. For now, back to holding companies.

The diversification advantage is obvious. In addition, by investing in one or more holding companies, a small investor is able to invest in several industries that might not otherwise be available due to sheer cost. As a case in point, a single investment in a holding company might automatically put you into the transportation, oil and gas, mining, hotel, real estate, logging, food, and iron and steel industries. This, too, is an obvious advantage of diversification.

Purchasing shares in an investment fund is the easiest and often the most practical method of diversifying investments. Generally speaking, an investment fund is a company whose business is the investing of its capital, raised through the marketing of its own shares, in various securities.

It is structured much like any other company, but instead of using its capital to build a plant, purchase raw materials and hire employees, it invests it in stocks and bonds of other companies with an eye to earning income in the form of dividends and interest, and making capital gains through timely switches in the securities owned. After administration expenses are paid from these earnings, dividends are distributed to the investment fund's shareholders or are re-invested.

It is obvious, then, how the investment fund differs from an operating company. What is not so obvious, though, is how it differs from a holding company. The distinction is that although the business of holding companies, such as Power Corp. and Brascan, is investing in other companies, they usually become substantially involved in the management of the companies whose shares they hold. Investment funds do not, primarily because they want to be able to dispose of their holdings quickly and completely on short notice, a move which would be inconsistent with the holding company concept.

Another distinction between the holding company and the investment fund is that the holding company's investments are not nearly as diversified nor do they cover as wide a range as those of an investment fund. And of course the investment fund's portfolio changes almost daily, whereas the holding company normally holds its investments for many, many years — in some cases, it seems, forever.

MAIN CATEGORIES OF INVESTMENT FUNDS

There are two main categories of investment funds: closed-end funds and open-end funds. The latter are more commonly referred to as mutual funds.

Both types of funds raise capital by selling their own shares and debt securities to the public. However, the closed-end fund raises a particular amount of capital and operates at that level, plus retained earnings, for an extended period of time, much like an operating company. If you want to buy or sell shares of a closed-end fund, you normally have to make the transaction with other buyers or sellers through a stock exchange or on the over-the-counter market.

Mutual funds, on the other hand, continually issue their own units to as many investors and in whatever numbers the market will bear. Similarly, the mutual fund will redeem its own units on demand. Therefore, the mutual fund's units are bought from and sold to the fund itself rather than from and to other unitholders.

Although the market price of the shares of a closed-end fund is obviously affected by the market value of the securities held by the fund in its own portfolio, the closed-end fund shares themselves usually trade at a level somewhat below their net asset value, because buyers and sellers must be found in the open market. This, too, is in direct contrast to the behaviour of mutual fund unit prices. The price of a mutual fund unit has a direct relationship to the net asset value of the fund's portfolio because the fund will redeem its own units on demand at a price based on its current net asset value.

Because investments in mutual funds are more common than in closed-end funds, the following comments on diversifying through the use of investment funds will be restricted to mutual funds.

MUTUAL FUNDS

There are four major types of mutual funds:

1. balanced funds
2. income funds
3. equity funds
4. specialty funds

Balanced funds, as the name suggests, represent the ultimate in investment diversification. Their portfolios are spread among common shares, preferred shares, bonds, debentures, and other commercial paper. A typical split — depending on current financial market conditions — might be: common stocks 60%; preferred shares 20%; bonds 7%; commercial paper 10%; and cash 3%.

Income funds concentrate more on bonds and debentures, with some high-grade preferreds but very few common shares. Their goal is high income and safety of capital.

The equity fund is a very popular type of mutual fund. It invests primarily in common shares, with the goal being growth of capital.

Then there are the specialty funds. These funds concentrate on a specific industry, such as oil and gas, gold, chemicals, or steel; or they concentrate on a geographical area, such as U.S., Japanese, or European investments. There are also specialty funds that concentrate on mortgages and others that deal exclusively in money markets.

To make the description complete, two other types of funds, though extremely rare and forming a small part of the present total fund picture, should be mentioned.

The first of these is the speculative fund, euphemistically referred to in some quarters as a "performance fund." These funds invest in high-risk, speculative common stocks. The poker table, the race track and Las Vegas may be better bets.

The other type of fund, once popular but now relegated to the weirdo class, is the fixed fund. In this fund, top-quality investments are chosen and just left there with little or no turnover. The advantage is minimization of management and administration costs. The obvious disadvantage, and no doubt the cause of their almost total extinction, is that things simply change too rapidly in this day and age to make that approach a sensible form of diversification.

The advantages of investing in mutual funds are diversification, having professional management of your investments, the ability to invest a small amount, and having the income tax implications of your investment activity administered for you. Each year the mutual fund will send you information slips telling you how much of what type of income (or loss — it's not always a one-way street) to report on your income tax return.

The main disadvantages of mutual funds are that they are usually over-hyped by high-pressure advertising, you have no control over your investment (other than to sell it), people usually buy and sell their mutual fund units at exactly the wrong times, and mutual funds are not good short-term investments.

Always remember the following points when considering an investment in mutual funds:

1. They are long-term investments, so be sure you aren't going to need your money back in a hurry.
2. Never borrow to invest in a mutual fund.
3. It's the net return that counts, so don't be turned off a particular fund simply because it charges a fee.
4. Management of the fund is the most important consideration, and it's very difficult for the ordinary investor to find out much about who makes the decisions for a fund.
5. What the fund results are *going* to be is more important than what they *have* been. But often past performance is the only yardstick available, so be sure it's *recent* past performance you examine.
6. When comparing the performance of various funds be sure the information is being reported on a similar basis. Be sure you aren't comparing apples and oranges.

Your mutual fund investment decisions should always be taken in the light of your investment goals and the degree of cost and risk you're prepared to incur to reach those goals. Whether you're a gambler, a speculator, or an investor, there are mutual funds to meet your requirements. Just be sure you're in the right one.

INVESTOR CONVENIENCE

If you're relying on investment income for your living expenses, you're going to want to receive dividend and interest payments spread throughout the year rather than all at once. This is another form of diversification and is usually accomplished in one of two ways: according to maturity dates or the distribution of income receipts throughout the year.

The value of a debt security at the time of its maturity is usually its par or face value. If debt securities' values always remained stable at their par or face value, maturity dates would be irrelevant. But that's not the way it is. Changing business and economic conditions cause interest rates to fluctuate, and the government often forces interest rate changes upon an unwilling market. When interest rates rise, bond prices fall and vice versa.

The closer a bond is to its maturity date, the closer its price will be to its par value, and it follows that its price fluctuation will be within a very narrow range. Also, short-term bond prices usually don't fluctuate as widely as do long-term bonds.

Because you can't tell with certainty what business and economic conditions will be at any particular time in the future, it makes good investment sense to vary maturity dates so that the bulk of your portfolio doesn't fall due at the same time.

Furthermore, the date of maturity is usually the date you will re-invest your money. Recognizing that the market may be especially good at one time and particularly bad at another, the ideal situation would be to have only a small portion of your portfolio coming due at any one time.

Although a minor consideration for many investors, for others the spreading of dividend and interest income as evenly as possible throughout the year is of significant importance. This is the case for investors who use their investment income for personal and living expenses, much like salary. For them a steady stream of income is essential.

Because interest payments on bonds are usually made semi-annually and dividend payments on both common and preferred shares range anywhere from quarterly to annually, it is possible, by exercising some care in security selection, to distribute income receipts fairly well throughout the year.

OVER-DIVERSIFICATION

Like all good things, diversification can be overdone. It should be kept within reasonable limits. What is reasonable in diversification, as is the case with so many investment decisions, depends entirely on an individual's particular circumstances. But there are some general comments which can be usefully made.

An important point to remember is to deal as much as possible in board lots when buying or selling stocks. An investor will usually have to pay a higher price (with a possible higher commission cost) for odd lots (less than a board lot). And it is a no-win situation. Paradoxically, an investor will usually receive less for an odd lot when selling. This happens because it's unlikely that there will be an odd-lot buyer available at exactly the same time as there is an odd-lot seller, so the price must go up or down depending on which party is compelled to sell or buy as the case might be.

Another key point is that the number of stocks you can know well and follow intelligently is limited unless you make managing your investments a full-time job. Not many people have the time and resources to achieve such a lofty goal.

A good rule of thumb is to limit investment in any one security to 10% of your total portfolio.

Then there is the administration aspect. A lot of capital spread over a large number of small investments requires a lot of careful supervision and is often inefficient in the long run.

For up to $100,000, ten different securities is an adequate and quite manageable diversification program, and it's hard to imagine an investment of less than $1,000 in one security making any sense. Of course, this particular rule of thumb doesn't apply to speculative purchases.

Although the really big investor who manages his or her own affairs could realistically be investing in 20 or more different securities, the 10% rule is really a good one for investors of all sizes.

The main point to remember is to avoid a portfolio that looks like a mini stock exchange. In these circumstances the investments will seldom do better in the long run than the market average — and that's not usually good enough.

BALANCE

As mentioned previously, it is impossible to maximize all of safety of capital, receipt of income, and capital growth within any one portfolio. What is possible, though, is to balance a portfolio to maximize one particular objective without completely sacrificing the other two.

The make-up of a portfolio can, and should, change from time to time as individual requirements and economic conditions change.

There are numerous examples in circulation of so-called illustrative portfolios. They serve a useful purpose as a starting point — but only as a starting point — in determining what your portfolio should look like. It is absolutely essential to fine-tune the portfolio to your own requirements and economic circumstances.

Chapter 39

Commodities, Collectibles and Precious Metals

COMMODITY TRADING

The commodity market — whether we are speaking of precious metals, or the more common commodities such as coffee, potatoes and grain products, or for that matter the esoterics, like pork bellies — is no place for the amateur or the faint of heart.

People must realize, before getting into it, that commodity trading is the most speculative market activity and is in no way an investment activity. The commodities market is dominated by experts in the various fields, and is a game in which the casual player can be wiped out very quickly.

In this book, in the chapters dealing with investments in securities, I pointed out that one of the important factors affecting the stock market is investor psychology. In the commodity field, *speculator* psychology is a major force — about on a par with earnings per share in the stock market. Add to this the fact that many commodity prices are affected by, of all things, the weather in various parts of the world, and you have some feeling for what you're up against. Can you really handle the strain of knowing that the safety of your money depends on what the weather is going to be like next fall in Brazil?

Does this mean no one should ever put money into the commodities market? Of course not. What it does mean, though, is that no one should get into commodities trading until he or she has acquired an in-depth knowledge of the particular commodities chosen and how the markets for those particular commodities work. You see, the commodities market is not just one market. It's many markets. Each commodity has its own market and its own market influences.

For example, let's get back to the weather in Brazil. If you decide you're going to trade in the coffee market, that's a commodity and that's a separate market. You don't really buy and sell coffee. What you buy and sell are contracts to purchase or sell coffee at some later date.

You might, for instance, buy a contract which allows the holder to buy or sell a certain amount of coffee a number of months from now. The price you will pay for that contract is based on the best guess by you and other players as to what coffee will be worth at that time. Your hope is that the price will move in whatever direction is needed to make your contract (either to buy or sell) worth more. Two things to remember here. First, the other players in the coffee market fall into two categories: speculators, like you or me, who are really guessing; and coffee dealers, the people who really buy and sell coffee as well as deal in pieces of paper as we would be doing, who probably have a lot better handle on what the price is apt to be than do you or I. Second, the whole deal may rise or fall on the coffee crop in Brazil. That, in turn, could depend strictly on the weather down there, or on the attitude of the Brazilian government.

It is no different if you're dealing in potatoes or wheat. Even professional climatologists have difficulty predicting the weather in Prince Edward Island and Saskatchewan, not to mention Idaho, Maine and Russia.

One thing you should understand about the commodities market, as already mentioned, is that you aren't dealing in the actual commodity itself. You *are* dealing with contracts to buy or sell it sometime in the future. That's why it's often referred to as the "futures" market. It works somewhat like the stock options market described earlier. It's hard to imagine what would have to go wrong before you'd end up with a truck dumping a couple of tons of pork bellies on your front lawn.

What is not difficult to imagine is the complexity of the markets and the tremendous odds the amateur player is bucking at all times.

The only thing certain about trading in commodities is that you should do so only with money you can clearly afford to lose. It's an area best left to experts. And you don't have just my word to take for it. One chairman of the Commodity Futures Trading Commission in the United States upon leaving office was quoted by *The Wall Street Journal*. He said, "I have never, ever, been in the futures market myself; I don't have the skill for it."

COLLECTIBLES

Much has been written and spoken in recent years about investing in collectibles — for example, works of art, stamp and coin collections, Persian rugs and china figurines.

The first point to remember about this activity is that it is not investing. It may be a business, it may be speculation, it may be spending money for the sheer enjoyment of the items themselves, but it is not investing.

There is absolutely nothing wrong with buying any of these items with a view to making a profit on them someday, as long as you realize that this is speculation. And, of course, there is nothing wrong with buying such items for their sheer enjoyment. If you make money on them later on, all the better.

There are four reasons why collectibles aren't investments. First, they don't provide any regular income. Bonds pay interest and many stocks pay dividends. Real estate can be used to provide rental income. But works of art and collections of any kind do not produce income. In fact, they cost money in the form of insurance premiums, storage fees, and income foregone on these costs.

Second, they are very illiquid; very hard to sell at a profit when you want to. When it comes to collectibles, it is almost always impossible to get the price you want when you want it, unless you are a dealer.

The third problem in the area of collectibles is the very high commissions you must pay, whether you are buying or selling.

Finally, there's the simple fact that collectibles are extremely sensitive to trends. The hot print or limited edition book of today may be tomorrow's garage sale item.

Now, none of this negative commentary means that you should never buy a piece of art or that you should avoid collecting things you enjoy. By all means do so if you have the money to spend and the personal interest necessary to understand and enjoy whatever it is you're collecting. But don't consider this to be a part of your investment activity. At best, it's speculation.

PRECIOUS METALS

As with the collectibles dealt with above, there has been a great deal said and written about making money by investing in precious metals, such as gold or silver, and similar commodities such as diamonds. Indeed, fortunes have been made by some people in these endeavours. But many more fortunes have been lost.

Again, like collectibles, and like commodity trading, this is really an area of speculation rather than investment, except, of course, for the professional trader — but then that's a business, not an investment.

Getting involved in the precious metal market is definitely not for the unsophisticated. Nor is it a sensible move for anyone who is playing with money that he or she can't afford to lose. In order to make money as a trader in precious metals you have to have a fair amount of money that you can clearly spare, because you cannot afford to have to sell at a time other than of your own choosing. The swings in the market for these commodities are so wide and unpredictable that you simply have to be able to wait out the bad times or you will lose your shirt.

The people who were buying gold at $60 an ounce were ecstatic when the price hit $350. But the poor wretches that bought it at $900 an ounce didn't share the same feeling when they had to sell at $350.

The odds are that you will be far better off to leave this one to the professionals as well.

Chapter 40

The Right Way to Play the Stock Market

Although many people lose money playing the stock market, a lot of others consistently make money playing it. The difference lies in how the market is played.

As explained in previous chapters, there are three types of market players: the investor, the speculator, and the gambler.

Although it's sometimes difficult to draw the line between the speculator and the gambler (other than to point out that speculating is smart gambling and gambling is stupid speculating), it is not difficult at all to identify the real investor. And it is only the real investor who consistently makes money in the stock market.

Investors make money by sitting, not trading. The in-and-out traders seldom, if ever, make money over any considerable period of time simply because they're devastated by commissions and the spreads between bid and ask prices.

The right way to play the stock market is to invest, not speculate or gamble.

There are some basic rules that, if followed religiously, will greatly enhance your profitability. At the very least they will significantly minimize your losses.

But before examining the rules for investing, let's look first at a few activities which constitute speculating (perhaps even gambling) even though many people think these activities constitute investing. Engaging in any of the following is *always* speculating:

1. Buying on margin (unless you're a professional market player).

2. Buying a "hot" issue, a new issue, or a fad issue. The best buy is rarely what the brokers are pushing.
3. Buying a stock just because it's gone up (remember, a drop of 50% completely wipes out a rise of 100%) or selling a stock simply because it's gone down. When investing, what's important is the future, not the past.
4. Following technical analysis.
5. Selling short.
6. Making an "investment" to earn extra income for living expenses. It's always better to use up *some* capital than to risk *all* of it.
7. Taking a risk you can't afford. It's always better to settle for a lower return.

So there are seven things you should *not* do if you intend to invest rather than speculate. However, again I remind you that speculating isn't of itself evil, so long as you don't confuse it with investing. Speculating should only be a hobby, never more. This means your speculative fund should never contain more money than you can easily afford to lose. You should never add to the speculative fund, and always take out any profits you might be lucky enough to make.

Now, back to the real investor. The real investor forgets about "the market." What's important to the real investor is the stocks that he or she owns. Real investors realize that a stock is a specific share of a specific business. It's how that business does that counts in the long run, not what "the market" is doing. The real investor will always remember the following rules:

1. Avoid investments that have little chance of being profitable.
2. Avoid investments that offer small gains compared to the possibility of large losses. Making bets at poor odds is speculating.
3. Don't look for a whole lot of *good* investments, look for a few *outstanding* investments.
4. Don't guess. If you don't understand an investment, stay out of it. Never despair about missing an "opportunity" you didn't understand.
5. Gross income is irrelevant when evaluating a company, and one year's earnings should never be taken too seriously.
6. Avoid non-convertible preferred shares.
7. Avoid non-voting common shares.
8. Bonds don't preserve capital.
9. Don't invest in a company unless you'd be content with it even if the stock exchanges closed for a year or two.

10. Any approach to the stock market that can be followed easily by a lot of people is too simple to be of any lasting value.
11. The market always makes mountains out of molehills.
12. The stock doesn't know you bought it.

Is there a perfect investment? Yes, I think so. It's the company that meets the following criteria:

1. Adequate size.
2. Strong balance sheet.
3. Dividends paid for at least the last fifteen years.
4. No losses in the past 10 years.
5. Price not more than 1½ times asset value.
6. At least a 10-year growth pattern.
7. Price/earnings ratio of not more than 15 based on the past three years.
8. Strong management.

Find that company and you won't go wrong in the long term. But, remember there is always short-term risk inherent in the stock market, no matter how good your stock is. The secret is being able to wait it out.

Patience, which is the child of knowledge and discipline, is the hallmark of the successful investor. If you know you're right, it's easy to wait.

Afterword

There you have it. Whether your income is large or small, whether your assets are meagre or substantial, you are bound to be better off if they are managed well. It doesn't really matter where the decimal point falls. You should take charge of your financial affairs and get the most out of your money.

By following the basic rules which are outlined throughout this book, applying a generous dose of common sense, and accepting the fact that you should live within your means, you can make your money count for far more than you ever imagined.

Making your money count is a day-to-day affair. Of course you will need professional help occasionally, but the smarter you get about making your money count, the less that help will cost you and the more beneficial it will become.

In the final analysis the responsibility to get the most for your money falls squarely on your shoulders. Remember, though, it's entirely within your capacity to handle that responsibility. You do not need to be a financier or a chartered accountant to get the most out of your dollar. Just manage it well. Don't read this book and then put it away. Refer to it from time to time as financial decisions need to be made.

Glossary

Annual Report:
The formal financial statements and report on operations presented annually by a corporation after its fiscal year-end.

Averages and Indexes:
Statistical tools that theoretically measure the state of the stock market or the economy, based on the performance of stocks or other selected criteria. Well-known indexes and averages include the Dow Jones Industrial Average, the Toronto Stock Exchange Industrial Index and the Consumer Price Index.

Averaging Down:
Buying more of a security at a lower price than your original investment in order to reduce the average cost per unit.

Banking Group:
A group of investment houses each of which individually assumes financial responsibility for part of a particular underwriting.

Basis Point:
1/100 of 1%

Bear:
One who expects the market or a stock to decline.

Bearer Security:
A stock or bond which does not have the owner's name recorded in the books of the issuing company or on the security certificate itself and which is therefore payable to the holder. See also "Street Certificate."

Bid and Ask:
A "bid" is the price a prospective buyer is willing to pay. "Ask" is the price a seller will accept. The two prices are usually referred to as a "quotation" or a "quote."

Blue Chip:
Well-established, nationally known common stocks, usually with a long and satisfactory dividend record and having all the attributes of a safe investment.

Blue Sky Law:
A slang term for laws enacted to protect the public against securities frauds.

Board Lot:
A regular trading unit (usually one hundred shares) which has been uniformly decided upon by the stock exchanges.

Board Room:
A room in a broker's office where clients may watch the quoted prices and sales of listed stocks as shown on a board, usually by means of electronic equipment.

Bond:
A certificate of indebtedness on which the issuer promises to pay the holder a specified amount of interest for a specified length of time, and to repay the loan on its maturity. Usually assets have been pledged as security for the loan. See also "Debenture."

Broker:
An agent who acts for both parties in a transaction.

Bull:
One who expects the market or a stock to go up.

Business Day:
Any day except Saturday, Sunday and legal holidays.

Buyer's Market:
When supply exceeds demand.

Call:
A transferable option to buy a specific number of shares at a stated price exercisable at a stated time. Obviously, calls would only be purchased by those who expect the subject stock to rise. See also "Put," "Option."

Callable:
Redeemable upon due notice by the security's issuer. For example, a

corporation might issue bonds which it could pay off and retire upon giving, say, three months' notice to the bondholders.

Capital Stock:
The ownership interest in a corporation, evidenced by the issue of share certificates.

Carrying Charges:
Usually refers to interest expense.

Central Bank:
A bank established by a national government to recommend and implement monetary policy on a national–international level. In Canada, it is the Bank of Canada; in the United States, the Federal Reserve Board; in the U.K., the Bank of England.

Certificate:
The actual piece of paper evidencing ownership of a stock or bond.

Closed-end Fund:
An investment company having fixed capital with no provision for the redemption of shares at the option of the shareholder. Shares must be bought or sold on the open market and not through the fund itself. See also "Open-end Fund."

Collateral Trust Bond:
A bond secured by collateral deposited with a trustee. The collateral is often the stocks and bonds of companies controlled by the issuing company, but may also be other securities.

Commercial Paper:
Short-term, interest-bearing, negotiable, promissory notes issued by corporations which provide for the payment of a specific amount of money at a stated time.

Common Share:
A synonym for common stock.

Common Stock:
Securities which represent ownership of a corporation and carry with them voting privileges. See also "Preferred Stock."

Conglomerate:
A company which directly or indirectly operates in a number of different industries which are usually unrelated to each other.

Consolidated Financial Statements:
The combined financial statements of a parent company and its

subsidiaries which present the financial position of the group as if it were one entity.

Consortium:

An association of independent organizations usually formed to undertake a specific project requiring special skills and resources not possessed by any of the participants individually.

Conventional Mortgage:

A mortgage which is not covered by a government-insured program.

Convertible:

A bond, debenture or preferred share which may be exchanged by its owner for common stock of the same company, in accordance with specific terms of the conversion privilege.

Coupon:

That portion of a bond certificate which entitles the holder to an interest payment of a specified amount, when clipped and presented to a paying agent (e.g. a bank) on or after its due date.

Cum dividend:

A quoted price which includes a declared but unpaid dividend. The purchaser of a share quoted cum dividend will receive the already declared dividend when it is paid. See also "Ex Dividend."

Cum Rights:

Shares owned from the day of an announcement that rights are to be issued until the date set for the shares to be traded "ex rights" (that is, when the rights and shares will trade separately). The owner of the shares in this period is entitled to receive the rights. See also "Rights."

Cumulative Preferred:

A preferred stock having a provision that if one or more of its dividends are not paid they accumulate and are added to the dividends which the preferred shareholders are entitled to in the future.

Current Yield:

The annual income from a particular investment expressed as a percentage of the investment's current value. For example, if income is $100 a year on an investment with a value of $1,000, the current yield is 10%.

Cyclical Stock:

A share in a corporation operating in an industry particularly sensitive to swings in economic conditions.

Day Order:
An order to buy or sell a security valid only for the day on which the order is given.

Debenture:
A certificate of indebtedness of a government or company, usually implying an unsecured obligation. See also "Bond."

Delivery, Regular:
Unless otherwise stipulated, those who sell securities must deliver the certificates on or before the fifth business day after the sale.

Discount:
The amount by which a security sells below its par value.

Discretionary Account:
An account established by a customer with a broker under which the broker has been specifically authorized in writing by the client to use his or her own judgment in buying and selling securities for the account of the customer.

Discretionary Order:
An order given to a broker by a customer specifying the security and the quantity to be bought or sold, but leaving entirely to the judgment of the broker the time and the price of the particular transaction.

Diversified Company:
A corporation engaged in a number of different lines of business either directly or through subsidiary companies.

Dividend:
Profits distributed to shareholders of a corporation.

Dow Jones Averages:
Stock price averages computed by Dow Jones & Company (who also publish *The Wall Street Journal*) giving average stock prices by class based on the highest, lowest, opening, and closing stock price averages for representative shares issued. The most commonly used average is that of thirty particular industrial stocks which are listed on the New York Stock Exchange, known as the Dow Jones Industrial.

Earnings Per Share:
A corporation's earning for a fiscal period divided by the number of shares outstanding at the end of the particular period which are entitled to full participation in those earnings.

Equity:

The ownership interest of common and preferred stockholders in a company, which is the difference between the company's assets and liabilities. If there are only common shares outstanding, "equity per share" would be assets minus liabilities divided by the number of shares outstanding. If there are preferred shares outstanding, it would be assets minus the total of liabilities and par value of preferred shares divided by the number of common shares outstanding.

Escrowed Shares:

Outstanding shares of a company which, although entitled to vote and receive dividends, cannot be bought or sold without special approval being obtained. Shares can be released from escrow only with the permission of relevant authorities such as the stock exchange or a securities commission. This is a technique commonly used by mining and oil and gas companies when treasury shares are issued for new properties.

Ex Dividend:

A quoted price which does not include a declared but unpaid dividend. When a person buys a share "ex dividend," the dividend will be paid to the seller of the stock. See also "Cum Dividend."

Ex Rights:

Without rights. The opposite of cum rights. See also "Cum Rights" and "Rights."

Extendible Bond:

A bond issued with a specific maturity date, but granting the holder the right to retain the bond for a specified additional period of time.

Extra:

Short for extra dividend. A dividend paid in addition to a regular dividend.

Face Value:

The value of a bond or preferred share appearing on the face of the certificate, usually the amount the issuing company promises to pay at maturity. It is no indication of market value.

Firm Bid:

An undertaking to buy a specified amount of securities at a stated price for a stated period of time, unless released from the obligation by the potential seller.

Flat:
A term meaning that the quoted market price of a bond or debenture is the total cost thereof.

Floor Trader:
An employee of a member firm of a stock exchange who executes buy and sell orders on the floor (trading area) of the exchange on behalf of his or her firm and its clients.

General Mortgage Bond:
A bond secured by a blanket mortgage on the issuer's property, but usually outranked by one or more other mortgages.

GTC Order:
Good-till-cancelled order. Same as an open order.

Growth Stock:
Shares of a company with excellent prospects for future increases in value.

Hypothecate:
To pledge as collateral for a loan.

Income Bond or Debenture:
A bond or debenture which promises to repay principal, but to pay interest only if sufficient income is earned.

Insider:
A director or senior officer of a corporation, or anyone who may be presumed to have access to inside information concerning the company. Anyone owning more than 10% of the voting shares in a corporation would likely be considered an insider in most jurisdictions.

Insider Report:
A report of all transactions in the shares of a corporation by those considered to be insiders of the company and submitted on a timely basis to the relevant securities commission.

Institutional Investor:
An institution, such as a pension fund, trust company or insurance company, which invests large sums of money in securities.

Investment Counsellor:
One whose profession is giving advice on investments for a fee.

Investment Company, Fund or Trust:
An organization which uses its capital to invest in other organizations. There are two principal types: closed-end and open-end, the latter

usually referred to as mutual funds. See also "Closed-end Fund," "Mutual Fund," and "Open-end Fund."

Junior Security:
A security having a lower priority of claims than another security of the same issuer.

Junk Bond:
A very high-risk bond characterized by very little security and a high interest rate.

Leading Indicators:
A selection of statistical data that indicate trends in the economy as a whole. Examples are levels of employment, capital investment, business starts and failures, profits, stock prices, inventories, housing starts and some commodity prices.

Leverage:
The borrowing and re-investing of money to produce a return in excess of the cost of borrowing.

Leveraged Buy-out:
The acquiring of control of a company by using borrowed money, often heavily financed by the issuance of junk bonds.

Limit Order:
A customer's order to a broker to buy at a stated price or lower, or to sell at a stated price or higher. The order can be executed only within the specified limits.

Listed Securities:
Securities which are listed on a stock exchange.

Long:
Signifies ownership of securities. If you are "long 100 shares of Bell common" it means you own 100 Bell common shares. See also "Short."

Margin:
The amount paid by a customer to a broker when securities are bought on credit, the balance being advanced by the broker against acceptable collateral.

Market Order:
An order placed to buy or sell a security immediately at the best price obtainable.

Marketable Security:
A security that can be easily sold.

Mutual Fund:
An open-end investment company which sells units or shares to investors. The mutual fund uses the proceeds of such sales for itself to invest in securities of various companies and governments. See also ''Investment Company,'' ''Closed-end Fund,'' and ''Open-end Fund.''

Net Worth:
A synonym for shareholders' equity.

No Par Value Stock:
Shares which have no par value. Most common shares are issued as having no par value because they are usually bought and sold on their market value, which reflects supply and demand; and if the company is wound up the common shareholders get everything that's left after all liabilities and preferred shareholders are paid off. See also ''Par Value.''

Odd Lot:
A number of shares less than the established board lot. See also ''Board Lot.''

Open-end Fund:
A synonym for a mutual fund. The opposite of a closed-end fund. Open-end funds sell their own shares or units to investors, buy back their own shares or units, and are not listed on a stock exchange. The capitalization of an open-end fund is not fixed. It will sell as many units as people want to buy. See also ''Closed-end Fund,'' ''Investment Company,'' and ''Mutual Fund.''

Option:
A right to buy or sell specific securities at a stated price within a specified period of time.

Over-the-counter:
Transactions in securities which are not listed on a stock exchange.

Paper Profit:
An unrealized profit. For example, when a stock purchased at $10 goes up to $15 but has not been sold there is a paper profit of $5.

Par Value:
The face value of a security. This is the amount which the holder is entitled to receive upon redemption of the security by the issuer. It is primarily used in connection with preferred shares and bonds. A

preferred share or bond with a par value of $100 would result in the holder thereof receiving $100 on its redemption. The par value is not representative of the security's market value, except immediately before redemption. Some common shares have par values assigned to them, but the par value of a common stock is meaningless, as described previously under "no par value."

Participating Stock:
A class of preferred stock which provides for payment of a dividend not less than that paid on the company's common shares. Occasionally, a participating stock will also share in the residual distribution of assets upon liquidation of a corporation.

Penny Stock:
Low-priced, speculative issues selling at less than $1 a share. Usually used as a derogatory term, even though some penny stocks develop into investment-calibre issues.

Point:
As applied to the price of shares, it means $1 per share. For bonds, it usually means 1% of the face value. If a stock goes up or down 2½ points, that means the price has increased or decreased by $2.50 per share. A $1,000 bond that dropped 2 points would have gone down in value by $20.

Portfolio Investments:
Long-term investments in corporations which are neither subsidiaries nor controlled by the investor.

Preferred Stock:
A class of share capital that entitles the holder to certain preferences over common shareholders, such as a fixed rate of dividend, or return of the stock's par value upon liquidation, or both. Preferred shares normally have voting rights only when their dividends are in arrears.

Premium:
The amount by which a preferred stock or bond sells above its par value. In the case of a new issue of bonds or stocks, the premium is the amount the market price rises over the original selling price. The term may also refer to the part of the redemption price of a bond or preferred stock in excess of par.

Price-earnings Ratio:
The market price of a common stock divided by the annual earnings per share for the preceding fiscal period.

Primary Distribution or Primary Offering:
The original sale of any issue of a corporation's securities.

Private Sector:
The sector of an economy consisting of individuals, corporations, firms and other institutions not under government control.

Profit Taking:
The process of converting paper profits into cash by selling the securities.

Pro Forma:
For illustrative purposes.

Prospectus:
A legal document describing securities being offered for sale to the public. A prospectus must be prepared in conformity with the requirements of the securities commissions in jurisdictions where the securities will be offered for sale.

Proxy:
A written authorization given by a shareholder to another person (who need not be a shareholder) to represent the shareholder and vote the shareholder's shares at a shareholders' meeting.

Proxy Battle:
A contest between two or more factions in a corporation in which each faction seeks to gain control of sufficient proxies to enable it to elect its candidates to the board of directors or win a decision in a particular vote at a shareholders' meeting.

Public Company:
A corporation whose shares are available to the general public.

Public Sector:
The sector of an economy consisting of government-owned institutions.

Put:
A transferable option to sell a specific number of shares at a stated price exercisable at a stated time. Puts are purchased by those who think a stock is going to go down. See also ''Call.''

Rally:
A brisk rise following a decline in the general price level of the market as a whole or of an individual stock.

Record Date:
The date on which a shareholder must be registered on a corporation's books in order to receive a dividend declared or to vote on the company's affairs.

Red Herring:
A preliminary prospectus, so-called because certain information is printed in red ink around the border of the front page. A red herring will not contain all the information found in the final prospectus. Its purpose is to determine the extent of public interest in a new security issue while it is being reviewed by the relevant securities commission.

Retractable Share:
A share having a fixed maturity date at a fixed price, at the option of the investor.

Rights:
Privileges granted to shareholders enabling them to acquire additional shares directly from the company.

Secondary Distribution or Secondary Offering:
The re-distribution to the public of a significant number of shares which had previously been sold by the issuing company.

Seller's Market:
When demand exceeds supply.

Senior Debt:
Debt having a higher priority of claims than other debt.

Senior Security:
A security having a higher priority of claims than other securities.

Settlement Date:
The date on which stock exchange transactions are due for delivery and payment. It is also the official date to be used for recording stock market transactions for income tax purposes. It is usually the fifth business day following the date of the transaction.

Shareholder of Record:
The shareholder in whose name shares are registered in the records of a corporation.

Shareholders' Equity:
The excess of assets over liabilities of a corporation.

Short:
Signifies that securities have been sold on your behalf, but you still haven't delivered them to your broker. See also "Short Sale."

Short Sale:
The sale of a security which the seller doesn't own. It is a highly speculative transaction done in anticipation of the price of a stock falling and the seller then being able to cover the sale by buying the stock later at a lower price, thereby making a profit on the transaction. You must advise your broker if you're selling short.

Stock Dividend:
A dividend paid by the issue of shares of capital stock rather than in cash.

Stock Option:
The right to purchase a stated number of shares of a corporation's capital stock at a fixed price at or during a fixed period of time. Such rights are usually given to officers and employees of the corporation.

Stock Split:
The division of the outstanding shares of a corporation into a larger number of shares without a change in value of the total shares outstanding. For example, one $100 share might be replaced by five shares each worth $20.

Stop-loss Order:
An order for the sale of securities designed to take effect as soon as the market price of the security reaches a specified amount.

Street Certificate:
A stock certificate registered in the name of an investment dealer rather than in the name of the individual owner, thereby making it easier to transact sales and purchases of the particular shares.

Stripped Bond:
A bond which has had all its interest coupons removed.

Subsidiary:
A corporation of which another corporation owns a majority of the voting shares.

Takeover Bid:
A bid to purchase shares of a corporation with a view to obtaining control of the corporation.

Treasury Stock or Treasury Shares:
Authorized but unissued shares.

Underwriting:
The term applied to the agreement by investment dealers to buy, at an agreed price, all of the issue of a securities offer. The investment dealer will then sell the securities to the general public.

Warrant:
A certificate giving the holder the right to purchase securities at a stated price within a stated period of time.

Wash Sale:
A sale which is immediately offset by an identical purchase.

Zero Coupon Bond:
A bond which pays no interest.

Appendix A

PERSONAL FINANCIAL PLANNING ANALYSIS

FOR ______________________________

This document serves as a starting point, whether used as a checklist by the planner or completed by the individual whose affairs are being reviewed. Certain personal questions are omitted because they may best be dealt with in other ways. All lists, schedules and other documents should be attached.

COMPLETED BY ______________________________

DATE ______________________________

GENERAL INFORMATION

Name in full ______________________________

Home address and telephone ______________________________

____

____

Business address and telephone ______________________________

____

____

Date of birth ______________ Place of birth ______________

Citizenship ______________________________

Domicile: at birth ______________________________

at marriage ______________________________

at present ______________________________

Marital status ______________ Date of marriage ______________

Does a marriage contract exist? ______________ (if so, attach copy)

State of health ______________ Insurable? ______________

Do you have a Will? ______________ (if so, attach copy)

Executors:

Name and address	Relationship to you

SPOUSE

Name in full ______________________________

Home address and telephone (if different from yours) ______________________________

____

____

Date of birth ______________ Place of birth ______________

Citizenship ______________ Domicile at marriage ______________

Occupation and business address, if any ______________________________

____

____

____

Details of divorce or legal separation, you or your spouse, if any ______________

____

____

Details of spouse's children, if any, from previous marriage ______________

____

____

State of health ______________________________

____

Estimated value and general description of spouse's estate, including source: ________

____

____

____

____

Does your spouse have a Will? ______________ (if so, attach copy)

SPOUSE (Cont'd)

Executors:

Name and address	Relationship to spouse

Could your spouse: run a business? ________________

handle own affairs? ________________

invest funds? ________________

Other Comments:

HEIRS

Complete Schedule II.

Do any of the heirs listed have physical or mental handicaps? If so, give details of any special assistance you may wish to give them.

____

____

Do you wish to give any other special assistance to any children, e.g. for education, to set up a business, etc.? If so, give details.

____

____

Do you wish to benefit any other persons such as business associates, employees, charities, friends, secret trusts, in-laws, parents or other relatives? If so, give details.

____

____

Could any of your children continue your business? ____________________

____

____

How much income will be required for your spouse and children after your death if you:

die before children are independent? ____________________

die after children are independent but before you retire? ____________________

die after you retire? ____________________

If any children have substantial property or income, provide details: ____________________

____

____

____

____

INCOME

Attach a list showing source, type and amount of all of last five years' income (or attach a copy of last five years' income tax returns for both self and spouse).

Indicate any significant changes in income expected in the current or future years:

How much disposable income do you require annually to live at your present standard of living?

Provide details of any settlement, trust, etc., to which you are a party:

Provide details of any substantial gifts or property transfers that you have made at any time:

INSURANCE, PENSIONS AND OTHER BENEFITS

Complete Schedules III and IV

Provide details of any other relevant matters:

ASSETS AND LIABILITIES

Complete Schedules V to VII (ignore reference to V-Day values on Schedules for assets acquired after 1971).

Have you elected to use V-Day values for capital gains tax purposes?

____

Complete Schedule VIII and ensure that all obligations are listed, including business and household debts, bank loans, income taxes (including potential liabilities), property taxes, mortgages, notes, etc.

Provide details of any guarantees or endorsements: ____________________

____

____

____

____

Complete the following summary using the detailed schedules:

	Present Value	Loans Against
CSV of life insurance		
Current value of pensions		
Current value of real property		
Current value of stocks, etc.		
Other assets		
Other liabilities		
TOTALS		

OBJECTIVES

At what age would you like to retire? ______

Where will you live when you retire? ______

How much income will you require when retired? ______

Are bequests to be free of death duties? ______

Do you want any special provisions to apply should your spouse remarry? ______

______

______

Are any other bequests to be contingent in any way? If so, give details.

______

______

Do you want control of any business to be retained by your estate?

______

Do you want control of any business to be transferred to any particular person?

______

Do you want your children to have:

income? ______

capital? ______

capital at a particular age, say 21, 25, etc.? ______

Is there any particular type of investment, business, or hobby in which you are interested, e.g., farming, real estate?

______

______

______

______

OTHER COMMENTS

DOCUMENTS

		Attached	To Follow	Not Applicable
Schedule I	List of Advisors	( )	( )	( )
Schedule II	List of Heirs	( )	( )	( )
Schedule III	Summary of Life Insurance	( )	( )	( )
Schedule IV	Summary of Pensions, etc.	( )	( )	( )
Schedule V	Summary of Real Property	( )	( )	( )
Schedule VI	Summary of Stocks, etc.	( )	( )	( )
Schedule VII	Other Assets	( )	( )	( )
Schedule VIII	Liabilities	( )	( )	( )
Last 1 2 3 4 5 years' income tax returns (circle)		( )	( )	( )
Wills	— self	( )	( )	( )
	— spouse	( )	( )	( )

Where are wills kept?

____

When were they last reviewed?

____

	Attached	To Follow	Not Applicable
Buy/Sell or partnership agreements	( )	( )	( )

Marriage Contract	( )	( )	( )
Other (Indicate)	( )	( )	( )
______________________	( )	( )	( )
______________________	( )	( )	( )
______________________	( )	( )	( )
______________________	( )	( )	( )
______________________	( )	( )	( )
______________________	( )	( )	( )
______________________	( )	( )	( )

PROFESSIONAL ADVISORS **SCHEDULE I**

	NAME	FIRM	ADDRESS	TELEPHONE NUMBER
ACCOUNTANT				
LAWYER				
BANK MANAGER				
LIFE UNDERWRITER				
TRUST COMPANY				
INVESTMENT COUNSEL				

HEIRS (attach separate lists if necessary)

SCHEDULE II

NAME AND ADDRESS	RELATIONSHIP	DATE OF BIRTH	MARITAL STATUS	NATURE OF BEQUEST

SUMMARY OF LIFE INSURANCE

SCHEDULE III

POLICY NUMBER	COMPANY	TYPE	FACE AMOUNT	OWNER	BENEFICIARY	ANNUAL PREMIUM	CURRENT CASH VALUE	POLICY LOAN
TOTALS								

COMMENTS: ____________________

____

PENSIONS, ANNUITIES, DISABILITY INSURANCE, ETC. **SCHEDULE IV**

DESCRIPTION	PREMIUMS	BENEFITS	AGE BENEFITS COMMENCE	CURRENT VALUE
TOTALS				

COMMENTS: ______________________________

SUMMARY OF REAL PROPERTY

SCHEDULE V

DESCRIPTION	PURCHASE DATE	COST	V-DAY VALUE	CURRENT VALUE	TYPE OF OWNERSHIP	DETAILS OF MORTGAGE
TOTALS						

SUMMARY OF STOCKS, BONDS AND MUTUAL FUNDS

SCHEDULE VI

DESCRIPTION	PURCHASE DATE	COST	V-DAY VALUE	CURRENT VALUE	DIVIDEND
TOTALS					

COMMENTS: ____________________

OTHER ASSETS

SCHEDULE VII

DESCRIPTION AND PURCHASE DATE	COST	V-DAY VALUE	CURRENT VALUE	COMMENTS
TOTALS				

LIABILITIES **SCHEDULE VIII**

DESCRIPTION	TERM	CURRENT BALANCE	INTEREST RATE	ANNUAL PAYMENTS (INTEREST & PRINCIPAL)	COMMENTS (WHETHER INSURED, ETC.)
TOTALS					

Index

Agents
  insurance, 71, 76, 79-80
  real estate, 105, 114-15
Annuities, 247-50
  certain, 249
  choice of, 250
  deferred, 248
  definition of, 247
  immediate, 247-48
  impaired life, 249
  joint and survivor, 249
  life with guaranteed period, 248
  life-only, 248
  specially guaranteed, 249
  variable, 249
Appraisers, insurance, 74
Assessment, income tax, 163-64
Assessment, property tax
  appealing of, 111-12
  checking of, 110-11
Assets and liabilities, 24
Auditors, income tax, 165-66
Automobiles. *See* Cars

Backing, equity, 228
Bank Act, 254
Bank of Canada, 251-54
Bank plans, 31
Banking
  family roles in, 23-24
  see also Swiss banks
Bears and bulls, 215-16
Bills, treasury. *See* Treasury bills
Bonds and debentures, 232-46
  Canada Savings Bonds, 246
  collateral trust bonds, 239
  convertible, 240-41
  corporate bonds, 186
  definition of, 232-33
  denomination of, 233
  extendible, 239
  government and municipal bonds, 186
  income, 238
  investment quality of, 243-46
  investor objectives with, 246
  issuers of, 234-35
  junk bonds, 243
  mortgage bonds, 235-37
  retractable, 239-40
  serial, 240
  sinking fund bonds, 238
  stripped bonds, 242-43
  yield of, 233
  zero coupon bonds, 242
  see also Debentures
Borrowing money, 4, 87-90
  compounded interest rate, 89-90
  for investment, 78, 179
  for RRSPs, 52-53
Budget sheet
  common errors in, 16
  preparation of, 15-16
Budgeting, personal, 6, 13-20
  for Christmas, 18-20
  for emergencies, 16-18
  family roles in, 14
  method for, 15-16
  myths about, 13-14
  for vacations, 18
Bulls and bears, 215-16

Canada Deposit Insurance, 82-84
  C.D.I.C., 82-84
  maximum amount of, 82-83

Q.D.I.B., 84
and RRSPs and RRIFs, 83
Canada Deposit Insurance Corporation (C.D.I.C.), 82-84
Canada Mortgage and Housing Corporation, 118
Canada Savings Bonds, 17, 187, 233, 246
Canadian and British Insurance Companies Act, 229, 245
Canadian Securities Institute, 228, 243-44, 246
Capital gains, 145-47, 188-89
Cars
insurance on, 72
leasing of, 27-29
purchase of, 91-96
Children
financial role of, 14, 24-25
life insurance on, 80
Christmas, budgeting for, 18-20
Clearing corporations, 257-58
Collectibles, 270
Commodity Futures Trading Commission (U.S.), 269
Commodity trading, 147, 268-70
Common shares. *See* Shares, common
Comparison shopping, 7
Contracts, marriage. *See* Marriage contracts
Coverage
asset, 244
dividend, 226-28
interest, 243-44
Credit, buying on, 4, 5, 19-20
Credit cards
as cash substitutes, 5
for Christmas shopping, 19-20
Credit unions, 89

Dealer Sponsorship, 229
Debentures, 237-38
defined, 232
subordinated, 238
with warrants, 241-42
see also Bonds and debentures
Debt, paying off, 5
Debt/equity ratio, 244-45
Diversification, 260-67
balance in, 267
holding companies, 262-63
investment funds, 262-65
for investor convenience, 265-66
mutual funds, 264-65
overdiversification, 266-67
reasons for, 260
risk reduction through, 261-63
Dividends, 204-7
coverage, 226-28
ex-dividend and cum-dividend, 205-6
payment record of, 228
re-investment plans, 206-7
regular and extra, 206
stock, 206

Economic outlook, effect on investment, 213
Emotion, effect on investment, 216
Equity backing, 228
Estate planning, 62-70
professional advisors for, 63-64
questionnaire about, 64-65, 291-302
tax considerations in, 69-70

wills in, 65-67. *See also* Wills
Executors, 67-68

Federal Trade Commission (U.S.), 116
Financial planning
assets and liabilities, 24
attitude and action for, 10-11
banking, 23-24
family roles in, 21-25
filing of records, 12
goals in, 11
handling vs managing money, 22
insurance, 23
mistakes in, 3-9
needs vs wants in, 11-12
wills in, 22-23. *See also* Wills
Funds
closed-end, 263
investment, 262-65
mutual or open-end, 264-65
Futures, 269-270

Gamblers, 185-86, 272
Gold, 270-71
Growth companies, 188-89

Holding companies, 262-63
Houses. *See* Real estate, investing in

Impulse buying, 7
Income tax, 129-68
after filing your return, 162-66
assessments, 163-64
auditors, 165-66
on business and professional income, 148-49
on capital gains, 145-47
on commodity trading gains, 147-48
discounters, 133
on dividends, 144-45
on employment assistance, 141
on employment income, 139-40
and estate planning, 69-70
evasion vs avoidance, 164-65
on family allowance, 141-42
filing your return, 131-38
on interest, 142-44
on pensions, 140-41
receipts exempt from, 149
on rental income, 148
shelters, 167-68
on tips, 140
see also Income tax credits; Income tax deductions
Income Tax Act, 37, 53, 54, 56, 132, 146, 238
Income tax credits, 150-61
child tax credit, 158-59
education credit, 155-56
pension income, 158
Income tax deductions, 150-61
alimony and maintenance payments, 152-53
charitable donations, 150-51
child care, 159-60
for commission salespeople, 160-61
for disabled people, 153-54
employment travel costs, 161
medical expenses, 151-52
moving (general), 157-58
moving (students), 156-57
for non-resident dependants, 154-55

tuition fees, 155
Insurance, 71-84
agent, choice of, 71
Canada deposit, 82-84
car, 72
disability, 81-82
family responsibilities in, 23
homeowners', 72-74
life. *See* Life Insurance
RRSPs, 47-48
Interest
amortization of, 105
compounding of, 4, 35, 47, 89-90
Intestacy, 66
Investment, 171-274
borrowing for, 7
objectives of, 187-89
vs speculation, 186
see also Diversification; Real estate, investment in; Securities, investing in; Stock market
Investment clubs, 173-79
rules of, 174-75
and income tax, 174
overview, 173-74
philosophy of, 175, 177-79
valuing an interest in, 175-77
Investment Dealers Association of Canada, 190, 197
Investors, 184-85, 272, 273-74
see also Bulls; Bears; Psychology, investor; Stock market, players in

Jobs, changing, 101-2

Lawyers
and appealing an assessment, 112
and estate planning, 63-64
and marriage contracts, 99-100
and offers to purchase property, 105, 113-14
and power of attorney, 86
and wills, 66,67
Leasing
financial lease, 28-29
operating lease, 27-28
vs buying, 26-27, 29-30
Leverage, 179
see also Borrowing money, for investment
Life insurance, 74-81
agents, dealing with, 76, 79-80
calculating necessary coverage, 75-76
changing policies, 81
chartered life underwriters (CLUs), 76
for children, 80
for non-smokers, 80
whole life vs term, 77-79
Living accommodation, renting vs buying, 5-6, 104
Loans. *See* Borrowing money
Lotteries, winning, 119-21
for $100,000, 120-21
for $1 million, 119-20

Market. *See* Stock market
Marriage contracts, 97-100
items to include, 98-99
legal advice on, 99-100
pitfalls of, 99
in Quebec, 97
reasons for, 97-98
Metals, precious, 270-71
Mortgage bonds, 235-37

Mortgage-backed securities, 118
Mortgage
holding, 118
long-term vs short-term, 32
paying off, 5
in your RRSP, 51-52
Mutual funds, 264-65

National Housing Act, 118
Needs vs wants, 11-12

Office of Interstate Land Sales Registration,U.S. Department of Housing and Urban Development, 116
Options, 256-59
call, 256
covered and naked writers of, 258
investment strategies for, 259

Planning. *See* Estate planning; Financial planning
Portfolios, balanced, 267
Power of attorney, 85-86
Preferred shares. *See* Shares, preferred
Price/earnings ratio, 211-12
Properties, purchase of. *See* Real estate, investing in
Property tax assessments, 110-12
Psychology, investor, 213-14, 268

Quebec Deposit Insurance Board (Q.D.I.B.), 84
Questionnaire, as estate-planning aid, 64-65, 291-302

Real estate, investing in, 103-18
country properties, 108-9
foreign, 116-17
mortgage-backed securities, 118
mortgages, holding, 118
principal residence, 103-6
property taxes, 110-12
recreation properties, 106-7
rental properties, 117-18
selling your home without an agent, 112-14
using a real estate agent, 114-15
using a real estate sales consultant, 115-116
Registered Education Savings Plans (RESPs), 59-61
Registered Retirement Income Funds (RRIFs), 56-58
deposit insurance on, 83
Registered Retirement Savings Plans (RRSPs), 33-55
and age of investor, 38-39
borrowing money for, 52-53
contribution limits, 36-37
deposit insurance on, 83
equity funds, 40-43
fixed income funds, 43-45
flexibility of, 37
guaranteed funds, 45-47
holding mortgage in, 51-52
insurance, 47-48
overview, 39-40
qualifications for, 35
reasons to have, 34-35
risk and return on, 37-38, 55
self-directed, 49-50
spousal, 51
as tax shelter, 34-35, 54-55
withdrawals from, 53-54

Rights, 208-9

Securities
bearer, 192
definition of, 180
investing in, 180-83
advantages of, 182
compared with real estate, 181
see also Diversification; Stock market
mortgage-backed, 118
registered, 192

Share certificates, 203
registered, 204
street form, 204
Shares, common, 203-20
consolidation of, 208
definition of, 203-4
dividends from, 204-7
factors affecting prices of, 210-11
factors to consider before buying, 211-15, 217-20
income tax on, 210
objectives in buying, 215-16, 220
rights, 208-9
speculation in, 220
splits of, 207-8
warrants, 210
Shares, preferred, 221-31
callable or redeemable, 224-25
convertible, 225
cumulative and non-cumulative, 224
dealer sponsorship, 229
definition of, 222-23
dividend coverage, 226-28
dividend payment record, 228
eligibility for insurance investments, 229
equity backing, 228
funding of, 230
issuer of, 230-31
market price vs call price of, 230
marketability of, 230
participating and non-participating, 224
protection of, 229-30
quality of, 225-26
reasons for choosing, 222-23
reasons for issuing, 221-22
retractable, 225
votes with, 223
Shopping, comparison, 7
Speculation, vs investment, 186
Speculators, 185, 272-73
psychology of, 268
Sponsorship, dealer, 229
Stanford Research Institute, 189
Stockbrokers, 190-93, 194-202
avoiding problems with, 196-200
how to choose, 194-96
Stock market, 180-83, 272-74
brokers. *See* Stockbrokers
common shares. *See* Shares, common
crash (October 1987), 7-8, 213
growth companies, 188-89
operating an account for investment in, 190-93
players in, 184-86
preferred shares. *See* Shares, preferred
sources of information on, 201-2

technical analysis of, 213-15
Stock options. *See* Options
Swiss banks, 122-26
advantages of, 124-25
disadvantages of, 125-126
numbered accounts in, 123-25
opening an account, 123-24
secrecy of transactions, 122-23
transfer of funds, 126

Tax, income. *See* Income tax
Taxes, property, 110-12
TransCanada Options Inc., 256, 257
Treasury bills, 17, 187, 251-55
auctions, 252-53
and Canadian money market, 253-54, 255
definition of, 251-52
history, 254-55

Wants vs needs, 11-12
Warrants, 210
debentures with, 241-42
Wills, 65-67
choosing executors, 67-68
dying without, 66
family roles in, 22-23
tax considerations in, 69-70
World events, effect on investment, 216
Writers of options, 257-59